WILLIAM G. DU
and friends as "G
health counselor
York (USA). He h
the Gospel of Thomas for over thirty-six years. His conviction that Thomas can be understood only in a non-dual context has been inspired and sustained by a variety of influences. These include a wide range of scholarly works on Biblical and non-canonical scripture, Christian mysticism, and the wealth of material from eastern traditions. As a boy in Cortland, New York, he attended a Catholic elementary and secondary school under the tutelage of the Franciscan Sisters of Allegany. He is a graduate of Syracuse University (BA) and the University of Toronto (BEd). He is a long-time associate member of the Westar Institute. When he is not thinking, writing, or speaking about the Gospel of Thomas, he is enjoying the company of his extended and extensive family, playing golf, or quietly walking the hills and valleys near his home in New York. His website is williamgduffy.com.

THE HIDDEN GOSPEL OF THOMAS

Commentaries on the Non-Dual Sayings of Jesus

WILLIAM G. DUFFY

Published in 2020 by SilverWood Books

SilverWood Books Ltd
14 Small Street, Bristol, BS1 1DE, United Kingdom
www.silverwoodbooks.co.uk

ISBN 978-1-78132-987-0 (paperback)
ISBN 978-1-78132-988-7 (ebook)

British Library Cataloguing in Publication Data
A CIP catalogue record for this book is
available from the British Library

Pages designed and typeset according to the author's creative direction

Happy birthday Char!

Love,
Mark, Lynda,
Joseph + Sophie
xxx

To Barbara Duffy Beigel
my friend and sister

Contents

Acknowledgments

In the ten years I spent on writing this book, I turned to and was supported by many people, both in person and in print. I wish to acknowledge my gratitude and affection for all those individuals who helped me with this project. Coming first to mind is the Inklings critique group of Corvallis, Oregon. Their encouragement and feedback on the early drafts were much appreciated. Likewise, the Utica Writers Club ably assumed this role when I moved back to central New York in 2017.

I want to thank my copy and line editor, Susan Hughes, for her sharp eyes and helpfulness. I am also grateful to Ann Beigel Kito, my niece, for her kind advice and helpful suggestions. For their lavish support and guidance, I am particularly grateful to the editors and staff of SilverWood Books.

I also wish to acknowledge Eve Taverne, my accomplished photographer of Poland, New York.

Last but not least, when my confidence slumped and the hours came slowly, there were many dear friends who appeared magically at my side. Among them were Todd and Diane Thompson, Gary and Diane Paape, Bob Gerding, Nancy Cochran, Kathy Walter, Abraham Likwornik, Paul and Pat Frishkoff, Marie Oliver, and C. Lill Ahrens.

Introduction

In December of 1945, a "lost gospel" was discovered buried in an earthen jar in Upper Egypt at a place called Jabal al-Tarif, not far from the right bank of the Nile River. It was found by Bedouin tribesmen along with 51 other documents that were bound together in ancient books called codices. It was the Gospel of Thomas, and ever since, it has both amazed and perplexed readers throughout the world. Not a narrative gospel like the four gospels of the Bible, it was a collection of 114 sayings of Jesus, about half of which were familiar from the New Testament. Most of the other sayings were entirely new. For nearly sixteen hundred years, this treasure of unseen aphorisms, dialogues, and parables remained buried and forgotten in its ceramic tomb. Even after it was found, it took years for it to be examined by scholars and for the word to get out that something extraordinary had been discovered. Indeed, it was not until 1959 that the Gospel of Thomas was first published in English. Complicating the matter, and somewhat eclipsing the news of this earlier find in Egypt, was the discovery of the Dead Sea Scrolls at Qumran (1946–1951). They were found in what is now the West Bank, the territory occupied by Israel in the 1967 Six-Day War. Often confused with these scrolls, the codices found at Jabal al-Tarif in Egypt, however, were quite distinct and were composed, for the most part, at a later time.

The Nag Hammadi Library

Although the story of the 1945 find at Jabal al-Tarif is submerged in contradiction and controversy, it was probably the enterprise of three brothers, Muhammad, Khalifah Ali, and Abu al-Majd, members of the Bedouin clan of al-Samman. Muhammad later reported that they were digging for *sabakh*, a natural fertilizer at the base of a cliff. There is speculation, however, that rather than fertilizer, they were seeking something of much greater value—funerary treasure. Indeed, it was rumored that graves had been found at this site and ancient tombs discovered in the caves above. In truth, a treasure was found, but one that was not fully appreciated until much later. A jar was unearthed by these men that when broken open revealed twelve codices[1] and part of a thirteenth. Scholars later realized that what emerged from that jar was a gold mine of information. The discovery immensely expanded the little that was known about the non-orthodox, religious environment of the early Jesus movement. Eventually, it answered questions that had long puzzled scholars of that period.

In content, the texts were quite varied, consisting mostly of proto-Gnostic, Gnostic, Jewish, and Hermetic works. There was also a barely recognizable fragment of Plato's *Republic*. Of the 52 treatises, 40 were previously unfamiliar to scholars. However, the most exciting find for many was the Gospel of Thomas. It was the only complete, though slightly damaged, copy of this gospel in existence. The codex in which Thomas was found, Codex II, contained seven treatises, among which were such works as the Gospel of Philip and the Apocryphon of John. These and all the works in this collection were written in Sahidic Coptic, an Egyptian language that employed an alphabet derived from and similar to Greek. An examination of the cartonnage[2] of Codex VII revealed letters dating to 341, 346, and 348 CE. This suggests that these books were fashioned sometime in the mid-fourth century. This does not necessarily mean that their authorship dates to that period, but only that their assemblage into books dates from that time. Since this find occurred not far from the modern city of Nag Hammadi, the entire set of codices has been called the Nag Hammadi Library.

Scholars soon realized, however, that there had been an earlier discovery, around the turn of the twentieth century, also in Egypt. It consisted of three, separate fragments of papyrus on which were written sayings of Jesus, this time not in Coptic but in Greek. At the time, they were described as remnants of two "unknown gospels." Little did they know that these scraps were fragments of this same Gospel of Thomas. Compared to the Coptic text, they consisted of about twelve percent (by word count) of that larger collection. They were found by the British team of Bernard P. Grenfell and Arthur S. Hunt in a series of excavations between 1896 and 1907. Unearthed under mounds of ancient rubbish near the ruins of the Roman city of Oxyrhynchus were thousands of such discarded papyri, ordinary documents, wills, deeds, letters and records of sale. Also discovered, though much less abundant, were remnants of classical literature such as plays by Menander and Euclid's *Elements.*

The realization that some of these Thomas sayings survived, not only in Coptic but also in Greek, helped scholars compare the documents for clues as to the gospel's meaning and what it suggested about its original language of composition. Although these earlier fragments were dated to between 200 CE and 250 CE, at least a hundred years earlier, it could not be determined conclusively which of these texts, the Greek or the Coptic, were more dependably authentic.

Past and present status

The history of this gospel is rather obscure. Some early Church Fathers made references to it, not in admiration but mainly to point out how peculiar it was. Such men as Origen of Alexandria, Hippolytus of Rome, and Eusebius of Caesarea alluded to it in their writings and histories of the emerging Church. Sometimes they associated it with heresies while referring to it as spurious and untrustworthy. Like other non-canonical works of that time, the Gospel of Thomas presented, in their minds at least, a Jesus who espoused unorthodox and unconventional teachings. Not surprisingly, it was judged inferior to the four gospels of the New Testament, and its use was discouraged. Eventually, all such writings were denounced, and Thomas was lost to history until its reappearance in 1945.

In contrast to the tendency of the gospels of Matthew, Mark, Luke, and John to comment on their sayings, in Thomas there are no commentaries or explanations, just the bare sayings. They are what scholars refer to as *logoi sophon,* or wisdom sayings, in the tradition of the Old Testament book of Proverbs. Thomas has almost no narrative, no background stories, no miracles, no crucifixion, and no resurrection. Its sayings were designed not to tell a story, as remarkable as that story obviously was, but solely to help the reader acquire spiritual awareness. Except for frequent catchword connections devised, it is thought, to aid in memorization, the sayings appear to lack any recognizable order. It is as if someone simply wrote them down haphazardly as Jesus spoke. That, of course, is what its prologue says Thomas did, Thomas being the ostensible compiler of the sayings. However, the truth is almost certainly more complicated than that. Collections of this sort were generally assembled over a period of time from various individuals or sources. Nevertheless, it is impossible to date the composition of this work with any certainty.

Some scholars—notably Stephen J. Patterson, Stevan Davies, and the late Helmut Koester—have suggested that the Gospel of Thomas dates from a time that preceded the four gospels or from the same span of years in which they were produced. They base this on a range of reasons. In his book *What Are They Saying About the Gospel of Thomas?*, Christopher W. Skinner writes a summation of the arguments of Helmut Koester for an early and independent dating of Thomas:

> First, Koester argues that Thomas and the sayings source Q are two examples of the earliest genre of Christian literature. Both documents consist of a list of sayings without a discernible logic, and both show evidence of an underlying wisdom gospel that was likely transmitted orally. Second, Thomas lacks a narrative structure and many of the overtly apocalyptic elements that are present in the canonical Gospels. Thus, Thomas is not interested in a future eschatology—a later development in Christian reflection and theologizing—but in providing the reader with a theological perspective rooted in the present. This observation is related to a third point: Koester believes that Thomas has an esoteric and undeveloped theology unlike what we see in the New Testament and in Christian and Gnostic texts from the second century. These three arguments support Koester's analysis of the text of Thomas, where he concludes that Thomas contains many sayings that appear to be more primitive versions of sayings that also appear in the synoptic Gospels.[3]

In response to these arguments, however, there are many scholars who maintain that the author or authors of Thomas borrowed half of its sayings from the New Testament and either invented the other sayings, borrowed them from unknown sources, or presented sayings that were possibly authentic but unfamiliar and unconventional. Scholars who agree with this general assessment are Mark Goodacre, Simon J. Gathercole, and

N. T. Wright. Additionally, some commentators have argued that in Thomas there are words and passages that are reminiscent of second-century Gnostic themes. Saying 50 is a prime example, with its references to the "elect" being questioned by a mysterious "they." This is similar to some so-called Gnostic descriptions of what is called the "ascent of souls" through the "spheres of the heavens." In such scenarios, these souls are interrogated by heavenly powers and expected to know passwords that allow them passage to higher realms. Some scholars further argue that it is significant that this gospel was discovered among a collection containing many other Gnostic works. Nevertheless, the view among most scholars in recent years is that the Gospel of Thomas is not Gnostic with a capital "G" or in the usual sense of the word. (See my commentary on the prologue and saying 50.) As for my own position, such questions of dating and dependence are not the focus of this book, and although I favor an early dating, I will not directly argue that point. It should be apparent, however, that my arguments for a non-dualistic Thomas find more support in the supposition of an early and independent origin. It appears unlikely that the non-dualistic perspective that we find in this gospel was attached at a later date to sayings that originated with Jesus, as many surely did. In fact, that perspective is fundamental to their understanding. I have in mind such sayings as 66 and 113.

My purpose in writing this book is not to date Thomas or "place" it within a historical setting. That examination is important, of course, but premature. First, I want to know what this curious gospel means. Without assuming anything about its author or anything about its relationship to the Bible, I want to know what the Jesus of this gospel considers important. My interest is focused on probing it for meaning. To my readers, I would caution you likewise to remain neutral about this particular Jesus. If, in response to a saying, you should say, "Jesus would never have said something like that," remind yourself that the Jesus of this gospel is not the Jesus of Matthew, Mark, Luke, or John. Sometimes he seems to be the same man; other times he appears quite distinct. Therefore, I advise you to suspend such judgments and approach this man as if you knew nothing about him. In this book, I make no claims as to who he is, whether he is the true, the authentic, Jesus or not. I leave that for others to argue. I do propose, however, that the Jesus of this gospel has a message and a unique point of view that is both internally consistent and deeply compelling. For that reason, I urge the reader to listen closely to his voice as it rises from these pages and test its truth. Or, as this Jesus would say, you should share his "yoke" (saying 90) and, as much as possible, allow the "hidden things" to be revealed (108).

Non-dualism

My first encounter with the Gospel of Thomas was in 1983, when I read an article by Stevan Davies in the journal *The Biblical Archaeologist*, entitled "Thomas: The Fourth Synoptic Gospel." I was fascinated by the possibility that this unfamiliar gospel might reveal new clues about Jesus and his teachings. But more than that, I was intrigued that some of the sayings appeared to reflect the philosophy of non-dualism. Was it possible, I asked myself, that the difficulty most readers have had with this gospel was due not only to its deliberate abstruseness, but also because most people were simply unfamiliar with this philosophy?

What is non-dualism? Non-dualism is the recognition that separation of any kind is unreal and that behind all illusions of duality is the fundamental truth of oneness. However, there is no single definition that is accepted by everyone. Moreover, trying to define non-dualism with words is nearly impossible. Oneness can only be experienced on the level of choiceless awareness. This is so because the intellect that attempts to capture this phenomenon in words, according to this philosophy, is, in itself, an illusion. The awareness of oneness, in fact, is more acute when the mind is quiet, when the intellect is profoundly still. In this way, the ego-mind, that part of the mind that judges and evaluates, recognizes its limitations. This, of course, is a rather insulting notion for the ego to accept and for the intellect to acknowledge. Yet, for the reader to understand the arguments that I propose in this book, this idea must be appreciated. Here, we use the intellect merely to suggest this point, that the ultimate character of man's being is ineffable. It is beyond words and concepts. It must be experienced on a deeper level. Man's task then, as this gospel intimates, is to prepare the soil of the mind and the loam of the heart for the seeds of this awareness.

My curiosity was particularly aroused when I read from Thomas the following saying:

> (22) Jesus saw infants being suckled. He said to his disciples, "These infants being suckled are like those who enter the Kingdom." They said to him, "Shall we then, as infants, enter the Kingdom?" Jesus said to them, "When you make the two one, and when you make the inside like the outside and the outside like the inside, and the above like the below, and when you make the male and the female one and the same, so that the male not be male nor the female female; and when you fashion eyes in the place of an eye, and a hand in place of a hand, and a foot in place of a foot, and a likeness in place of a likeness; then will you enter the Kingdom."

Reading this, I was immediately struck by its resemblance to certain traditions native to India and the Far East. This passage from Thomas reminded me of the non-dualist philosophy of Advaita Vedanta, a school of Hinduism, and, in a broader way, of the teachings of Buddhism and Taoism. Yet, I saw no cause-and-effect significance to this resemblance. That is to say, I was not aware of any convincing evidence that the Jesus of this gospel was a Buddhist or Taoist or indeed had any knowledge of these traditions. However, my growing knowledge of non-dualism compelled me to realize that something profoundly divergent was going on in this saying that could not be explained without reference to this philosophy. Here in saying 22, the two are made one, and the fundamental dualities of nature are utterly extinguished. In fact, these differences are nullified to such an extent that it is insufficient to refer to this singularity, as some commentators have, as a merging of the two. In such a merge, qualities are mixed together, but the result remains a mix, a combination of two qualities. Even an amalgam or alloy can be reduced to its component elements. Moreover, how does one merge inside and outside or above and below? No, what is suggested here is that to enter the Kingdom (of the Father) one must fully accept the idea that anything outside of oneness is meaningless, that duality itself is meaningless. If that is true, if Jesus is indeed stating the non-dualist proposition that to enter the Kingdom, to be enlightened, one must understand that oneness is the fundamental reality of everything, then separation itself must be meaningless and, therefore, an illusion. As strange as this may seem, this is what non-dualism, in its most consistent expression, proposes and what this gospel appears to support. Indeed, 22 may be considered almost a dictionary definition of non-dualism.

Having made this connection between saying 22 and non-dualism, I wondered if I could detect additional evidence in Thomas of this worldview of oneness, for that is what it is. It is not just a philosophy but a comprehensive alignment of the mind with oneness. With this understanding, I have analyzed each of the 114 sayings and discovered that, when exposed to the light of non-dualism, most of what seems impenetrably obscure not only becomes accessible to reason but powerfully insightful. Contrary to what some commentators have concluded, I believe that the Gospel of Thomas is not incomprehensible. Within its shaded interior are strong clues and distinct patterns that point to an understanding of life that, though unconventional, is nevertheless coherent and meaningful. It is like a picture puzzle that when purchased lies in pieces. But when someone who loves puzzles finds a way to connect all the pieces, something beautiful can appear. What distinguishes this from other books on Thomas is the recognition that within this assemblage of seemingly random and nonsensical segments, there are patterns to be found that, when carefully studied and compared, reveal an impression that is shockingly profound yet instinctively recognizable. One can spend a lifetime studying the shape of each piece of a puzzle and get lost in the minutia of it all, failing to see the forest for the trees. But sometimes it takes someone with a literary eye to see this forest while others see only individual trees. This is why my literary analysis of this gospel is justified.

Comprehending the incomprehensible

I ask the readers of this book to maintain an open mind. Non-dualism is not an easy concept to understand. Therefore, I will attempt to explain it as simply as possible. Non-dualism denies that separation is real, and in spite of what the five senses *appear* to report to the brain, distinct objects of perception do not truly exist. This applies to everything perceived in the world. Even space and time are expressions of separation, and therefore, illusory. This, of course, sounds insane. It seems that only a dysfunctional mind could conceive of such a thing. But wait a minute, perhaps there is something dysfunctional about the way minds perceive the world. Perhaps there is something within our minds that purposely distorts or invents perceptions that are simply not real. Present-day psychologists generally agree that there is such a component of ordinary thinking. They call it the ego. It is the controller that dictates its own version of the truth in every situation. It is that which reacts, judges, and rules over our understanding of reality. Moreover, it is this ego that proclaims non-duality a joke, an absurd idea, and actually, fears it as a dangerous threat to its existence. That threat is the reason it embraces separation and denies anything that would jeopardize its hold on the mind. Yet the ego is nothing more than a complex of beliefs. In itself, it is really nothing. It is a cloak, if you will, a defensive garment that appears to protect the wearer from physical danger. However, in non-duality, as its advocates understand it, danger is an illusion, as is the body itself. They in fact maintain that there is no danger, only the ego's belief that there is. When these egoic beliefs are challenged, the true, the benevolent, the spiritual nature of man emerges in consciousness. His oneness with his "creator" is remembered and separation is dismissed. In fact, as saying 22 states, to appreciate the Kingdom one must see the inside and the outside as the same. One must understand that everything experienced is not two but one. And to do that, to cross that invisible line of understanding, all that is needed is a change of mind about what is real and what is not.

Non-dualists often describe perception as the projection of the ego upon the blank screen of awareness. They compare it to the projection of a film upon a movie screen. Just as it is absurd to confuse the images of people on a movie screen with real people, it is absurd, they maintain, to confuse the world, as reported by the senses, with reality. The world is merely a projection of the mind upon the screen of awareness and, according to non-dualism, it is nothing more than that. More accurately, it is a projection of that part of the mind that is dominated by the ego. This ego-mind is the source of all fear and self-loathing, and it projects these attack thoughts outward to further justify their reality. Consequently, when these thoughts are projected outward, the world is seen as a place in which everything is insecure, attack is natural, defense is wisdom, and nothing escapes the inevitable march to death.

As for awareness, in the view of non-dualists, it is a state in which nothing actually happens. When it is free of distracting thoughts and impressions, it consumes the ego not by doing anything, not by attacking error, but in allowing the light of truth to shine it away. Thus, in this peaceful and natural way, mistakes are corrected and illusions are dispelled. In the context of this gospel in which God is affectionately referred to as the "Father," what remains is the naked awareness that God is a loving God, and that man is not separate from Him but an extension of Him. From this non-dualist perspective, nothing is ever born, nothing suffers, and nothing ever dies. Like his Father, man is eternal and divine. From this viewpoint, separation is folly. It is a foolish dream and nothing more than that. In this gospel, Jesus never uses the word "dream," although he suggests this idea in numerous ways. In saying 28, he hints that he awakened to a fresh perspective; he "stood to my (his) feet," as if after sleeping, and found his fellow man intoxicated, blind, and empty.

In this way of looking at life, man is never separate from God and, therefore, loss of any kind is impossible. When he awakens from his dream of separation, he will thus know his identity as a child of God (3b). To be clear, however, there are many descriptions and interpretations of non-dualism. This is just one of them. Nevertheless, this is one perspective that explains quite well the "hidden" mysteries in Thomas. I am convinced that this particular key, this frame, this way of looking, when applied to this gospel, brings light to these sayings instead of more darkness.

The Gospel of Thomas views the world as an impossible idea. In saying 56, Jesus calls the world a "corpse," something dead. It is not something that once was alive and is now dead but something that, in its very essence, is dead. To a non-dualist, the world is a manifestation of the belief in separation. This is why it is dead; it is unreal. There is no meaning in the push and pull we call everyday life. Yet, to a mind that sleeps and dreams of separation, the world appears very real. Therefore, anything seen on the screen of awareness that even hints of separation should be understood in this way. In contrast, the realm of the "Kingdom" is a place of life. Those who "live from the living one," according to the Jesus of this gospel, are immortal (11a and 111). For mystics who seek, above all else, union with the divine, indifference to the push and pull of everyday life is a precondition of waking up. In this gospel, Jesus reveals himself to be a mystic. He is the "bridegroom" who, among others, finds his oneness in the "bridal chamber" of the Kingdom (104). He is the ultimate mystic who, having found the "bubbling spring" of truth for himself, measures it out to others, as he does to Thomas in saying 13. This is the non-dualistic theology of this gospel: Man's reality is oneness in spirit with his Source, and everything outside of this oneness is unreal and unworthy of his attention. When he discovers this oneness, he is "astonished" (2), and then, identifying with his Source, he comes to know himself as a child, or extension, of the Father (3).

The particular quality of non-duality in Thomas

I respectfully ask the reader to bear with me a little longer on this subject of non-duality. Important distinctions need to be made. The form or brand of non-duality in Thomas is unique. One cannot simply describe its features in terms of Advaita, Buddhism, *A Course in Miracles,* or any other model. There are clear similarities among all of these expressions, but they are not identical. In Advaita, there are no strict dogmas or universally accepted definitions. Even among individual gurus, there are often subtle differences in their teachings of theory and practice. But for the most part, teachers of this tradition adhere to an understanding that goes back centuries.

The word Advaita in Sanskrit means "not two." Advaita Vedanta denies the fundamental duality of such seeming opposites as body and soul, male and female, good and evil, and heaven and earth. That is to say, it understands the duality of these things to be illusory in and of themselves. What this means is that although man incorrectly perceives duality in the world, both halves of these dualities are manifestations of Brahman, the divine principle and ultimate reality. So, ultimately, such qualities as good and evil both have their roots in the oneness of Brahman and are expressions of that reality. This idea apparently arose from the belief that man could simply not conceive of such basic abstractions out of nothing. Therefore, such ideas must have originated in Brahman. Thus, imperfection has its roots in perfection. This appears to present a problem in logic, although I admit that I am not an expert in the fine points of Advaita Vedanta. Furthermore, whether it is logical or not, this appears to be a complicated explanation for what should be simple and straightforward. Anyone may observe that the ego cherishes complication and, therefore, any explanation that can be characterized this way must be, at least, suspect. On the other hand, what must be perfect, that is, Brahman or ultimate reality, must be uncomplicated and clear. That is why clarity and spiritual vision arise in a mind at peace and in a state of choiceless awareness. Another way of saying this is that within the dream of separation everything is complicated, nothing is clear. Awareness of the truth is found only within the Kingdom of the Father in which there are no complications or contradictions.

There are no sayings in Thomas that appear to support this particular component of Advaita philosophy, that within perfection, imperfection can arise. Saying 29 says in part that "if the flesh came into being because of spirit, it is amazing." It is amazing, or incredulous, in the sense that it denies the principle that from perfection only perfection can arise. If this is true, then ultimate reality, which must be perfect to be divine, could hardly be the source of anything that is limited, mortal, or imperfect. If it did, it would not be perfect. It would harbor within it the seeds of imperfection. Therefore, as an aid in making sense of the non-duality in Thomas, I am inclined to favor the less complicated and more consistent understanding of non-duality elaborated in *A Course in Miracles.* That is to say, as spirit, man is perfect and merely dreams of imperfection. His only task then is to wake up from this dream and realize his absolute perfection. I base this preference mainly on saying 29 and the lack of any contrary evidence in this gospel.

In Buddhism, particularly in Zen, the tendency is to stress the idea of no-mind, a mental state in which the mind is not conscious of itself. The Gospel of Thomas, on the other hand, seems to stress the Platonic notion of a split mind, the two parts being the divine mind and what might be called the ego-mind, represented by the lion in saying 7. The divine part in Thomas appears to be whole, true, and shared with God and all of creation. The lion-mind or ego-mind is the part that believes the ego's lies. Its seeming power and significance is evident only to the extent that the whole mind is willing to surrender power and significance to it. Nevertheless, the seeming difference between no-mind and whole mind is probably rhetorical. In any case, it may not matter, as both appear to be experienced in much the same way. What really matters is not the words used to describe such an experience but the quality of limitless peace and silence found within it.

Some practitioners equate non-dualism with monism, the philosophy that states that everything that exists does so as one. Others have said that monism is a *concept* of oneness; whereas non-dualism is the *experience* of oneness in which all concepts are abandoned, including the concept of oneness. For the purposes of this book, I speak of oneness as both a concept and an experience that defies definition. It is generally the case that people must first understand the concept before they can go beyond it. Consequently, this is a book in which the sayings of this gospel are defined and explored, but also one in which a way out is suggested that extends beyond the sayings to the indescribable reality to which they point.

When I refer to *A Course in Miracles*,[4] I am alluding to that modern spiritual classic of non-dualism that was published in 1976. It presents an understanding of this philosophy that, in my estimation, is both internally consistent and psychologically sound. It was written by Helen Schucman, a professor of Medical Psychology at Columbia University's College of Physicians and Surgeons in New York City. Aside from her belief that it was not she who wrote the book but Jesus writing through her,[5] it would be hard to find, in either an ancient or modern work, a more accessible and cogent explanation of non-dualism. I have used this book's insights where applicable to explain key concepts such as separation and its roots in fear and guilt. Particularly striking is the resemblance of what these two works have to say about the incompatibility of the two kingdoms or realms of being, the Kingdom of the Father and the realm of the world. In Thomas, this incompatibility is metaphorically portrayed in the parables of absurdity, the wise fisherman (8), the merchant (76), and the lost sheep (107). In each parable, the preferred professional decision is absurd as judged by the world. Similarly, in the world, the spiritual realm of the Kingdom is absurd as judged by the ego. Actually, it works both ways. The two realms of being, the Kingdom of the Father and the kingdom of the world, are incomprehensible to each other. Likewise, in *A Course in Miracles,* there is no communication between the thought systems of the Holy Spirit and the ego. While all of its ideas may not have occurred to the Jesus of this gospel, the sayings in Thomas suggest the same attributes of mature and persuasive metaphysics that *A Course in Miracles* thoroughly explores. Nevertheless, I have not relied on any one description of non-duality to explicate Thomas but have borrowed ideas from a variety of traditions, both old and new.

As mentioned before, my goal in this book is not to imply a causal relationship between Thomas and other non-dualistic teachings but to demonstrate how a coherent philosophy, with all its implications, can bring life to Thomas when everything else fails. This is the "key" that fits the lock. This is what works. And while I generally am opposed to analyzing ancient works in terms of modern ideas, non-dualism is not a modern idea. In India, it was an ancient concept even by the first century CE. The ancient Greeks argued its merits as well, although not precisely in the same way. The Presocratic, Eleatic schools of Parmenides and Zeno, both of Elea, and Melissus of Samos were proponents of non-dualism in the sixth and fifth centuries BCE. Moreover, non-dualism is not a complicated philosophy—radical, yes; challenging, yes; but not complicated. It could appear anywhere without precedent, among men or women of any culture devoted to finding the true nature of their being. Wherever mystics are found, which could be anywhere, some form of non-dualism is practiced. Wherever separation is questioned and silent unity embraced, the key to that experience is non-dualism.

In this book, I have attempted to join the author of this gospel in the place where he is. I have submitted to the reader, as best I could, not only his point of view but also the implications of his teachings. Additionally, some subjective input is essential to allude to what is not of this world but of the spiritual Kingdom. After all, the proof of this Kingdom's existence is not found in the world. It is unavoidably found in the deeply personal experience of it in the mind and nowhere else. Therefore, in writing this book, I quite deliberately chose to present my arguments for a non-dual frame of reference in Thomas fairly but sympathetically. Just as the best and most carefully nuanced books on Zen Buddhism are invariably written by experienced advocates of Zen, so too does non-dualism require a special treatment. It requires someone with a spiritual awareness of the Kingdom, however imperfect, to guide the reader, subjectively as well as objectively, as best he can. The objective discernment of literary patterns in the text must be augmented by a subjective understanding of what is unnamable and beyond the mortal mind to experience and appreciate.

Hidden versus secret

It should be obvious that these sayings are very challenging. They were written in a cryptic style and crafted to be intentionally difficult. They conceal allusions that are "hidden" and implications that require considerable reflection. To emphasize this point, the Coptic word for "hidden" appears many times in Thomas. Yet, most scholars have translated this word as "secret," an acceptable translation. However, it is one that cannot be consistently applied in all instances where the word appears. That translation appears particularly inappropriate in the prologue where the sayings may be described as either "secret" or "hidden." From all the available evidence found *within* this gospel, these sayings were not secret; they were hidden. They were hidden in the sense that they were difficult to understand. But more significantly, they were hidden because in Thomas, the Kingdom is hidden within the mind. This is a recurring theme in this gospel. Yet, since in Thomas, inside and outside are meaningless distinctions, the Kingdom is everywhere (22). So in saying 5, we have:

> Jesus said, "Recognize what is in front of your face, and that which is hidden from you will become plain to you. For there is nothing hidden which will not become manifest."

For those who favor the translation of "secret," it is argued that this was a time in which secrecy and mystery were widespread preoccupations. In the period in which the Gospel of Thomas was written and circulated, secrecy was highly valued particularly among religious factions and those who perceived themselves as exclusively special. However, in contrast, the Gospel of Thomas does not support such exclusiveness. Critics point to sayings 23, 49, and 50 as evidence that Thomas was elitist. In those sayings, the Coptic word for "choose" or "chosen" gives the impression that the followers are special, having been specifically chosen either by Jesus or by God. Indeed, the word "chosen" is sometimes translated as "elect." However, my commentaries on these sayings demonstrate that the focus of sayings 23 and 49, despite their surface appearances, is fixed on the essential wholeness of man's being, not on his specialness in isolation. As for 50, before being "chosen," the disciples had to wake up, the restored translation being "stood to our feet," a code phrase for being enlightened. The implication is that before waking up, they were like anyone else; they were unaware of their spiritual identity. But in choosing to wake up, they were chosen. In the light of non-dualism, the dichotomy of "choose" and "chosen" falls away. In union with God, all forms of separation cease to have meaning.

There is no internal evidence that the Thomas sayings were intended to be kept secret, excluding everyone except for a select few. They are cryptic, but their mystery is not imposed as a bar to anyone. As we shall see, the very idea of specialness, the idea that some people are special and therefore separate from ordinary people, is completely alien to Thomas. In a gospel that teaches the oneness of life, it would be contradictory to deny this oneness by restricting sayings to only a select group of followers. It is, rather, an open invitation to witness the truth to those who are willing to question their basic values and assumptions. Its strangeness arises from its brilliantly conceived metaphors designed to frustrate the conventional understanding of reality while suggesting a spiritual alternative.

In the Gospel of Thomas, the "Kingdom of the Father"[6] is hidden. In its direct application and by the use of synonyms, the concept of hiddenness permeates this gospel, while secrecy does not. There are no winners and losers in Thomas, and anyone who realizes his identity as a child of the Father (3b), who earnestly seeks the Kingdom, will find it. No one is excluded except those who exclude themselves (99). By the use of metaphor and allegory, the Kingdom is compared to the situation in saying 96, in which leaven is *concealed* in dough, and in saying (109), in which treasure is *buried* in a field. More broadly, the Kingdom is hidden in the peculiar behavior of a fisherman (8) who tosses overboard a boatload of small marketable fish in favor of one large but unmarketable fish that he keeps. It is hidden within the strange story (107) of a shepherd who abandons his flock of ninety-nine sheep to search for the one sheep that he wants. When one steps back and looks objectively at all of these allusions to what is hidden in Thomas, it becomes apparent that what is hidden is truth, and where it is hidden is within the mind. In other words, what the Jesus of this gospel is interested in is the treasure of spiritual truth that lies buried within the mind of every man and woman. As I shall show in my commentaries, this is where he points; this is where the treasure lies, and according to the Gospel of Thomas, this is where the focus of man's attention must be. The Kingdom is found not by manipulating the world for whatever reason but in seeking the hidden oneness of spirit that connects all minds with the mind of the "Father." That is where true safety abides, and that is the non-dualistic teaching of this gospel. Throughout the sayings, this theme of one-versus-many represents the primacy of spiritual oneness over separation. In saying 42 (Leipoldt/Schoedel translation), when one comes into being as he passes away, it is the awareness of oneness that comes into being within the mind and the false identification with separation that passes away. Awareness of the Kingdom replaces the illusion of the world.

In Thomas, the Kingdom is not hidden by an angry god or demiurge but fearfully suppressed within the mind by man himself. It is precisely because the Kingdom is so tenaciously hidden that, although present everywhere, man does not see it (113). Nevertheless, as saying 5 states, "There is nothing hidden which will not become manifest." The Gospel of Thomas reveals the truth to those who are willing to open their eyes to it (62). The word "hidden" is mentioned in nine separate sayings in addition to the prologue. Indeed, the thematic importance of this idea in Thomas may explain why the prologue makes special mention of it. One scholar, Marvin Meyer, even speculated that the prologue might provide an earlier version of the title: *The Hidden Sayings of Jesus*, changed later to *The Gospel of Thomas*.[7]

The influence of Plato

In these commentaries, I will describe the "mind" not in the modern sense of the brain being the absolute source of all thoughts, and not necessarily as I understand it myself, but in the Platonic sense in accord with what this Jesus seems to take for granted. The Greek philosopher Plato (427–347 BCE) had an enormous influence on Greek and Roman culture for centuries after his death. In the first century CE, any man who aspired to philosophy would be expected to address how his ideas squared with Plato's. This gospel, of course, never mentions the great philosopher. Yet, this was a time in which interest in Plato had revived. It has been called the Middle Platonism period (first century BCE to the second century CE), and although this Jesus does not appear to subscribe to all of Plato's ideas, and probably never read his works, his conception of the mind has the stamp of Plato all over it. In Plato's *The Republic* (588b–589b), the mind is envisioned as tripartite: in addition to having a spirited part and an appetitive part, it has a higher, immortal part (nous) that is not of the body but divine. This higher part has been compared to the true Self, since it is not directly linked to worldly perception. It represents the part of the mind concerned with truth rather than with appearances. In saying 7, this higher Self is what Jesus calls the "man." In that saying, the man has the potential to consume the "lion." This may be compared to the light of awareness that consumes or shines away the false beliefs of the ego. Or it might be compared, in the Platonic sense, to the "nous," or divine mind dominating or ruling over the two lower parts, the spirited and the appetitive parts. In Thomas, both of these lower parts are represented by the lion. This general idea of a contested mind appears to be the concept that Jesus supports in this gospel.

One cannot assume that Jesus lived in an intellectual bubble and had no contact with men educated in Greek philosophy and contemporary, philosophical trends. This gospel certainly reflects an interest in Platonic ideas and Plato's conception of the divine mind versus lower order thinking. There is also an echo here of Plato's reflections on the contrast between truth and illusion as explored in his allegory of the Cave (*The Republic*, 514a–520a). Among the leading scholars in the field of Thomas studies is Stephen J. Patterson. In 2017, he wrote an impressive, two-part article in the journal *The Fourth R* entitled "Plato's Gospel." Of the dialogues of Plato, Patterson writes, "This is the tradition that animates the more speculative and mysterious sayings of the Gospel of Thomas." Furthermore, he affirms the influence of Plato's ideas in Thomas when he writes, "In the hands of the Middle Platonists, it (the maxim 'know thyself') became an affirmation of the divine element dwelling within each human being. 'Know thyself, that you are divine.'"[8] This Platonic idea is clearly expressed in saying 3b of the Gospel of Thomas. However, while I agree with him that Thomas assumes an appreciation of Platonic ideas, this gospel goes much further than Plato does to delineate an entirely distinct realm of being, a spiritual realm characterized by oneness that Jesus calls the "Kingdom of the Father." Fundamentally, Thomas is non-dualistic. It is concerned with making the "two one," or as Jesus rhetorically says to his disciples in 72, "I am not a divider, am I?" On the other hand, Plato is generally considered dualistic. Plato would have never stated what is promised in saying 111 to the seeker of truth, that the "heavens and the earth will be rolled up in your presence" and that "the one who lives from the living one (God) will not see death" (111). Unlike Plato, this Jesus does not focus his attention on creating a good and just society but on realizing the "roll-up" or end of the false perception of a physical universe. So perhaps instead of calling this Plato's gospel, we might call it the mystic's gospel with Platonic assumptions.

To appreciate the chain of meaning that runs through Thomas, the reader must be patient. No saying alone makes plain the interpretation of the whole. Key principles are buried throughout its rich soil of metaphor and allegory that, with a little attention, rise to the surface. In my commentaries on this gospel, I trace these hidden rhizomes of meaning to reveal and explain the philosophical basis of the work as a whole. Scholars are fond of saying that Thomas either means something or it means nothing. My view is that it means something and that the outlines of this something can be charted. For example, if two sayings are represented on a chart as bisecting lines, the point at which they meet can be understood as that place in each saying in which a common, significant understanding is expressed. That these two sayings intersect at all may be by chance. If a third saying is added to the chart in the same way and if it intersects the other two on precisely the same point of agreement, then the prospect of this being by chance would seem unlikely. As I demonstrate in this book, there are dozens of sayings in Thomas that, in their support of a non-dualistic worldview, intersect at that precise point of agreement. Except for a few sayings that are marginally supportive or not supportive at all (saying 12), most of the sayings in the Gospel of Thomas can be seen as supporting a non-dualistic worldview. This clearly cannot happen by chance.

If one has a key to a room that has never been opened, and that key works to open this room when all other keys have failed, then that key should be retained and not tossed away. Such is the key of non-dualism. Until now, the obscurity of Thomas has prevented readers from entering and appreciating the contents of that wonderful room. But now, its doors can be thrown open, and the light of comprehension can again reveal its long-neglected interior.

Text presentation and orientation

Each of my commentaries is preceded by a translation of a Coptic saying found in the Gospel of Thomas. This is, broadly speaking, the generally accepted or standard translation of the text found at Jabal al-Tarif in 1945. Following this on the page is a translation, where available, of the same saying in Greek from the earlier Oxyrhynchus find. Of the first thirty-nine Coptic sayings plus the prologue, twenty of these have Greek versions from the Oxyrhynchus fragments. Some, however, are either so incomplete or so nearly identical to the Coptic versions—saying 1, for example—that I have not included them among the introductory translations. Consequently, I have selected ten sayings (plus the prologue), translated from the Greek fragments, to contrast with their Coptic equivalents. For the remainder of the book, I present only the Coptic translations. For further contrast, I have included one version of saying 2 from the writings of Clement of Alexandria and an occasional quote from the synoptic gospels.

In addition to these translations, I have included, where applicable, literal translations of certain words and passages based on the interlineal translations of Michael W. Grondin and the late Thomas Paterson Brown to whom I am immensely grateful. Also, in some cases, I have presented my own, restored versions of the sayings, which are always intended as suggestions rather than as established facts. I use the word "restored" in the sense that it restores, as well as I am able, a word or phrase to a saying that appears to have been changed or omitted by a scribe in antiquity. One can trace these scribal intrusions throughout the text and see that they repeatedly assume the function of correcting a view of Jesus that was deemed too ordinary, too human, or perhaps not as exalted from the perspective of an orthodox-leaning scribe. There are other reasons for restoring a saying as well. Complicated sayings tend to degrade, becoming, in the hands of scribes, even more complicated over time. Hence, mistakes are not only repeated, but because the sayings are misunderstood, rather drastic "corrections" are made to make sense of them. An example is saying 30, in which a statement about the primacy of oneness (one over two or three) in the Greek version devolves over time into a plug for the Trinity, of "three gods," in the Coptic. In addition, some modern translators have a tendency to translate a word as it might be translated in the Biblical version of the same saying. Sometimes that works; sometimes an equivalent word works better. Thus, what appear to be scribal errors, or more often, scribal intrusions, are detected and, where possible, repaired. This is always a risky business, but I believe that my suggestions regarding restored sayings are reasonable and hopefully helpful.

Language, being a form of communication that depends on symbols, always fails to convey accurately that which is spoken of or written about. This is because symbols are not the things themselves. In the non-dualistic realm of the Kingdom, language fails utterly, and virtually nothing can be described. Even God Himself is lost in the effort to translate the ineffable into what can be grasped by the human mind. So we call God "Him," though He is not a male, a female, or a thing. Still, we must use the familiar literary conventions in order to be understood at all. So, with this in mind, and for the sake of clarity, I have referred to God generically as "He" and "Him." Likewise, "man," meaning humankind, is also by convention consigned a generic "he" and "him," though "she" and "her" would be just as appropriate. Remember, however, that in non-duality, there is no male and no female.

In both the Greek and the Coptic versions of Thomas, there are lacunae or gaps in the text where translators have attempted, where possible, to suggest a word or phrase for that which is missing. Sometimes, the parallel saying in the Bible provides the likely restoration, but sometimes not. With such considerations as the context and the precise number of letters needed to fill the gaps, scholars have done their best to identify the missing words. It should be mentioned, however, that these are always just best judgments, not facts. In earlier drafts of this book, I had displayed these gaps, particularly in the case of the Greek Oxyrhynchus version where the three papyrus fragments were extremely fragile and damaged. Consequently, some sayings would have so many ellipses, pointed and square brackets, that the average readers to whom I showed my copy were, from my point of view, needlessly confused. I therefore decided to present these texts in my book without this added difficulty. As for the Coptic text, I retain these marks when necessary. Nevertheless, I encourage those who are interested to examine the Oxyrhinchus translations on the internet and draw their own conclusions.

Symbols

( ) Parentheses enclose a word or phrase not in the manuscript but suggested by the translator or commentator to clarify or inform.

< > Pointed brackets enclose an element implied in the saying but supplied by the translator.

[ ] Square brackets indicate a lacuna or break in the text or material that is uncertain.

{ } Braces indicate a nonessential word or letter added by a scribe.

---

1 A codex (singular) is an assemblage of manuscript pages stitched together to make the earliest form of a book. Although such books were written on papyrus, they replaced, by this time, the use of papyrus scrolls.

2 This refers to discarded papyrus used to thicken and strengthen the leather covers of each codex.

3 Christopher W. Skinner, *What Are They Saying About the Gospel of Thomas?* (New York/Mahwah, NJ: Paulist Press, 2012), 35–36.

4 Foundation for Inner Peace, *A Course in Miracles*, 2nd edn. (New York, Viking, 1996).

5 It is interesting to note that in the words of this "Jesus:" T-6.I.15.2, he denies he ever said, "I came not to bring peace but a sword," a quote from Matthew 10:34. The Thomas version (16) quotes Jesus as saying that he will cast "fire, sword, and war" upon the earth. Since this general idea of bringing or casting a sword upon the world is attested to in both gospels, the evidence is quite strong that Jesus did indeed say something like this. The task at hand, then, is to determine what he meant by it.

6 The Thomas version of the Biblical "Kingdom of God."

7 Marvin Meyer, *The Gospel of Thomas, The Hidden Sayings of Jesus* (San Francisco: Harper, 1992), 67.

8 Stephen Patterson, "Plato's Gospel, part 1," *The Fourth R 30*, no. 1 (January–February 2017): 5–6, 21–24; Patterson, "Plato's Gospel, part 2," *The Fourth R 30*, no. 2 (March–April 2017): 5–10, 24–25.

Text and Commentary

Prologue

(P) "These are the hidden sayings that the living Jesus spoke and that Didymos Judas Thomas wrote down." (Coptic version)

(P) "These are the hidden sayings that the living Jesus spoke and that Judas, who is also Thomas, wrote." (Greek Oxyrhynchus version)

It was not uncommon in ancient times for a body of work, whether Greek or Roman, to have a prologue which briefly explained the material that followed. This particular prologue is brief, although it conveys a significant amount of information.

Above, we have two translations, the Coptic and the Greek. In the first line of both, we have a word that is generally translated as "secret," despite the fact that it is commonly translated as "hidden" where it appears elsewhere in the Coptic version. Some commentators have made the point that "secret" is appropriate here because its use reinforces their position that this is a Gnostic gospel. Strictly speaking, however, it is not a Gnostic gospel. The Gospel of Thomas does not share the same interest in cosmology and ritual as do the so-called Gnostic texts. For example, in Thomas, there are no upper or lower aeons, secret hand-signs, evil archons, mystery rites, etc. In Greek, the word "gnosis" means "knowledge," and indeed, it can be said that Thomas is gnostic with a small "g." Thus, by *knowing* the truth of his oneness with God, man will understand his true nature. This is an idea repeatedly found in this gospel. But what is not found is any evidence that the Gospel of Thomas fits neatly into this wide-ranging and probably later development of the Jesus movement.

Why in this prologue is Jesus called the "living Jesus?" There is no clear evidence regarding this. It may refer either to Jesus before his death or, as some commentators have proposed, to Jesus after his resurrection. It may refer to Jesus as living because he lived in the minds of those who took his words to heart and embraced his wisdom. It seems more likely, however, that the writer of the prologue mistook the "Living One" in sayings 59 and 111 as referring to Jesus. The "Living One" in those sayings, however, almost certainly refers to the "Father" (God), not to Jesus. (See my commentary on saying 59.)

This brings us to another question: who wrote this prologue? It was evidently not authored by Jesus or even by Thomas, since it refers to both men in the third person. Its author is unknown. Whoever it was, he or she seems to have had some reason to think that Thomas was the compiler of this collection of Jesus sayings. Specifically, he identifies Thomas in the Coptic version as Didymos Judas Thomas. "Didymos" is the Greek word for "twin," just as "Thomas" is the Aramaic word for "twin." The man's name was Judas, although his nickname was apparently "the twin." Presumably, the word was repeated in Greek and Aramaic forms to clarify his identity among those familiar with one designation but not the other. Compared to other explanations for this duplication, this seems the most likely. The name of Thomas, of course, is recognizable from the New Testament gospels, particularly in John where there is mention of the Apostle "Thomas called Didymus" (John 11:16, 20:24, 21:2).

There is another voice in this gospel, that of the narrator. The narrator may, in fact, have been the same individual who wrote the prologue. It is impossible to say. His function is to make these sayings accessible to the reader. He is the one who introduces most of the sayings with "Jesus said."

Lastly, some commentators have made the point that since half of these sayings were previously unknown, it is therefore reasonable to conclude that someone other than Jesus was the author of this gospel. This unidentified writer, they propose, borrowed half of the sayings from the synoptic gospels, slightly altered some of them, and came up with the rest somewhere else. He is the one, they argue, who should be considered the "author" of the Gospel of Thomas. That being the case, they further argue that the prologue should be considered the work of this unknown author (or authors). This last assumption is significant because it means that, if he wrote both the prologue and the sayings, the phrase "living Jesus" might indeed identify Jesus as the "Living One" found later in sayings 59 and 111. As the author of both, he would certainly know to whom this phrase referred. However, this appears to be a rather complicated explanation. We should instead appeal to Occam's razor, which maintains that "among competing hypotheses, the one with the fewest assumptions should be selected." The explanation with the least assumptions is that the Gospel of Thomas is precisely what the prologue says it is—a collection of Jesus sayings that begins where the prologue ends. Whether or not all of these sayings are authentic is another matter. The least complicated explanation for the prologue is that it was written to identify the author as Jesus and the compiler as Thomas. Nevertheless, this introduction to the sayings may have been composed in the early days of the Jesus movement or many years later. That question remains unanswered.

Saying 1

> **(1) And he said, "Whoever finds the interpretation of these sayings will not taste death."**

It appears that no one knows precisely where the prologue ends and saying 1 begins. Many scholars have questioned the conventional practice of enumerating this saying as saying 1, rather than seeing it as an extension of the prologue. They have argued that "he" in this saying more likely refers to Thomas than to the usual candidate, Jesus. Indeed, it seems peculiar that a set of sayings, presumably collected by Thomas, would be introduced by Jesus himself. If, however, this collection existed as a written composition during Jesus's lifetime, it is not impossible that he also composed this introduction. In any case, we may never know who wrote this line, whether it was Jesus, Thomas, or someone else.

This brief introduction establishes the idea that the sayings of this gospel need to be interpreted. There indeed is nothing straightforward about them. They were composed mostly in a cryptic style. Their meaning is hidden like a treasure in a field, and like the field of saying 109, each saying must be plowed and carefully turned over before the treasure is revealed. Thomas is like an intricate and obscure poem. Each word and phrase must be weighed and measured in the context of the gospel as a whole. What makes these sayings particularly difficult is their use of highly metaphorical terms and strange allusions. And although the language seems incomprehensible at times, there is an allure about this gospel that is undeniable. Indeed, many commentators have expressed a fascination with Thomas while admitting that, for them, some of its sayings make no sense at all.

Perhaps the most confounding assertion found anywhere in Thomas is the one about death that we find here—that if one finds the hidden meaning of these sayings, he "will not taste death." The significance of this line has been much debated by scholars, without consensus. It would seem that if the author had literally meant that whoever unlocked the meaning of these sayings would live forever, he would have said so unambiguously. He says instead that he who finds it will not "taste" death. The implication is that he will consume death but not taste it. Some maintain that this is simply a colorful choice of words. In Thomas, however, words are notably lean and stark. There is little color in this gospel and few flourishes. An alternative way of looking at this is that man will eventually shed his body, as a thing no longer needed, but not taste death or experience death as the termination of anything real or significant.

Such expressions, as found in this introduction, reveal the non-dualistic character of this gospel. In that view, man is created as spirit, yet mistakenly believes himself to be flesh. Throughout his life, he will live as a body and eventually set it aside. But a body, this philosophy maintains, is not what he is. If he identifies with the body, he will experience its pain, its decay, and its death. However, if he can shake off this attachment to it and wake up to his true identity as spirit, everything in his experience will reflect that decision. He will not suffer loss or "taste" the bitterness of death. At the end of his days, his body will seem like the skin of a molting serpent. He will slough it off and be glad that something inessential to his being is gone.

I will have more to say about this philosophy in later commentaries. Suffice it to say that for now the interpretation of these sayings points clearly to an understanding in which the physical world is seen as a corpse-like realm (see saying 56) and not man's true home. If the reader of these sayings is faithful to this understanding, he will experience life in all its astonishing fullness; if not, he will "taste" death in all its various forms. That essentially is the premise of these sayings. For more on what it means in Thomas to taste or see death, see my commentaries on sayings 18, 19, 85, and 111.

Saying 2

> **(2) Jesus said, "Let him who seeks not cease seeking until he finds. When he finds, he will become troubled. When he becomes troubled, he will be astonished, and he will reign over the all." (Coptic version)**

> **(2)** Jesus says, "Let the one seeking not stop seeking until he finds. And when he finds, he will be astonished, and being astonished, he will reign and reigning, he will rest." (Greek Oxyrhynchus version)

> **(2)** *"He who seeks will not cease until he finds, and finding he will marvel, and having marveled he will reign, and having reigned he will rest." (Clement of Alexandria, Stromata, 2.9.45 and 5.14.96)*[1]

The "seeker" of this saying seeks truth—not relative truth, but the fundamental truth of his being. It is only this that could account for the profound experiences that follow from his search. It is only in this quest for ultimate truth that the Jesus of this gospel appears interested.

I have cited three versions of this saying, the standard Coptic translation from the Nag Hammadi codex, the Greek Oxyrhynchus translation, and a version written by Clement of Alexandria from his Stromata, circa 198–203 CE. In all three, the relentless search for the truth results in finding. In the Coptic translation, there is something unsettling about this discovery. The seeker is "troubled." This only happens here. The other versions omit this word and proceed directly on to "be astonished" or "marvel." This omission of the word "troubled" in the earlier constructions does not necessarily mean that it is not authentic or original to this saying. Indeed, if the seeker is not quite ready to have his ego thoroughly challenged by truth, he might be drawn into fear and temporarily troubled. Nevertheless, when the truth is found—unambiguously found, as it apparently is here—one would expect a more immediate and overwhelming consequence, which is astonishment.

In this saying, Jesus describes what happens as a result of conclusively finding the Kingdom, which in this gospel is equivalent to finding a treasure. It is a glorious, life-changing experience. All struggles are left behind, and in one brilliant breakthrough, what previously seemed unimaginable is found. Its effect is astonishment comparable to nothing ever experienced in the realm of the world (17). After such a revelation, there is no going back and no room for doubt. Some translators of both the Coptic and the Greek have used the word "marvel" instead of "be astonished." This is an acceptable translation, but it is too weak in this context. The implication of the following saying (3) is that the seeker is fundamentally mistaken about who he thinks he is. In that state of not knowing, he "dwells in poverty." So when his true identity as a child of God is revealed to him, he will not merely marvel; he will be utterly astonished. Here, in saying 2, the same extraordinary benediction is the result of faithfully seeking.

After being astonished, all three versions maintain that the seeker then reigns. In the Coptic construction, he reigns over "the all," also translated as "everything." Reigning suggests a force of power over something. This power is specifically alluded to in saying 106 where, metaphorically, it moves a "mountain." The implication of that saying is that this power is spiritual, and its function is to deny reality to the world of limitations, represented by a "mountain." Unlike worldly power, spiritual power, as understood by non-dualists, does not force, suppress, or manipulate. It does nothing. It simply reveals the truth that the world has no real power. Then, only when this is recognized, when the limitations of the world are laid aside, is complete rest possible.

The final stage, then, is "rest." It is not found in the Coptic version but would seem to follow naturally from "reign." To rest in this ultimate sense is to be so certain of one's identity as a child of God (3b), and so clear about one's freedom from the world of struggle and limitation, that nothing can disturb its peace.

The seeker of truth does not seek what the ego seeks. The ego seeks ways to make separation the overriding rule of its domain. Within its world of separation, it strives to optimize pleasure and avoid pain, though often confusing one for the other. The ego changes and rearranges the world in defense of what it perceives as threats to its existence. In contrast, the seeker of truth seeks by aligning himself with what is peaceful, joyful, and loving. He seeks by joining rather than by erecting barriers to joining. To help him see, he has a light, the light of truth (24). This light shines away the darkness like a laser cutting through the fog of the ego. The only cure for darkness is light, but the darkness of fear and guilt must first surrender to the light to allow it to penetrate every dark and hidden corner of the mind. When the ego is sufficiently weakened to permit this to happen, oneness and clarity are gradually restored to consciousness. Then finally, when the last vestiges of ego are consumed by the light, something astonishing is found. It goes by different names: the truth, the bubbling spring of living water, or the Kingdom.

---

1 In his comments on this saying, Clement of Alexandria stated that it came from the Gospel of the Hebrews, a lost gospel, unknown except for fragments quoted by later writers. What relationship this gospel had with the Gospel of Thomas is unknown.

Saying 3

> **(3a) Jesus said, "If those who lead you say to you, 'See, the Kingdom is in the sky,' then the birds of the sky will go before you. If they say to you, 'It is in the sea,' then the fish will go before you. Rather, the Kingdom is inside of you, and it is outside of you.**
> **(3b) When you come to know yourselves, then you will become known, and you will realize that it is you who are the Sons of the Living Father. But if you will not know yourselves, you dwell in poverty, and it is you who are that poverty." (Coptic version)**

> **(3a)** Jesus said, "If those pulling you say to you, 'Look, the Kingdom is in the sky,' the birds of the sky will go before you. Or if they should say that it is under the ground, the fish of the sea will precede you. The Kingdom of [God] is within you and outside you.
> **(3b)** Whoever knows himself will find this (the Kingdom), and when you know yourselves, you will know that you are Children of the Living Father. If however you will not know yourselves, you are in poverty, and you are the poverty." (Greek Oxyrhynchus version)

Just as saying 2 describes what happens when one seeks and finds (one is astonished, rules, and rests), this saying describes where it happens (inside of you and outside of you), and how it happens (by knowing yourself). One has the feeling that if these two sayings could be fully understood and applied, all the other sayings in this collection would likewise be understood. Indeed, Jesus appears to offer here a road map as to where he intends to take his listeners.

In 3a, the phrase "those who lead you" can be taken narrowly or broadly. It can refer to the spiritual leaders of the day or to anyone who pulls the seeker in one direction or another. The literal translation of this phrase in the Greek version is "those pulling you." The implication is that these "leaders" are pulling the seeker away from his natural inclinations or insights. They are saying, in effect, that the Kingdom is not here and now; it is out there somewhere, beyond one's reach. They point to the sky and beneath the ground as if to say, "Ignore what you feel within and look outward; your god is a distant god, a remote god, a god who made the world and then withdrew." In his characteristically witty fashion, Jesus points out the absurdity of this idea and says instead, "The Kingdom is inside of you, and it is outside of you."

Two questions then arise: What is the Kingdom, and how can it be both inside and outside? In the Gospel of Thomas, the Kingdom is neither a place nor a future period of time. It is never defined precisely, although its properties are hinted at in sayings that begin: "The Kingdom is like..." From another angle, it is often compared to what it is not like. It is not something treasured by the world, yet is immensely valuable. It is not something separate but distinguished by its quality of oneness. Several times, Jesus says that the Kingdom can be seen only when man makes the "two one." Additionally, it cannot be localized in space and time. In saying 113, Jesus says of it: "It will not come by watching for it. They will not say, 'Here it is' or 'There it is.' Rather, the Kingdom of the Father is spread out upon the earth, and men do not see it." It is not a thing, not a physical thing, so, of course, men cannot see it with their physical eyes. But, in the way that spirit experiences spirit, it can be seen everywhere.

This saying states, "The Kingdom is inside of you, and it is outside of you." In saying 22, Jesus makes the seemingly contradictory point that to enter the Kingdom you must make the "inside like the outside and the outside like the inside." This is another way of saying that to enter the Kingdom of the Father, one must realize that such dualities as inside and outside are meaningless. Indeed, this understanding of dualities is a fundamental teaching of this gospel. That means that the statement here, that the Kingdom is both inside and outside, is not a contradiction. This is simply a way of saying that it is not "here" or not "there" but everywhere. It is a description not meant for enlightened minds who understand the meaninglessness of dualities but for those who are bound by language and temporarily unable to see beyond the limitations of worldly concepts. Likewise, in Luke 17:21, the Kingdom is "within," and seeking it there is legitimate and helpful, but it is also outside in the sense that it is not confined to the body. There is no body. There is no world. That is the hidden truth of this gospel. The fundamental feature of the Kingdom is wholeness in which separation is impossible. What Jesus is suggesting here is that the Kingdom is everywhere because the Kingdom is all there is. It is spiritual, dimensionless, and all-inclusive; and everything else is an illusion. Only in this way can the Kingdom be here and now.

In the Greek Oxyrhynchus version above, 3b can be seen as an expansion and explication of the Kingdom in 3a. In 3b it says, "Whoever knows himself will find this..." The word "this" refers to the "Kingdom" in the previous paragraph (3a). In the Coptic version, this link word is missing, so this connection between the Kingdom and knowing oneself is also missing. Instead, the Coptic 3b has, "When you come to know yourselves, then you will become known..." A dichotomy is introduced here: "know" and "become known," which is somewhat like the previous "inside" and "outside," but in this case, the same word (to know) is presented in both the active and passive voice. The fact that this dichotomous expression does not appear in the earlier Greek version does not necessarily rule out its authenticity. It can be understood as making the same point as was made for "inside" and "outside," and therefore not contradictory to the gospel as a whole. Just as "inside" and "outside" are meaningless dualities within the Kingdom, so are "know" and "become known," the active/passive duality. In the oneness of the Kingdom, there is no doer separate from what is done. In the Kingdom, there is only knowing. So, in this saying to truly know is to know that which is beyond the duality of "know" and "become known."

Despite this difference between the Greek and Coptic texts, both make essentially the same point: "When you know yourselves, you will know that you are Children/Sons of the Living Father." This is an admission that man is fundamentally mistaken about his identity. He believes that he is a child born from other bodies, existing in a world of space and time. But, in fact, he is a child of God, born of spirit. He thinks he is a creature limited by the laws of this world. But, in fact, he is unlimited just as his Father is unlimited. This saying provides further evidence of the mystical, ecstatic quality of this gospel. Here, the physical world as an idea is not supported but farcically dismissed. The Kingdom does not abide in duality but in the realization of oneness.

The saying concludes that "if you will not know yourselves, you dwell in poverty, and it is you who are that poverty." Knowing one's identity is compared to wealth, and not knowing to poverty. This wealth/poverty comparison, of course, does not refer to monetary values. It refers to the presence or absence in the mind of unlimited peace and joy. This is true wealth. Further, it is an experience that must be accepted within the mind on behalf of everyone. In the New Testament, Jesus is presented as the "Son of God," to the seeming exclusion of all others. Here, that identity is shared with all the "Children/Sons of the Living Father." In a sense, everyone is anointed; everyone is a messiah, not just Jesus. Furthermore, everyone is one; the wholeness of creation is the Messiah. To experience such grandeur, one must forgive and release every trace of separation that appears to come between God and all of life. In this awareness of wholeness is found the Kingdom of the Living Father.

Saying 4

> **(4) Jesus said, "The man old in days will not hesitate to ask a small child seven days old about the place of life, and he will live. For many who are first will become last, and they will become one and the same." (Coptic version)**

> **(4)** Jesus said, "A person old of days will not hesitate to ask a child seven of days about the place of life, and he will live. For many of the first will be last and the last will be first, and they will become one." (Greek Oxyrhynchus version)

In this saying, we have an old man and an infant. In the Greek of the Oxyrhynchus version, the man is "old of days" who *without hesitation* will ask a child "seven of days" about the place of life. It is well known that in the culture of the time, elderly men were respected for their knowledge of the world and considered wise in years. It would hardly have seemed likely, in that setting, that such a man would ask an infant about the place of life. Nor would he seek this wisdom from an infant who cannot speak. The situation is absurd. The absurdity is heightened by the man's lack of hesitation. He will not "hesitate" to ask.

This is not the only instance in Thomas where a scenario of absurdity forms the basis of a saying. In the parable of the lost sheep (saying 107), the shepherd abandons his ninety-nine sheep to look for his one lost sheep. When he finds it, he speaks to it and tells the sheep that he wants him more than he does the other ninety-nine. In the parable of the wise fisherman (8), the fisherman, "without difficulty," tosses back into the sea his entire catch of small but marketable fish and keeps one large, unmarketable fish instead. Both actions are absurd, as no shepherd or fisherman could behave this way and remain in business for very long.

To comprehend what Jesus is saying here, the reader must understand the function of absurdity and hyperbole in these sayings and how they relate to the principal themes in Thomas. They dramatically showcase the upside-down world in which man customarily lives. In this so-called real world, the recognition of wholeness and innocence is denied, while the belief that God's children were created to be either first or last is fully accepted. The truth is seen as absurd, while the absurdity is seen as real. In his parables and aphorisms, Jesus playfully casts doubt on this accepted order and offers an alternative to separation and worldly standards of wisdom. That alternative is oneness, represented by the "Kingdom."

There is a suggestion in this saying that the infant is a male child. He is seven days old, and in the Jewish world of that time, a male child would have been circumcised on the eighth day. But, for the Jesus of this gospel, circumcision is a needless and foolish custom (saying 53). And before this foolishness of humankind can touch him, this seven-day-old infant shines in the light of his purity. But more than that, he represents a state of mind in which separation is minimally experienced. His eyes are yet unfocussed on differences, so the child sees his mother as an extension of himself. In 22, Jesus compares infants being suckled to those who enter the Kingdom. Again, the image is one of union with Source. The infant's message to the elder is not conveyed verbally but expressed in his state of innocence and oneness. The message is this: The "place of life" is found in the awareness of unqualified oneness.

The word "place" is often used in Thomas as a code word for the Kingdom or a mind at peace, the place where the Kingdom is experienced. Other examples are sayings 24, 50, 60, 67, 68, and 86. In this saying, the elder wishes to know about the "place of life," that is, about that state of mind where life is fully experienced. The infant represents that state of mind. He is in full contact with it. By aspiring to be as simple as an infant, to abandon the frantic activity of the adult mind and allow the awareness of oneness to be his one goal, the old man "lives." In that awareness, he is brought into contact with his essential Self, his undivided spirit-Self, which is his true identity. He "lives" because God the Father lives. The Father is referred to in sayings 3 and 50 as the "Living Father." Life is associated with divinity throughout these sayings. Likewise, the old man lives because in realizing his oneness with God, he becomes aware of his own divine nature and that of the infant.

The final sentence of the Greek version reads, "For many of the first will be last and the last will be first and they will become one." Although the surface reality of this encounter of the elder with the infant is one of inversion, the roles of teacher and student being reversed, the true reality is that in the awareness of the Kingdom, there is no teacher and student duality. In that awareness, all sense of separation dissolves. That realization knows nothing of teacher and student or infant and elder.

An essential step in the development of that state of mind, however, is the willingness to look beyond the accepted order of the world. "Many of the first" reminds the reader of the many small fish of saying 8 and the many sheep of saying 107, which in both cases were exchanged for the "one." Such inversions remind us that within the Kingdom, the notion of "many" has no meaning. A determined seeker must ignore what "many" do, or "many" think, and look for the truth wherever it is. To that part of the mind dominated by the ego, this will always seem absurd, because the ego knows nothing of oneness and indeed nothing of the Kingdom. To the mind free of the arrogance of the ego, however, the oneness of spirit will always arise in innocence and truth.

Saying 5

> **(5) Jesus said, "Recognize what is in front of your face, and that which is hidden from you will become plain to you. For there is nothing hidden which will not become manifest." (Coptic version)**

> (5) Jesus said, "Know what is in front of your face and that which has been hidden from you will be revealed to you. For there is nothing hidden that will not become clear and nothing buried that will not be raised." (Greek Oxyrhynchus version)

In his book *The Gospel of Thomas, Annotated and Explained*, Stevan Davies comments about this saying, "If what is hidden is the Kingdom, as saying 3 seems to indicate, its location is here in the present world. The Kingdom is everywhere now."[1] Indeed, saying 5 builds on the theme introduced in saying 3, that the Kingdom is not remote and separate but is "inside of you and it is outside of you." Its non-dual presence is not separate but intimately a part of the one who seeks it. It is "in front of your face." It is there to be recognized and known. This saying does not claim that it is there sometimes or there under the right circumstances, but simply that it is there. It is always there. If such is the case, then how can it be "hidden?" The paradox is that the Kingdom is both in front of your face and hidden. The answer to that riddle is that it cannot be hidden, except by the individual who refuses to look at it. By this refusal, he hides it from his own eyes. He buries it within his mind in a fearful scurry of denial.

This refusal to recognize what is "in front of your face" is echoed in saying 51: "What you look forward to has already come, but you do not recognize it." It is also referenced in sayings 37 and 91. In 113, it says, "The Kingdom of the Father is spread out upon the earth, and men do not see it." This gospel does not say anywhere that the Kingdom can be acquired by praying for it, by fasting for it, or by earning it through deeds of public charity. All of these pious practices deny that the Kingdom is already present and that nothing else is needed. As this gospel sees it, the Kingdom is an ever-present treasure and a refuge—beyond location, beyond time, and beyond thought entirely. Between one thought and the next, it is present. Between all efforts to see it elsewhere, it is here and now.

The earlier Greek version of this saying has an additional phrase: "...and nothing buried that will not be raised." The final word, lost in a gap in the text, is generally assumed to be "raised." Further support for this restoration comes from a linen burial shroud, also from Oxyrhynchus, dated to the fifth or sixth century, on which is written: "Jesus said, 'Nothing is buried, which will not be raised.'" Although the words "buried" and "raised" imply a physical resurrection, their presence in this saying suggests something else. It suggests that even though the truth seems dead, it is not dead; it merely lies within a mind asleep. When that mind awakens to the fact that the Kingdom is always present, the truth is "raised" to consciousness, and then it "recognizes" its true nature, which is bliss.

---

1 Stevan Davies, The Gospel of Thomas, Annotated & Explained (Woodstock, Vermont: Skylight Paths, 2003), 6.

Saying 6

(6a) His disciples asked him and said to him, "Do you want us to fast? How shall we pray? Shall we give alms? What diet shall we observe?"
(6b) Jesus said, "Do not tell lies, and do not do what you hate, for all things are plain in the sight of heaven.
(6c) For nothing hidden will not become manifest, and nothing covered will remain without being uncovered." (Coptic version)

(6a) His disciples questioned him and said, "How should we fast and how should we pray, and how should we do charitable giving and what will we observe concerning food?"
(6b) Jesus said, "Do not lie and do not do whatever you hate, for before the truth everything has cause to appear.
(6c) For there is nothing hidden that will not become clear." (Greek Oxyrhynchus version)

The Greek version of this saying has significant gaps, and the missing words are restored based partially on the Coptic version. It is clear, however, that there are small but significant differences between these two renderings. In the Coptic, the disciples ask Jesus, "Do you want us to fast?" In the earlier Greek, they assume that fasting is beneficial and ask instead, "*How* should we fast?" In the Coptic version, it is "Shall we give alms?" In the Greek, it is "*How* should we do charitable giving?" The Greek version consistently asks "how" or "what," whereas the Coptic does so only half the time. Because of this consistency in the Greek version, the reply of Jesus is more unexpected. It may even seem that he is evading the question. In the Greek version, the disciples' assumption is that Jesus would not disagree on the basic value of these practices. When his answers imply that he does, the contrast is more pronounced and perhaps more troubling.

In a later saying (14), all four of these pious acts are examined in greater detail. Some scholars believe that 14 was originally the response to 6a and that somehow the two sayings became detached from each other. Although both sayings support each other, this does not exclude the possibility that saying 6, as it appears here, is complete and faithful to the original intention. Actually, sayings 6a, b, and c work well together to advance a compelling message and one that is consistent with the entire gospel. They address the question of pious acts from a broader perspective than what is customarily assumed. The disciples would naturally expect specific answers to their specific questions. When Jesus does not respond so, a silent invitation is advanced to the reader to enter into the conversation. The reader is asked to bridge the space between the questions and his answers, between the dissonance of the dialogue and its resolution.

In Mark 12:28-31, Jesus is asked to identify the greatest or most important commandment. His answer does not include any of the Ten Commandments, as one might expect. He responds instead with a broader and deeper answer, one that goes to the heart of the matter: "Hear, O Israel: The Lord is one. Love the Lord your God with all your heart and with all your soul and with all your mind and with all your strength. This is the first commandment. The second is this: 'Love your neighbor as yourself.'" In the saying at hand, Jesus also goes to the heart of the matter. He passes up the easy answer for one that points out what all four of these practices have in common.

The common link between these practices of fasting, praying, giving alms, and observing the dietary laws is that each presupposes that God and His creation are separate, requiring elaborate formulas to bridge the gap. In truth, these formulas are attempts to buy favor from God with sacrifice, to win something at the expense of something else. The common assumption about fasting in the religious sense is that one does this to atone for sin. Jesus is not speaking here of fasting as a means of purifying the body, which can sometimes be helpful on the physical level. The aim of religious fasting is soul purification, the removal of that which taints the soul, which is sin. This is the kind of fasting that Jesus is opposed to and to which he specifically connects in saying 104 with atonement for past sins. But in Thomas, the Kingdom is not entered by purchase. It is entered by releasing the blocks to its awareness. Jesus says, "Do not do what you hate." By this he means, do not accept the idea that God demands suffering in exchange for man's freedom. Performing a hateful practice has no intrinsic value. If it did, then this kind of fasting would amount to nothing more than the purchase of favor in exchange for pain.

The "prayer" referred to here is the prayer of supplication: if you ask reverently, God will grant you something that you do not have. Again, this understanding of prayer is consistent with saying 104 where, like fasting, it is linked to atonement for sin. Such prayer is not consistent with the Gospel of Thomas. First, it denies that the truth is right in front of your face, as saying 5 affirms. It denies that what you seek is already in your possession. Secondly, supplication puts you in an undeserving posture, one that says to God, "I do not deserve to be one with you. I am outside and separate from you. But if you would grant this sinner my earnest request, I will be your loyal servant." In the context of this gospel, true prayer is a grateful affirmation of what you have, not a plea for what you think you do not have.

As for giving alms, it need not be a sacrifice to give to those who temporarily have less. In 25, Jesus says, "Love your brother like your soul." The implication of that saying is that true loving is not a matter of judging who is worthy of your love and who is not. One loves because the receiver of that love is "like your soul." Loving is a communion of souls; so too is giving. In the Kingdom, there is no distinction, no duality, between the giver and the receiver. The intimacy between giver and receiver explains why giving unconditionally is the same as receiving. That is why it is not a sacrifice. However, giving alms to curry favor with God is not giving; it is a business deal. One favor is exchanged for another. Likewise, refraining from eating certain foods which the scriptures deem unclean is an obsequious practice, having little practical value at all except to brandish one's devotion to one's religion. That practice then becomes a goal in itself, and God is lost in the bargain.

We are told in this saying, in effect, that sacrifice is not the way to God. God is the way to God. Stratagems and gambits are not the way. So when Jesus says, "Do not lie," he is saying do not lie to yourself. Do not attempt to convince yourself that you are so unworthy of the Kingdom that you need to bargain your way into God's favor. This is a lie; it is not true. Instead, embrace the Kingdom without subterfuge. "Do not do what you hate" means that no payment is required. Admittance to the Kingdom is free. Loving God is not hard. The way or yoke that Jesus proposes is "easy" (90). The Kingdom has its own laws, but these laws ensure that all things worthy of finding are found in stillness and ease.

The Greek Oxyrhynchus version retains a word not found in the Coptic. The Coptic translation says, "All things are plain in the sight of heaven." The Greek says, "Before the *truth*, everything has cause to appear." In the light of truth, everything appears as it is. There is no need to lie. The "truth" is what Jesus is talking about here. There is no mention anywhere in Thomas of a judgmental God who looks down from the heavens to favor or condemn. Here, an ancient scribe apparently changed the word "truth" to "heaven," perhaps to support his own orthodox bias. In contrast, Jesus pokes fun at the notion of the Kingdom being in the sky in 3a.

The Greek version ends with essentially the same promise as does saying 5: "For there is nothing hidden that will not be made clear." Acts of piety do not reveal the Kingdom; they hide it. They obscure it and make it seem remote and impossible to achieve. If the seeker of truth is honest with himself, he will not attempt to make deals with God, but seek Him directly. He will refuse to engage in meaningless stratagems of sacrifice and manipulation, but instead place all his trust in realizing the oneness of existence. By doing only this, the hidden truth will "be made clear."

The additional statement in the Coptic, "and nothing covered will remain without being uncovered," adds force to the preceding statement.

Yet, because it is missing from the earlier Greek version, it may conceivably be a later attachment. Nevertheless, because it perfectly finishes off the saying in a typically Thomasine manner and style, I am inclined to think it is original.

Saying 7

> **(7) Jesus said, "Blessed is the lion that becomes man when consumed by man; and cursed is the man whom the lion consumes, and the lion becomes man." (Coptic version)**

> ***(7) Jesus said, "Blessed is the lion that becomes man when consumed by man; and cursed is the man whom the lion consumes, and the man becomes lion." (My restored version)***

It is widely agreed that this saying is not referring to an actual man or lion but that these words are used here as metaphors. However, there is little agreement among scholars about what these metaphors mean. In my view, the encounter portrayed in this saying between the man and the lion represents an inner encounter, an encounter wholly within the mind. I also believe that the word "man" may be equated with other metaphors in Thomas that function in the same internal way. Such metaphors, among others, are the "seeker" of saying 2 and the man who slays the powerful man in 98.

The "man" is that part of the mind that strives for wholeness, knowing that what it seeks is not of this world. This striving for wholeness entails no sacrifice. It is the yoke that is "easy" in saying 90 and the "movement" of saying 50 which, paradoxically, arises in "rest." It merely looks for that which is its own essence. The "man" is both the seeker and that which is sought, for what it seeks is to know and love itself. It is the true Self, although the full knowledge of this fact is temporarily hidden from its awareness. Conversely, the lion represents the false self, the inauthentic self, or what might be called the ego-self.

This saying suggests that the mind of man is split in allegiance between two diametrically opposed identities. One, the true Self, has given up a part of its mind to the other. It has accepted into its consciousness the false idea of separation, and this idea has crystallized into the belief structure we call the ego. The ego-self was born of fear and guilt, and to maintain its hold on the mind, it imagines a world in which these emotions are the glue that holds it together. It appears to be powerful and loud, like a lion, while the true Self is quiet though potentially far more powerful. The part of the mind that is governed by the ego attacks, while its counterpart extends love. In general, man identifies almost exclusively with his ego-self, assigning his true mind or Self the task of picking up the pieces of devastation that result from the ego's rule. So we have the expression, "I was not in my right mind when I did that." Inevitably, these two thought systems must vie for dominance, though for the present, an unstable truce may prevail.

The sage and the mystic live for the truth. They learn to tame their ego-selves and render them quiet through meditation and insight. For them, the wholeness of life is known only when the ego-self is seen as meaningless, barren, and illusory. And while the ego, like the lion, consumes by attacking, the true Self consumes by shining its light of love and forgiveness on everything. It does not oppose; it responds to fear with love and guilt with forgiveness. And knowing that the ego is fueled by fear, it denies fear's sway and thus denies the ego its source of strength. The "man" consumes the "lion" by realizing its own peaceful and innocent nature. It succeeds by freeing itself of all obstacles to the realization that it is, as saying 3 asserts, the Son of the Living Father. Thus, the "man" becomes aware that it is the true Self, with a capital "S," not something separate but one with all of life and with its Source.

In Plato's *The Republic* (588b–589b), these aspects of the mind are represented by three metaphors: the man, the lion and the many-headed beast. In Plato's view, the lion and the many-headed beast are representations of the lower or baser side of man's nature. By taming these aspects of the mind or by exposing the mind to finer, more ennobling, ideas of justice and moderation, these lesser parts are brought into union with the whole. The inner man, what Plato calls "the divine ruler" or the "divine man," will then rule over his inner realm. It is not known, of course, if these passages were known to Jesus or if they had any influence on the composition of this saying. *The Republic* was certainly well known in his day. It would have been familiar to anyone exposed to classical Greek culture and philosophy. So this connection is possible. It is interesting to note that among the

Nag Hammadi trove of texts, of which the Gospel of Thomas is one, was found a rather battered and corrupted copy of precisely this section of Plato's *The Republic.*

If we replace the word "lion" with the word "ego," the saying becomes, "Blessed is the ego that becomes man when consumed by man." When the divine part of man's mind emerges to dominate its shadow counterpart, the ego, all belief in littleness and separation falls apart. It should be remembered that the ego is simply a set of false beliefs. It cannot survive the light of truth. So when the ego falls apart, the true mind, called "the man" by Jesus, becomes fully aware of itself and fully awake. The mind, previously dominated by thoughts of alienation, is now free of this darkness and indeed blessed. It has consumed the ego.

If, however, the fear and guilt of the ego are allowed dominion over the mind, then it can be said that the lion consumes the man. The "divine man," to borrow Plato's term, is submerged in that other identity. Then indeed, the man becomes lion. It becomes indistinct and hidden, its energy absorbed by the ravenous beast. So the final line should read, "Cursed is the man whom the lion consumes, and the man becomes lion." The Coptic text has reversed this final phrase in this way: "...and the lion becomes man." Most scholars agree that this was an error in transmission. It makes no sense otherwise. Some commentators have attempted to wrench meaning out of this reversed order of "man" and "lion,"—unsuccessfully, in my opinion.

Seen as metaphors, "man" and "lion" are perfect descriptions of those thought systems of the mind which vie for ascendancy. They are diametrically opposed to each other, and one must consume the other to freely reign. Usually, an unstable truce is maintained between the two. However, it needs to be stressed that the ego is a set of false ideas which stubbornly holds that man is separate from his Source and that oneness is ultimately impossible. This gospel does not support that position. There is no idea more alien to the Jesus of this gospel than that. In this saying, the fierce beast, the lion, for which a defenseless man would ordinarily be no match, is, in the final line, overcome. As a representation of the ego, the lion is seen as vulnerable and capable of being consumed by the light of truth. In essence, this is the Eucharist; the body/ego is consumed in remembrance of Jesus and in remembrance of man's true identity. Indeed, the message of the Last Supper may well have been just this. When Jesus said, "This is my body. This is my blood," he was symbolically reminding the disciples that the idea of a separate body consumed by an enlightened mind was the crucial idea he wanted to leave them on his last night. Every time they consumed bread and wine, they would think of this saying and remember the lesson of the Last Supper—that the vital choice was to consume the body/ego or be consumed by it.

Saying 8

> **(8) And he said, "The man is like a wise fisherman who cast his net into the sea and drew it up from the sea filled with small fish. Among them, the wise fisherman found a fine large fish. So, he threw all the small fish back into the sea and chose the large fish without difficulty. Whoever has ears to hear, let him hear."**

The fisherman in this parable is compared to "the man." The original comparison, however, was probably to "the Kingdom of the Father," a phrase that introduces five other Thomas parables similar to this one (57, 76, 96, 97, and 98). An ancient editor may have made this change to stress the connection of "the man" in the last saying (7) to the "fisherman" in this one. Nevertheless, that substitution does not seem to have substantially affected the meaning of this parable.

To discover that meaning, we need to recognize the similar wording of two other Thomas parables, the parable of the merchant (76) and the parable of the lost sheep (107). In all three, the one is preferred over the many. The many are rejected, exchanged, or abandoned for the one. Furthermore, in all three parables, this rejection of the many is something that no practical man would ever do. As judged by the world, an absurd choice is made, and yet we are told that the man in each case is either shrewd, loving, or, as in this parable, wise. These resemblances must be taken into account as a first step in understanding this parable.

In the first century CE, as well as now, the typical small fish in the Sea of Galilee was the Kinneret bleak or lavnun (Acanthobrama terraesanctae). This freshwater fish, similar in appearance to the sardine, was caught in vast numbers. It swam near the surface in extensive schools.[1] It was certainly possible for a lone fisherman, using a cast net, to fill his boat with bleak. At that time, the largest fish in the Galilee was the African catfish or sfamnun (Clarias gariepinus). It could grow to more than four feet in length and weigh over a hundred pounds. The problem with the catfish, however, is that it had no scales. As such, it was considered unclean and forbidden for Jews to eat (Leviticus 11:9-12).[2] The suggestion that the large fish of this parable is a worthless catfish adds a second layer of irony to this already ironic story.

The absurdity of tossing a net full of highly marketable bleak back into the sea while keeping the large and worthless catfish is obvious. That this fisherman should be called "wise" raises the level of absurdity to that of a farce. To his fellow fishermen, he would have been thought a fool. And that is precisely the point. In these sayings, Jesus teaches Kingdom awareness, a major theme in this Gospel. The Kingdom is that realm of existence that is, and always will be, considered foolish in the eyes of the world. The world knows profit and loss; it knows responsibility and irresponsibility, and it operates within the dimensions of space and time. However, within the Kingdom of the Father, there is no loss; it recognizes only one responsibility, to the truth, and as spirit, its home is not in space and time but in dimensionless eternity. To the world, this is absurd. The two realms appear in stark contrast to each other. This is so because the Kingdom and the world are mutually exclusive. One represents the oneness and fullness of life, while the other represents separation and mortality. Neither have points in common with the other. From either viewpoint, the other is completely absurd.

In this saying, the "wise fisherman" is a metaphor for the seeker of wisdom who encounters the small and the many. He rejects them. Among them, however, he finds a "fine large fish," a metaphor for the oneness of the Kingdom. Unlike the things of this world, the Kingdom is not seen by the eyes or heard by the ears but experienced directly by the mind. Its impact there is ineffable and incomparable to anything found in this world. It is nothing less than the awareness that man and God are one. That experience of union with God is also the "treasure" of parables 76 and 109. It is what is sought in sayings 24, 60, 92, 94, and 107. It is what astonishes in saying 2. In contrast, nowhere in Thomas is the world accorded such value.

Commentators have suggested a variety of meanings for this parable. Some say it represents the sorting out of the righteous and the wicked for assignment to heaven or hell. The version in Matthew (13:47-50) indeed endorses this idea. Others, inclined to see Thomas as a Gnostic text, see the fisherman as God. In that role, He singles out for favor the true Gnostic, metaphorically throwing the rest of humanity back into the sea. Still others see the fisherman as essentially a conservationist, returning the small fish to the sea so that they may grow naturally into fine large fish. What all of these interpretations have in common is that they ignore the similarities within Thomas, mentioned above, and instead look outside the text for its meaning. Some commentators have even suggested that the Gospel of Thomas in its entirety has no discernible meaning at all. It is merely a jumble of nonsensical and unrelated ideas. Yet, for those who understand its non-dualistic frame of reference, it comes alive, and its message is fresh and vital.

There are patterns here that cannot be ignored. But to see these patterns, one must have an open mind. The final line of this parable says, "Whoever has ears to hear, let him hear." Jesus encourages the reader to look again at this, to look beyond his usual assumptions, to be willing to open his mind to another way of thinking, however strange that may seem at first.

The implications of this parable are quite profound, yet practical. All men and women are fishermen. They all have their nets out to capture what they can of life's bounty. Mostly what they catch are small and meaningless things—meaningless attachments and meaningless possessions. When they recognize and discard from their minds these small "fish" as meaningless, then, what is truly meaningful comes into view. This is the fine large fish, the Kingdom, which man shares with God and with all of His children. When experienced, the awareness of this Kingdom is so overwhelming that nothing else seems worthy of keeping. The fisherman chooses the larger fish, and, for him, nothing can ever be the same. It is important also to realize that this metaphorical fisherman, who represents the seeker of wisdom, makes his choice "without difficulty." This means that once the Kingdom is recognized, choosing peace over the many and insignificant things of this world is easy.

1 Goren, Fishelson & Trewavas, 1973, "Acanthobrama telavinensis," Fish Identification – FishBase, https://www.fishbase.de/summary/Acanthobrama-telavivensis.html#.

2 Mendel Nun, "Fish Storms and a Boat," Jerusalem Perspective, https://www.jerusalemperspective.com/2456/.

Saying 9

> **(9) Jesus said, "Now the sower went out, took a handful (of seeds), and scattered them. Some fell on the road, and the birds came and gathered them up. Others fell on the rock. They did not take root in the soil and did not produce ears. And others fell on thorns. They choked the seed(s) and worms ate them. And others fell on the good soil and it produced good fruit: it yielded sixty per measure and a hundred and twenty per measure."**

Several Thomasine themes come together in this parable. Again we see the absurd situation. A sower takes up a mere "handful" of seeds and scatters them indiscriminately over the ground. No farmer in the ancient world would have sown his precious seeds this way. He would have cast far more and done so carefully, choosing only the good soil in which to plant his crop. Clearly what this man is doing, by the standards of the world, is not rational. There are other such parables in Thomas. They appear to be rational at first glance, but on closer inspection, reveal a situation that is quite insane. The parables of the wise fisherman (8), the shrewd merchant (76), and the lost sheep (107) are additional examples. The reader must ask why; what is the purpose of portraying the world in such a manner? The purpose of this is to suggest that, indeed, sanity can only be found in the realm of the Kingdom and *nowhere* else.

To many readers, this will seem quite a harsh and sweeping statement to make. And certainly, nowhere in Thomas does Jesus say precisely this in so many words. However, it should be quite apparent that in this gospel, everything is hinted at, suggested, or illustrated in bizarre parables and challenging aphorisms. Nothing is spelled out. It must be kept in mind that

Thomas is a non-dualistic work, and in non-dualism the world is a mental construct, a projection of guilt and fear in which the concept of separation is made real. It is not real, but it is seen as real. This is why it is insane. It is a cosmic joke. The sage and the mystic do not take the world seriously; therefore, their minds are free and clear of the insane conflicts and limitations that the world represents.

The alternative to the world, presented in this gospel, is an entirely different realm called the "Kingdom." This is a realm presided over by a loving God, whose laws and principles are likewise loving and wholly unlike the laws and principles of the world. In this parable, these characteristics are metaphorically represented by a farmer (God) sowing his seeds. From the perspective of the Kingdom, everything this farmer does is rational. For example, his seeds are distributed evenly, nothing is held back, and no one is denied. This contrasts with the world where nothing is completely free, everything is limited, and where separation guarantees that some individuals will prosper while others will suffer loss. In the realm of the Kingdom, however, it is only the readiness of the mind to receive, represented by the condition of the ground in this parable that determines what is received and what is not. It has nothing to do with who or what God favors. It simply comes down to this: if one's mind is aligned with the Kingdom, one will know its fullness.

The philosophy of non-dualism does not necessarily require a divine father figure. One could be religious or not and yet be a non-dualist. One could even be an atheist and still have the insight to distrust the promises of the material world. Non-dualists who accept this idea of divinity, however, invariably believe that such a divine being can have no favorites. No one is denied God's gifts. It is only the willingness and openness of the recipient that determines the value of His bounty. God gives all to all. His unqualified generosity of spirit is integral to who He is.

In this parable, God is the metaphorical sower, and the blessings of His love are the seeds. They are scattered freely, and no one is denied. The ego, however, fears God's love because it denies the reality of separation. Complete acceptance of that love would mean the ego's dissolution. Consequently, its path is the worldly path, represented in this parable by the "road." Such a road is so trodden down by the egocentric standards of humanity that nothing can grow on it. Only the "birds" are there to scoop up the seeds. The allusion to the metaphor of the "birds" appears to represent the intervention of some religious leaders, perhaps the Pharisees and the scribes mentioned in saying 39. They consume what is meant to germinate naturally in the minds of those prepared to receive it. They hinder this natural process instead of serving and guarding its development.

Other seeds fall on rock. The rock represents a quality of mind so hardened by denial and encrusted with fear that nothing can penetrate it. On this rock, nothing can sink its roots and ripen to maturity. Likewise, in minds overgrown with meaningless thoughts, the seeds of God's blessings are choked as if by dense thorns. Such are the obsessive patterns of thought that tyrannize the mind and block its path to clarity. Then worms, reminding the reader of the worm of death in saying 76, come to destroy what is left.

It is only in the good soil, the prepared soil, that the seeds of love can sink their roots. Here they grow and multiply. They produce "sixty per measure and one hundred and twenty per measure." These numbers merely represent the idea of great bounty. It is as if Jesus is saying, "It was an excellent crop of sixty per measure. No, it was an enormous crop, double that size, a full one hundred and twenty per measure!" To the receptive mind, to a trusting and quiet mind, this bounty cannot be limited. It goes on blessing and growing until all willing minds are infused with its message of love. Once given space and fertile ground in which to grow, the seeds of God's love flourish beyond measure.

There is another familiar theme here. In the realm of the Kingdom, that which appears to be minuscule and meager can produce or promote enormous harvests of vigorous life. So it is with the "mustard seed" (20) and with the "leaven" which, when concealed in dough, produces large loaves of bread (96). In this saying, it is a mere "handful" of seeds, of which only a portion finds good soil. From the perspective of the ego-mind, these seeds seem diminutive and pathetic. In fact, everything about this process seems impossibly bizarre to the ego. But given a receptive mind in which to grow, the potential of God's gifts is unlimited. God gives freely, but only a mind that is free of fear and made permeable by trust can hear His call and embrace His love.

Saying 10

> **(10) Jesus said, "I have cast fire upon the world, and behold, I am guarding it until it blazes."**

It should be repeated here again that in the Gospel of Thomas there are two realms: one is the Kingdom of the Father; the other is the world. The world may be thought of as a kingdom with a small "k." It is the realm of the "lion" (saying 7) or, in common parlance, the realm of the ego. In contrast, the Kingdom of the Father is the awareness of oneness. It is experienced when man sets aside all dualistic thinking and embraces his divinity. In saying 22, Jesus compares this embrace to "infants being suckled." Yet, the Kingdom has nothing to do with the body; it is formless. It cannot be experienced by the senses nor can it be reduced to mental concepts (17). It cannot be defined but only experienced.

The realm of the world utterly denies this oneness and this identification with divinity. Within its domain, man believes himself to be separate from his fellow creatures and separate from his Source. And although it is not stated directly, it is evident from the context of these sayings that one of these realms is real and the other is not. (See my commentaries on sayings 11a, 29, 40, and 56.) The Jesus of this gospel teaches that the Kingdom is man's true home, while the world is a false idea, clung to by man in a kind of drunken stupor (28). He further teaches that this world that he clings to is a corpse (56), something totally without life. Only the Kingdom has life, and so it is the Kingdom which must be chosen unequivocally. Man must free himself of his attachment to that false idea that he calls the "world."

In this saying, when Jesus states that he has cast fire on the world, he means that he has endeavored to end the world's hold on the mind of man. It is this *idea* of a world, rather than the physical world, with which he is concerned. This is not the apocalypse of Revelation. His intention is only to destroy the world as an *idea*, the belief that man is at home in separation. The fire he casts is not the world's fire but the fire of truth and light. It is the same fire in saying 82, where Jesus says, "He who is near me is near the fire." It is the fire of love that is the only thing that can end separation. Everything else only adds to it.

Jesus sets this idea of a world on fire, and now he guards it until it blazes to extinction. In everything he does, in every word he utters, there is this focus and determination to end, once and for all, the illusion of a realm without God. He has found the Kingdom for himself, and because he loves his brother like his soul (25), he wishes to share with him this discovery. Consequently, he will not cease to guard these flames until the idea of separation is utterly reduced to ashes. (See also my commentary on saying 71.)

Saying 11

> **(11a) Jesus said, "This heaven will pass away, and the one above it will pass away. The dead are not alive, and those who live will not die."**
> **(11b) "In the days when you consumed what is dead, you made it what is alive. When you come to dwell in the light, what will you do? On the day when you were one, you became two. But when you become two, what will you do?"**

Sometimes in Thomas, a "Jesus said" is left out, as in 11b, and two sayings are mistaken as one. Saying 11 appears to be such a case. With that said, however, both 11a and 11b deal with the same issues of the temporal versus the eternal and the false versus the true. In 11a, Jesus vehemently declares that what is fleeting, presumably the world, will pass away, and what is alive is alive forever. Saying 11b is about consequences. The consequences of allowing the true to prevail over the false and the false to prevail over the true are contrasted. A question is then asked about each decision. I will examine 11b in a separate commentary.

In 11a, a distinction should be made between passing away and dying. Jesus says, "This heaven will pass away, and the one above it will pass away." The Greek loan word used here for "pass away" is *parage*. It is not the same word generally translated as "die." It is, however, the same word used in saying 42 (Leipoldt/Schoedel translation): "Come into being as you pass away." In that saying, to "pass away" is likewise not to die physically, but to let identification with the ego pass from the mind so that the true Self might be experienced. Extending that same concept to this saying, "this heaven…and the one above it" is a phrase describing something that will pass away as an *idea*, not something that will die in the physical sense.

The heaven that is above the lower one should not be confused with the spiritual heaven of Christian tradition. In antiquity, the sky was divided into layers or "heavens." In 2 Corinthians 12:1-4, Paul equates the third heaven with paradise, the spiritual place where God abides. This presumes that there were two lower heavens. The first heaven is described in Genesis as the atmosphere in which birds fly and extends to the firmament or arc of the sky. The second heaven presumably includes the sun, the moon, and all the stars. These two heavens refer to all the *physical* objects in the sky. For Jesus, this was the physical universe. One can envision him extending his hand around in a sweep while speaking of "this heaven" and "the one above it." For him, these were not spiritual realms. Nowhere in Thomas does spirit pass away, and therefore, these "heavens" cannot refer to a tenuous spirit realm likely to pass away. It is a vision, repeated in saying 111, where "The heavens and the earth will be rolled up in your presence." Both sayings refer to the physical world that will be rolled up or pass away when exposed to truth. In other words, the world will "pass away" as a false idea. Again, the meaning here is consistent with that same meaning in 42. The world will not die or come to a destructive end but pass from the mind, the way all illusions do when exposed to truth. The world is an illusion. The idea that it is real is the one that Jesus proposes waging war against in 16. He does not stand for the physical destruction of the world but only for its dissolution as a false idea.

What are we then to make of the second statement, "The dead are not alive?" Consistent with the non-dualistic nature of this gospel, the dead are not alive because there is no such thing as death. What appears to be dead is an illusion. There is only life—not physical life but spiritual life. Since Jesus has just claimed that the world is a mere idea that will pass away as a false idea, anything *of* the world, such as bodies, must likewise be illusory and eventually pass away as a false idea. Jesus is saying in this second statement that not only is the world not alive or real, neither are bodies alive or real as manifestations of that first, fundamental error.

In the final statement comes the conclusion: "those who live will not die." In Thomas, "the living" is always associated with spirit, as in the phrase, "the Living One" (37, 59, and 111). Those who know themselves as spirit will never experience death in any form. Their bodies will appear to die, but they will never experience death as a loss of anything real. From their perspective of spirit, the entire world of limitation and separation has passed away, and they have awakened as if from a dream.

When man comes to understand that what God created is life, not death, then he can begin to let go of everything that is not of life, transitory, and unreal. The Kingdom of the Father is the true realm and home of man. It is a spiritual realm in which what lives was never born and can never die. For Jesus, this is his reality. It is utterly beyond dualism. There is no "heaven" below or "heaven" above; there is only the Kingdom of Heaven.

Saying 11B

> **(11b) "In the days when you consumed what is dead, you made it what is living. When you come to dwell in the light, what will you do? On the day when you were one, you made the two. But when you become two, what will you do?"**

Although choice within the dream of separation is meaningless, as is everything else within that dream, man is free to wake up from dreaming, as daunting as that enterprise may be. This is the extent of free will, to be awake to the truth or to block the truth by dreaming an impossible vision of exile. In this saying, the experiences of oneness and "light" are either acknowledged or blocked, and questions are asked about the consequences of those choices. The first line reads, "In the days when you consumed what is dead, you made it what is living." Again we have an allusion to eating. The reader is reminded of the man who consumes the lion in saying 7. As I explained in my commentary on that saying, the "lion" represents the ego-self, the fearful and guilt-ridden self, which when consumed by the "man," becomes man. The words and implications of 11b are nearly identical to what we find in the opening line of 7. What this saying adds, however, is the assertion that this ego/lion-self is dead. Like the world, the ego-self is a corpse (56). As the hero of the dream of separation, it is a false identity.

There is nothing true about it. Yet, as in 7, it can be made into "what is living." It can be made true, by being consumed, and it is consumed by being challenged. Again, the ego is merely a set of false beliefs that appears to confirm a separate self. When those beliefs are confronted by the truth, they dissolve, and the truth is finally acknowledged.

Though never expressly stated, the underlying premise of Thomas is this: If God is real, as this gospel appears to affirm, then what God created must also be real. What He did not create must be an illusion. God did not create separation, it being a denial of love. Therefore, it is not real. For God to have created separation, He must have rejected love and created something that existed outside Himself. However, to be Himself, to be true to Himself, God must be wholly loving, omnipresent, and all-inclusive. To be perfect, He must be unlimited and, therefore, divine. On the other hand, the ego-self, or "what is dead" in this saying, is separate, and being separate it must be unreal. Jesus refers to it as "dead" because it is devoid of life. It is imaginary. With this realization comes the willingness to embrace "what is living" and let go of what is dead. The wholeness of life is then clearly seen, and the light of truth shines again in the mind of man. And so, the answer to the question "When you come to dwell in the light, what will you do?" is apparent. There is nothing left to do but to experience its power and its peace. The question is also answered in saying 2. It says there that after finding the truth and being astonished, you will "reign" and you will "rest."

The next set of lines presents the opposite course of action with the opposite consequence. "On the day" can be seen as the first day in time when inexplicably the thought of separation emerged out of oneness. As an event in time, it seemed to happen in the past. However, just as separation is impossible, so is time. Everything that happens, or seems to happen, happens in the present moment. Therefore, the choice for oneness or separation, truth or illusion, and love or fear is always present. On this day, "you" fall into a kind of drunken stupor (28) and choose to see yourself as separate. On this day, you "make" the illusion of duality. In other words, on this day you become lost to your own identity. Consequently, oneness seems to you like an impossible abstraction. But in truth, nothing has changed. You merely sleep (102) and dream a dream of separation. Separation from God is impossible, but on this day you believe in "two;" you believe in the reality of the many. The inclusiveness of "one" is exchanged for the exclusiveness of "two."

Notice that the key word here is "made," not "created." In the Gospel of Thomas, the word "made" is repeatedly used to represent man's choice to experience illusion over truth or truth over illusion. Choice can work both ways. So in saying 22, what is "made" or chosen is the vision of non-duality. That is a positive choice. In this saying (11b), it is a negative choice. Duality and separation are chosen, and a world of conflict and struggle is made and supported. Chaos replaces order. And what is the consequence of this making? The saying asks, "What will you do?" You will not reign, nor will you rest, as you did when you dwelled in the light. You will suffer. In the words of 3b, as a consequence of not realizing your divine connection with the Father, "you dwell in poverty."

Saying 12

> **(12) The disciples said to Jesus, "We know that you will leave us. Who is to be our leader?"**
> **Jesus said to them, "Wherever you are, you are to go to James the Righteous, for whose sake heaven and earth came into being."**

This saying is perplexing, not for what it says but for what it omits. Apart from naming James the Righteous, also known as James the Just, as Jesus's eventual successor, there are no insightful comparisons or hidden treasures of wisdom here. Since this is a collection of wisdom sayings, one would expect to find some evidence of either explicit or implicit wisdom. Instead, its message is prosaic and common. The disciples worry that they might be leaderless after Jesus is gone, and Jesus responds unequivocally: "Go to James." His reply leaves no room for doubt that James is his preferred choice. That, in itself, from the viewpoint of this gospel, is surprising.

This saying is incompatible with the Gospel of Thomas in multiple ways. At the very least, it is curious that Jesus should suspend his thoughtful and enigmatic sayings here to turn his attention to the business of his succession. The emphasis is not on acquiring wisdom but on assuring his disciples that they will not be left leaderless. The emphasis is on the future, but nowhere else in Thomas does Jesus show the least bit of interest in the future. In sayings 18, 36, 51, and 113, he urges his disciples not to worry but to trust in the present and recognize that all that they seek in the future is already here. In other words, nothing worth finding is found in the future. In this saying, Jesus seems to overlook his own teaching. Furthermore, what kind of a future does this saying propose? It is a future entrusted to James rather than to Thomas. Yet, this is the Gospel of Thomas, not the Gospel of James. Why would this gospel specifically promote James over Thomas? For these and other reasons, I believe that this saying is not original to this collection of Jesus sayings.

Consider the way the saying begins. The disciples reveal their anxiety about the future. They ask, "Who is to be our leader?" The literal translation of this line is, "Who is to be made great, up over us?" The irony of this question is that in saying 3, Jesus ridicules "leaders" who teach that the Kingdom is in the sky and in the sea, external to man. It suggests instead that truth is uncovered not by blindly following leaders but by realizing the truth about one's self. In 13, Jesus tells the apostle Thomas that he is not his "master," suggesting that he is not his authoritative teacher or leader. But it is Thomas himself who has drunk from the "bubbling spring," which Jesus has simply measured out. It is Thomas who has become intoxicated by the wonder of what he finds. In the words of saying 2, the point of these sayings is that he "who seeks" must continue to seek until he finds. He alone must do the seeking. He alone will find the treasure within. No one can do this for him. Even one who is "great, up over us" cannot accomplish this for him. It seems, therefore, unlikely that such a saying as this one, which concerns the leadership of the Jesus movement, would be included originally in this collection.

Historically, James was reputed to be a brother of Jesus and a leader of the movement after his brother's death. However, in this gospel, James is only mentioned once, here in this saying. He is not mentioned in saying 13, where Thomas is raised in prominence over Simon Peter and Matthew. In 99, he is presumably among the "brothers" of Jesus, who, along with his mother, are excluded from a meeting between Jesus and his disciples. Of those who remain inside, Jesus says of them that "those here who do the will of my Father are my brothers and mother." This mention of his family in 99 leaves the impression that James was not even a disciple, at least at this stage. Indeed, in John 7:5, all of the brothers of Jesus are said to "not believe in him."

Very little is known about James. We cannot be certain that he was the author of the New Testament letter written in his name. Paul describes him as a leader of the early church, as does Luke in Acts. He quite possibly was, yet he is nowhere listed among the twelve apostles. In the New Testament gospels, all that is said of him is that he was the brother of Jesus—curiously little information for someone who apparently succeeded him.

How then are we to understand the next line of this saying in reference to James? He is someone "for whose sake heaven and earth came into being." Such a phrase would seem to be a compliment and nothing more. As scholars have stated, this was a typical way of praising someone in ancient Jewish literature. However, in the light of this gospel's unique philosophy, this phrase is highly ironic, and this irony cannot be overlooked. What it calls "heaven and earth" is the world, and the world is not regarded particularly highly in this gospel. In saying 56, it is a "corpse." In 11, it will "pass away." In 111, it will be "rolled up," and in 10, Jesus "casts fire" upon it. So, with this in mind, the question must be asked: In the context of this gospel, how exactly could this phrase be seen as a compliment? If it was for James's sake that the world came into being, how then could he be considered worthy of leading the disciples? Clearly, Jesus would not have uttered these words. Whoever did, meant it as a compliment, but it seems unlikely that the Jesus of this gospel would have.

My analysis of saying 12 points out the inconsistencies it has with the gospel as a whole. Its appearance in this collection of wisdom sayings is irregular. The Jesus of Thomas shows no interest in organizational problems. His typical answer to every problem is the "Kingdom." Yet, if James did succeed his brother in the emerging Jesus movement, as he evidently did, it would not be out of character for a scribe more aligned with the orthodox side of the movement to inject this saying into Thomas. The intent would have been to promote and protect the authority of James and the authority of those who followed him in the leadership of the Jesus movement.

Saying 13

(13a) Jesus said to his disciples, "Compare me to someone and tell me whom I am like."
Simon Peter said to him, "You are like a righteous angel."
Matthew said to him, "You are like a wise philosopher."
Thomas said to him, "Master, I am wholly incapable of saying whom you are like."
Jesus said, "I am not your master. Because you have drunk, you have become intoxicated from the bubbling spring which I have measured out."
(13b) And Jesus took him and withdrew and told him three words (statements). When Thomas returned to his companions, they asked him, "What did Jesus say to you?"
Thomas said to them, "If I tell you one of the things which he told me, you will pick up stones and throw them at me; a fire will come out of the stones and burn you up."

This logion contains two distinct segments. One is seemingly an authentic Jesus saying; the other is seemingly not. The first has Jesus asking the question, "Whom am I like?" Simon Peter responds, "You are like a righteous angel." It is the spiritual qualities of Jesus that he appreciates, in contrast to Matthew who sees his teacher as a "wise philosopher." Jesus is apparently like an angel in the sense that he is devoted to serving God. The Greek loanword for "righteous" is the same word that is used to describe James in the previous saying (12). This suggests that both men, Jesus and James, have a reputation for being virtuous. So, according to Simon Peter, Jesus is a virtuous man devoted to serving God. There is nothing about this description that seems unreasonable. Nevertheless, Jesus says nothing.

Next, Matthew says, "You are a wise philosopher." Clearly, Jesus is wise, and his unconventional ideas on the non-dualistic nature of reality reveal his regard for both spirituality and philosophy. Matthew apparently sees this philosophic side of Jesus more clearly. But again, Jesus says nothing.

He then turns to Thomas, who says, "Master, I am wholly incapable of saying whom you are like." For Thomas, his reverence for Jesus is so great that he finds it impossible to compare him to anything. However, even *his* answer does not satisfy Jesus. Thomas uses the word "master," and Jesus denies that label emphatically: "I am not your master. Because you have drunk, you have become intoxicated from the bubbling spring which I have measured out." The word "master" is sometimes translated as "teacher," although "master" suggests not only one who teaches but the additional connotation of one who teaches with authority. Thomas sees Jesus as deserving of this elevated position of authority, above the level of ordinary men. However, Jesus denies this implication of specialness and suggests instead that the focus should not be on himself, but on the "bubbling spring."

This "bubbling spring" may be a reference to the inspiration of the Holy Spirit (44) or to the innate source of wisdom described in these sayings as the "light." In either case, Jesus describes himself as one who simply "measures out." What he measures out is transformational truth, which has a profound effect on Thomas. Jesus tells him that he has become intoxicated, or perhaps disoriented, as if from a sudden surge of awareness. Such an experience would have produced in Thomas an enormous feeling of awe for his "master." However, the point remains that Jesus is an ordinary man who simply "measures out" or points to what is vital without pretense, without being above or separate from ordinary men.

Some may argue that Jesus did indeed claim to be special, as evidenced in saying 77: "It is I who am the light which is above them all." However, as I have argued in my commentary on that saying, the "light" is the same light that exists in everyone. The light that "is above them all" may be translated as the light that "falls on everything" or even the light that "shines on everything." Thus, Jesus is a man of light, one who identifies with the light that shines on everything. Indeed, in saying 24, a man of light may be anyone, not exclusively Jesus. Possessing light is the birthright of the all-inclusive Self and therefore beyond specialness. It is the truth about the light that Jesus has "measured out."

In this saying (13), neither Simon Peter, Matthew, nor even Thomas has it quite right. Jesus insists that he is not special. He cannot be compared to anyone else because he is not separate from anyone else. In this gospel, oneness is everything, and therefore, the light that Jesus possesses is the same light that his disciples possess, though they are unaware of it. Additionally, the source of his wisdom, symbolized by the bubbling spring, is freely available to everyone, and it is this that is real and vital, not the exterior qualities or persona of Jesus.

In 13b, Jesus pulls Thomas aside and tells him "three words," sometimes translated as "three things" or "three statements." It is misleading to identify these as magical words or incantations, as some commentators have. Nowhere in Thomas is there any evidence of the use of magic or the esoteric power of words or numbers. True, numbers are mentioned in Thomas but only in ways that can be explained in the context of each saying. When Thomas returns to his companions, he reports to them that if he were to tell them even one of the things that Jesus told him, they would throw stones at him. Stoning was the penalty, at that time, for a wide variety of offenses, including blasphemy. He further tells them that "a fire will come out of the stones" and burn them up. This, of course, is metaphorical language that needs to be explained.

One should be very suspicious of 13b and its allusion to "three words." It is not an extension of the saying. It has nothing to do with the preceding dialogue. That exchange ended with the words, "bubbling spring which I have measured out." At this point, Jesus and Thomas are still together, but their conversation has ended and, properly speaking, the saying has concluded. What follows as 13b appears to be a second logion tacked on to 13a. It is actually a narrative consisting of a brief dialogue between Jesus and Thomas followed by one between Thomas and his companions. It is not a Jesus saying in itself but an allusion to the lines that immediately follow in saying 14: "If you fast, you will bring forth sin for yourselves and; if you pray, you will be condemned and; if you give alms, you will do harm to your spirits."

Here are the three statements that are particularly provocative and incendiary. Nowhere else in this gospel do we find anything so seemingly antithetical to the beliefs and culture of the time. They dramatically challenge core religious practices that were revered not only by first-century Jews but by most religious groups everywhere. To a contemporary Jew, they might well have seemed, if not blasphemous, irreverent in the extreme. But seen in context, all three of these statements are consistent with this gospel's philosophy. (See my commentary on saying 14.) Nevertheless, it is hardly surprising that such "words" would produce, in some quarters, talk of stoning and fire. Of course, 14 refers to a fourth pious practice, that of adhering to the strict dietary laws. It is this Jesus challenges when he instructs his disciples to "eat what they will set before you." However, it is the first three of these practices that are boldly targeted for particular scorn.

My suggestion, which is admittedly speculative, appears to be the best explanation for this mysterious commentary in Thomas. It is that these final lines (13b) were not a part of the original saying. They were amended to 13a by a scribe reacting negatively to these three extraordinary statements in saying 14. There is a pattern in Thomas that supports this interpretation. In at least 18 of these sayings, a scribe (or more than one) felt obliged to alter or inject words into these sayings that reflected his orthodox bias. His hand can be seen throughout this gospel, mostly altering a single word or two, but sometimes interfering in a major way. Such was the case here.

For this scribe, unfamiliar with the subtle wording of this gospel, these three assertions in 14 fell on his sensitive, orthodox convictions like hammer blows, and it was more than he could accept. He could have expunged this saying (14) from his copy, but that would have probably been noticed. So he inserted the subtle suggestion between sayings 13 and 14 that these three statements were so hot that they were blasphemous. To avoid seeming to attack Jesus, he had Thomas speak of committing blasphemy. His apparent intention was not to condemn Thomas but to use his name as a metaphor for the Gospel of Thomas itself. He is saying here that if the truth about these three statements were exposed, the Gospel of Thomas would be seen as blasphemous. Likewise, he uses the "companions" as metaphors for this gospel's potential victims, representing future readers. In metaphorical terms, if these statements were known to the general public, the Gospel of Thomas would be condemned, and the fire from its blasphemy would burn or harm its readers. This, in fact, is a subtle attack on the Gospel of Thomas itself by a confused and shocked scribe. Subsequently, no one caught on to this, and these confusing lines remained in place—perhaps inevitably in a gospel replete with many confusing lines.

Saying 14

(14) Jesus said to them, "If you fast, you will bring forth sin for yourselves; and if you pray, you will be condemned; and if you give alms, you will do harm to your spirits. When you go into any land and walk about in the districts, if they receive you, eat what they set before you, and heal the sick among them. For what goes into your mouth will not defile you, but what comes out of your mouth—it is that which will defile you."

In the New Testament gospels, there are many examples of Jesus challenging the cherished beliefs and practices of his day. He has been called an iconoclast, one who attacks the current icons of religious veneration. This was done not to abuse anyone but to put straight what has been abusive to both man and God. Such an iconoclast is no less present in the Gospel of Thomas and perhaps more so. In this saying, his words seem blunt and extreme, but his intention is to arouse his disciples, not to console them with soothing platitudes.

In a previous logion (6), Jesus responded to questions about the same pious acts that are mentioned in this saying with the line, "Do not tell lies, and do not do what you hate." In my commentary on that saying, I argued that fasting as a religious obligation is essentially a business deal, an attempt to trade one thing for another. The discomfort of going without food is endured in exchange for God's favor. If done purely for health reasons and in moderation, it is harmless. But as a religious practice, as saying 6 suggests, such fasting conceals a "lie." This is so because it entails subterfuge. It involves striking a bargain with God to get something that is otherwise thought unobtainable. It assumes that God's love is something that can be purchased. The currency of this purchase is suffering. Whatever form it takes—self-flagellation, self-imposed poverty or fasting to please God—it is an attack on oneself with the hidden purpose of currying favor with the divine.

Furthermore, to bargain with the divine is to deny that one is already united with the divine. As this gospel repeatedly affirms, oneness with God is man's enduring reality. (See 22, Greek version of 30, 48, 61, 75, and 84.) Therefore, to attack oneself for whatever reason, is to attack God. Neither one can be attacked without attacking the other. As a consequence, an unconscious acceptance of guilt cannot be avoided. He who denies his oneness with God, who attempts to manipulate Him and who attacks what is one with divinity, will unavoidably see himself as sinful. In this saying, this is how he will "bring forth sin" for himself. Yet, in the philosophy of non-dualism, guilt and sin do not exist, since God in His infinite love could not have created either. Nevertheless, it is inescapable that man will believe himself guilty and sinful as long as he insists on manipulating God to obtain something in return.

Likewise, when one prays for anything, with the possible exception of inner guidance, he dictates to God what he, in his limited awareness, believes to be true. In effect, he tells God that he lacks something external to himself and that he must have it to be complete. No matter how humble he sees himself or how effacing are his pleas, this insistence on knowing what his true needs are is both arrogant and presumptuous. As this gospel suggests, he has everything he needs. (See the Greek version of 36, 41, 70, 88, and 113.) He would know this if he would accept his oneness with God and feel its power. In this saying, Jesus says that by praying this way, he will be "condemned." And so he will, not by God but unconsciously by himself. His insistence that he is not complete, that he needs something that God is withholding, appears to support the idea of a distant and wrathful God. The result is the acceptance of unjustified guilt. Again, this is merely a judgment by man, not by God. In actuality, nothing has changed. He is still one with his Source. It is precisely because of this oneness with Source that God does not condemn. To do so, would be to condemn Himself. In truth, He is one with His creation, and His love for His child is unconditional and unassailable.

Giving alms can also be harmful. As Jesus apparently understands it, giving freely from the heart is not giving alms. What he speaks of here is the pious practice of exchanging money for ego-inflating advantages. For example, such giving could be for the approval of others, for the atonement of "sins," or even for the comforting feeling of giving. If it ignores the real needs of the disadvantaged; that too could be an ego-inflating activity. The difference comes down to how and why one gives. True giving is spontaneous.

It is an expression of oneness. The spirit soars when such giving is practiced but is attacked when pious almsgiving takes its place. Jesus says here that almsgiving does "harm to your spirits." The literal translation of this phrase is "doing an evil to your spirits." The implication is that almsgiving will bring forth evil as fasting brings forth sin. Evil, like sin, is experienced as a consequence of denying one's oneness with God. But, neither evil nor sin is real, and neither has real consequences. (See my commentary on saying 45.) It is not God's will that man should experience anything that is not of God. And what is not the will of God must be unreal (40). But the one who indulges in these pious practices will suffer their phantom consequences nevertheless. As long as he denies his oneness with God, he will experience his illusory projections of guilt and fear, and, consequently, his own attacks on himself.

Next, Jesus takes on the dietary laws (kashrut), which have their origins mostly in the books of Leviticus and Deuteronomy. Among these laws are prohibitions against eating pork, shellfish, and of consuming meat mixed with milk products. It is probably only in the outer "districts" where a Jew might be offered a meal heedless of these laws. In such circumstances, Jesus says "eat what they will set before you." Eat what they eat. Do not make an issue of your differences with them or that which makes you separate from them. Join them, and in your joining heal them. By saying this, he not only dismisses the dietary laws but offers an alternative, which is to heal. At that time, healers or doctors addressed themselves to the whole man, more than they do today. Healing was not just for the body but for the mind and spirit, as well. In this saying, Jesus is suggesting that there is a higher law, above all of man's laws. That higher law is to "love your brother like your soul" (25) and to recognize the oneness of the Kingdom. In that frame of mind, the healer will always do the right thing and say the right thing.

Finally, Jesus says, "For what goes into your mouth will not defile you, but what comes out of your mouth—it is that which will defile you." Food does not defile. But any unloving expression, whether uttered from the mouth or arising from a practice that divides and isolates, will defile what is holy. Man is holy, being a child of God (3b). Therefore, he must safeguard this holiness with love and let this be his only law.

Saying 15

> **(15) Jesus said, "When you see him who was not born of woman, fall on your faces and worship him. That one is your Father."**

God is the womb of life. In the realm of the Kingdom, there is no other womb but His. So in saying 79, when it says, "Blessed is the womb that has not conceived and the breasts that have not given milk," it is God's womb to which it is referring. Therefore, in this saying, "he who was not born of woman" is the one who was born from the womb of God, the one who was created as spirit, not as flesh. This one is God's true creation. The body that is "born of woman" is fundamentally an illusion. As understood non-dualistically, the body is actually nothing. It is a meaningless dream. On awakening in the realm of the Kingdom, the spirit-mind recognizes this fact and accepts its oneness with the Father.

When the mind conceives of the body and believes it to be real, it directs the body's senses to confirm the reality of that belief. That is how the illusion of the body, as well as the world, is maintained. So in this saying, when this one "who was not born of woman" is seen, he is seen not with the body's eyes, but being spirit, with the mind's eye. In truth, he is the oneness of life, consisting of both Father and Son, wholly inseparable from one another. Jesus says, "Fall on your faces and worship him. That one is your Father." The Son is an extension of the Father and, like the Father, is worthy of complete love and devotion. He is God's creation in union with Himself. To see every man and woman in this way is to see them as they truly are.

When man is willing to forgive his fellow creatures and himself for believing that they were ever anything less than this, then he will "see" this pristine Self in union with his Father. He will "worship" him in the sense of acknowledging the indwelling God. In India, for thousands of years people have greeted each other with the word "namaste." This means: I profess the divine in you; I see the Brahman in you. It acknowledges the Truth in the other, that which is real, vibrant, and beyond all appearances of limitation. That one is the Father, inseparable from His creation.

Saying 16

> **(16) Jesus said, "Men think, perhaps, that I have come to cast peace upon the world. They do not know that I have come to cast dissension upon the earth: fire, sword and war. For there will be five in a house: three will be against two, and two against three, the father against the son, and the son against the father. And they will stand as solitary ones (whole ones)."**

Nothing in Thomas will make any sense until it is understood that all appeals in this gospel are appeals for vigilance, not on the level of the world, but on the level of the mind. Its focus is on understanding the world as it is, having the right thoughts about it, rather than changing it for whatever purpose. When the word "world" appears in Thomas, it nearly always is presented as an *idea*, not a fact. This pattern can be observed in saying 10, one similar to this one: "I have cast fire upon the world, and behold, I am guarding it until it blazes." Jesus does not literally set fire to anything. Rather, he sets fire to the idea of a world and what the world represents. In the context of this gospel, the world represents separation. Likewise, in this saying, the casting of "fire, sword and war" is directed not at an actual world but, again, at the *idea* of a separate world. Its violent rhetoric is intended not to inflame the passions or promote hatred but to urge his listeners to resolutely make a choice. The choice is to join Jesus in opposing the idea of a separate world or, ironically, to acquiesce in the same violence and hatred this saying incorrectly seems to support.

Irony, hyperbole, and code words are literary tools that are all present here. This is a difficult saying, but the reader must be patient. He should remember how other sayings in this gospel use challenging words to disturb and arouse. In the first line, Jesus appears to deny his devotion to peace, but notice that in appearing to do so, he acknowledges his reputation as a peacemaker. He says, in effect, never mind that the focus of my teachings is on peace and unity; my real teaching is "dissension." To his intimate disciples, such a statement would immediately send a signal to their minds—be careful. Listen to what he is saying. He seemingly is refuting everything he stands for, yet his devotion to peace is incontestable. So, what is he up to?

That is precisely the question he wants his listeners to ask themselves.

He says that he has come to "cast dissension" upon the earth. In the same way that he "cast fire" on the world in saying 10, here he hurls "fire, sword and war." It is the idea of a world in which everything is separate from everything else that provokes his opposition. That includes man from man as well as man from God. He opposes this idea and forcefully confronts it. Indeed, for the non-dualist, separation is an idea that is inconsistent with a loving God and, therefore, inconsistent with the object of God's love, which is the wholeness of life.

In the next line, a house of five is split apart, three against two, two against three, father against son, and son against father. These five are "in a house." We will see this word "house" used again in other sayings in Thomas. It is one of three code words found in this saying. It is a metaphorical house. It represents a thought structure or fundamental way of understanding reality. Such houses in Thomas may be well built, supported by a cornerstone of truth (66), or they may consist entirely of false beliefs, supported by illusions. In this false sense, the word is used in sayings 21, 35, 48, 71, 97, and 98. Used here, it represents the false belief that separation is real. To support that belief, the ego-mind will always promote separate interests and separate loyalties. Thus, within a mind so aligned, conflicts are inevitable. The two/three conflicts represent man against man; the father/son conflicts represent man against God. To the ego, such conflicts are natural, based as they are on the supposed reality of separation. Yet, separation is not real, and conflicts are not natural. That is the idea on which Jesus casts his fire, sword, and war. In a parallel saying (71), Jesus says essentially the same thing: "I will destroy this house and no one will be able to build it [up again]."

If one takes this saying literally, he will assume quite understandably that Jesus is displaying a side of his personality that is violent or even maniacal. By assuming this, the reader would miss the context in which his disciples experience their master. From the overwhelming evidence of this gospel, he is a peaceful man, a loving man. But he clearly burns with the conviction of oneness and is eager to lead his disciples to that place of oneness he calls the Kingdom. Further, if one accepts the literal interpretation of this saying, it will lead to the erroneous conclusion that Jesus does not wish to confront separation but seeks to divide people from each other and from

God. One would also assume that experiencing division to the fullest extent is the unavoidable price of being his disciple. But this ignores saying 72, in which Jesus firmly says, "I am not a divider..." Indeed, he is not a divider. From the evidence of this gospel, the man-against-man/man-against-God analogies describe how the ego perceives the world, not how Jesus knows it. In his view, it is not a place of hopeless fragmentation and conflict. It is simply unreal, a dream from which man needs to awaken. It is a vast illusion. In his teaching, only oneness is real, and that is why Jesus confronts the very idea of the "world" and the inevitability of strife.

When so confronted, the idea of separation gradually loses its hold on the mind. The final line in this saying expresses that idea, but requires some explanation: "And they will stand as solitary ones." There are two other code words here that have a special meaning in Thomas. The first is "stand," or as it is literally written in the Coptic, "stand to their feet." That phrase, also found in sayings 18, 23, 28, and 50, implies waking up, as in standing to one's feet after sleeping. In each of these sayings, it suggests a waking up to a totally new understanding. It suggests the idea of being enlightened or reborn to a vision beyond human thought and concepts.

The other code word in this saying is "solitary." The Greek loanword used here is *monachos* which means "single ones," or "whole ones." The word has been translated both ways, though clearly the implications of these translations are quite distinct. Understood as "whole ones," the word may be seen to describe those who live and act from a place of oneness or wholeness. Their minds are undivided, and therefore, their vision of reality is clear and unclouded by thoughts of separation. In Thomas, there are two other sayings which use the Greek form of this word (49 and 75) and three which use a similar Coptic phrase which means "one alone" (4, 22, and 23). The difference between "single one" and "one alone" is not significant, and in all six sayings which employ these words, the interpretations of "one who is whole" and "they will become whole" work powerfully in the non-dual context of this gospel. So rather than monachos alluding to one who is alone and isolated, it alludes to one who is joined in wholeness and in full contact with all that is real.

In this logion, Jesus is saying that he has come to utterly destroy the belief in separation, where man is separate from his fellow man and separate from his creator. This separation is illustrated by the "three against two" and "two against three" allusion. It is only in this "house," or structure of egoic beliefs, that such divisions exist. It is this idea of separation that he has come to destroy. As a consequence of his teaching, man will learn that there is no "two" and no "three." There is only one. He will wake up (stand to his feet) as one who is whole (monachos) and experience the glory of the Kingdom. (For more on "two" and "three," see my commentary on saying 30.)

Saying 17

> **(17) Jesus said, "I will give you what no eye has seen, what no ear has heard, what no hand has touched, and what has never occurred to the human mind."**

The Chinese sage, Lao Tzu, lived some 500 years before the birth of Jesus. His verses, known as the *Tao Te Ching*, have been translated many different ways. Among them is this translation of verse 14, which reads in part:

> Eyes look but cannot see it.
> Ears listen but cannot hear it.
> Hands grasp but cannot touch it.
> Beyond the senses lies the Great Unity–
> invisible, inaudible, intangible. (Translation by Jonathan Star)[1]

Clearly, Jesus did not originate the idea of the Kingdom, described by Lao Tzu as the "Great Unity–invisible, inaudible and intangible." There were others before him who pointed to this ineffable treasure beyond the senses. But to this idea, Jesus added another. The oneness of the Kingdom is not only beyond the reach of the senses to experience it; it is beyond the reach of the mind to conceive of it. In this saying, he says of his gift: it "has never occurred to the human mind." Indeed, the human intellect cannot comprehend it. It is not an intellectual concept at all but a profound knowing which actually comes into focus when conventional thinking ceases. If man is to know it, he cannot receive it through his senses or through the common workings of his human brain. It cannot be categorized, analyzed, or even remembered to the extent that it was originally experienced. It must be known entirely in the moment, free of any connection with the world of perception, of thought, of past associations or future expectations.

To give anything away, one must first have it. By giving the Great Unity to others, Jesus demonstrates that he has it himself. In saying 24, his disciples say to him, "Show us the *place* where you are, as it is necessary for us to seek it." They are not asking for an intellectual discussion. They do not expect to join with him on that superficial level. Rather, they look to the man himself. More specifically, they look to the "place" where he is. As elsewhere noted, the word "place" in Thomas is used as a code word for the Kingdom. So in saying 24, the disciples are, in fact, asking Jesus to share with them the Kingdom, to share with them what Lao Tzu called "the Great Unity." In his reply, he tells them that within a man of light there is a light with which he lights up the whole world. In other words, they need not acquire anything. To know the Kingdom, they need only achieve stillness and extend the light which is already present within their minds.

The gift of Jesus to his disciples is the gift of awareness. By his teaching and example, they become aware of their place in the Kingdom. They become aware of their identities as children of God (3b). His gift to his disciples is the invitation to awaken to the reality of the Kingdom and remember that their birthright as children of God is waiting within to be claimed. Jesus provides the key that unlocks and releases what was always there.

When ultimate freedom is encountered in anyone, it cannot be ignored. Its attraction is palpable. The disciples cannot resist this quality that they see in Jesus, but for them it remains a mystery. Jesus provides the key to their understanding, and in doing so, opens a door that might not have been opened without his help. With patience and the deftness of a great teacher, he leads his disciples to that *place* where he is. He leads them *within* to discover a treasure that is beyond anything they could ever have conceived of with their worldly brains.

---

1 Jonathan Star, *Tao Te Ching, The Definitive Edition* (New York: Penguin, 2001), 27.

Saying 18

(18) The disciples said to Jesus, "Tell us how our end will be." Jesus replied, "Have you discovered the beginning, so that you look for the end? For where the beginning is, there will the end be. Blessed is he who will take his place in the beginning. He will know the end and will not taste death."

The disciples are fearful and confused. They ask Jesus about their future: "Tell us how our end will be." Rather than answer their question directly, he replies with a question of his own: "Have you discovered the beginning, so that you look for the end?" His answer reminds us of how a Zen master might reply to such a question. As in all of these sayings, Jesus's intention appears always to dive into fearless questions and bottomless mysteries.

The sense of his response suggests that before the disciples can have a clear understanding of the end of man, they must understand how man came to be in the first place. Jesus speaks abstractly: "Have you discovered the beginning?" That is the pivotal question of this dialogue. What is man's beginning? We, the readers of this gospel, have an advantage over the disciples in this regard. When we look ahead to sayings 49 and 50, we see that for Jesus, the "beginning" is synonymous with the "Kingdom" and also with the "light." In saying 49, he says that the "solitary and elect" are from the Kingdom. By "solitary and elect," he means those who have realized their true, spiritual identity. (See saying 49 in regard to this translation.) He says, "You are from it and to it you will return." In 50, the disciples are told unequivocally that they "came from the light." It is evident then that in this saying Jesus is not referring to physical or historical origins; he is speaking of spiritual origins equivalent to what he means by the "Kingdom" and the "light."

In the next line, he further explains: "For where the beginning is, there will the end be." The literal translation of this line is, "For in the *place* which the origin (is), there the end will be." As previously noted, the word "place" is often employed in Thomas as a code word for the Kingdom. It is used here to further make clear that the "beginning" cannot be found in the world, but only in the Kingdom, in the realm of the spiritual. The idea of finding the end where the beginning is comes up in another saying, the Schoedel/Leipoldt translation of saying 42: "Come into being as you pass away."

There, the idea is presented, as well, but more succinctly. To "come into being" has essentially the same meaning as to take one's "place in the beginning," as in our present saying. Both phrases urge the reader to find or return to the Kingdom. In Thomas, the Kingdom is man's true home. It is the truth that lies hidden behind the illusion of separation. To find it again, man must abandon his belief in separation. He must die to everything that supports and defends that belief. In short, he must let his ego, the belief structure responsible for the conception of separation, "pass away." This is what it means to "pass away" in saying 42 and what it means to "know the end" here. To experience the beginning (the Kingdom), man's identification with the ego must come to an end. As one's ego identification passes away, what comes into being is the awareness of one's true identity—not a separate self but the wholeness of creation, undivided and inseparable from its Source.

The disciples are concerned with their future. They ask Jesus what their end will be. By this, they apparently want to know what will happen to them after they die. Their "end," as they understand it, is the end of the body. In Thomas, however, the body is already dead. In saying 56, Jesus calls the world a "corpse." And in 80, the body is like the world, suggesting that the body is also a corpse, a thing without true life. His reply here in saying 18 suggests that what begins and ends in any significant way is not the body. What actually begins is the awareness of one's true identity. It is the moment when man discovers he is not a body but a spiritual being, a child of God and one with his Father.

In this saying, the "beginning" is a symbol for eternal life. In the context of the world, it is a fresh change, but in the context of the Kingdom, it is a return to a place where nothing changes. In that place, there are no dualities; there are no beginnings and no ends. So when man "takes his place in the beginning," he will know the "end" of all concepts, feelings, and sensations of anything that characterizes separation, even space and time. In a sense, he will return to the moment of creation in the eternal now. The experience is one of utter bliss. This is the ultimate answer. This is how Jesus responds to the fear of his disciples. Their thinking is on a wrong track, but with this suggestion they are offered his alternative to fear.

Some commentators have suggested that this saying represents a reality that is cyclical, reflecting the cyclical patterns in nature. There was certainly much interest in that idea in antiquity. However, in Thomas, reality is not natural; it is supranatural. It cannot be cyclical because to be so, it must exist in time. It is supra-existent. It is not pre-existent, post-existent, or anything in-between. It exists beyond the illusion of space and time. Cycles in nature, therefore, are not what Jesus is speaking of here.

Further evidence of this is found in the next line: "Blessed is he who will take his place in the beginning. He will know the end and will not taste death." The literal translation from the Coptic is this: "A blessed one he who shall stand to his feet in the beginning, and he shall know the end, and he shall receive taste not of death." Here again is that key phrase in Thomas, "stand to his feet," which unfortunately is reduced by most translators to merely "stand" or "take his place." In all the other sayings in which it is found (16, 23, 28, and 50), it suggests a waking-up event, a condition of wholeness or ultimate awareness of the Truth. Since "beginning," as we have seen above, is synonymous in Thomas with the "Kingdom" and with "light," to "discover the beginning" is to wake up to the Kingdom and be filled with light. It is to be enlightened to the wonder of God's love. Thus, every time man makes this discovery, he returns to the creation of his soul in timelessness. He wakes up from his space-time dream to "discover" his timeless creation. As I explained in my commentary on saying 1, he then will not "taste" death when it comes. He will not experience it as a loss. The answer Jesus gives his disciples is direct and uncompromising. In response to their fear, he tells them that when they wake up to the Kingdom, they will know with certainty that there is nothing to fear.

Saying 19

> **(19) Jesus said, "Blessed is he who came to be before he came to be. If you become my disciples and listen to my words, these stones will serve you. For there are five trees for you in Paradise which remain unchanged in summer and winter and whose leaves do not fall. Whoever knows them will not taste death."**

The Jesus of the Gospel of Thomas is no ordinary, first-century Jewish reformer. Nor is his gospel Gnostic with a capital "G." (See my commentary on the prologue.) As we have seen in these sayings, his perspective is that of non-dualism. In this saying, hidden within a maze of seeming contradictions and mysterious allusions, is a non-dualistic version of the Genesis creation story. As evidence of this, there are four features borrowed here from that story. There is the phrase, "he who came to be before he came to be." This is an allusion to the creation of man, the first creation, but in this case, as we shall see, it is followed by a second creation or pseudo creation. Next, there is the promise that, "If you become my disciples and listen to my words, these stones will serve you." This reminds us of Genesis 1:26 and 1:28, where God granted Adam dominion over the earth and all its creatures. In this saying, the word "stones" is used as a metaphor for the world. Then, there are the "five trees" in Paradise, which bring to mind the trees of "life" and "knowledge" in the Garden of Eden. Lastly, there is the promise that whoever knows these five trees will "not taste death." This is a promise of eternal life which contrasts with the punishment of mortality meted out to Adam and Eve. So already we see that the "Fall" of man in Genesis is here being supplanted by an invitation. It is an invitation to rise to true dominion over the idea of a separate world and, by doing so, experience immortality once again.

The first statement, in the form of a beatitude, presents a paradox that can be explained by seeing the first "came to be" as the real creation and the second "came to be" as an attempt by man to create himself, to substitute the real with the unreal and the truth with the dream. This second coming into being may be further explained as a fall into a dreamlike state brought about by a single thought. That thought was, "I am separate." For the Father, nothing changed, since He understood that separation was impossible. For man, however, overwhelming guilt and fear resulting from this thought, the thought of spurning God's will, enveloped him like a shroud. To escape this intensity of self-inflicted pain, he fell asleep and dreamed a dream of separation. It was totally unreal, and yet, as all dreams do, it appeared solid and beyond doubt. Without realizing what he had done, he thus had made for himself the perfect refuge to escape from what he imagined was the wrath of God. He had made the physical universe, consisting of nothing, yet seeming to be everything. It was just a dream, but within this dream, he could lose himself and hide his shame for what he fantasized was the unforgivable "sin" of rejecting God. But again, nothing actually had changed. God's wrath was likewise a component of the dream. God's love for his Son remained constant and unlimited. There was no need for God to forgive his Son, as his Son had simply fallen asleep. There was no legitimate cause for man's guilt, and, therefore, there were no real effects. God's love of His creation remained unchanged, but for man everything seemed to sink into an endless nightmare. On that illusory first day of his newfound refuge from God, form and change were made, struggle and violence overwhelmed peace, and everything was divided against itself. Life was splintered into immeasurable parts, and behind this dream of chaos always loomed guilt and fear, fueling the dream and driving it onward. He saw himself as fragmented into separate bodies, bodies condemned to suffer pain and die ingloriously as if in a prison made of iron. Yet, because of man's "original sin" of believing he was separate from God, he also believed that pain and death were his due punishments for this "crime." Consequently, his "just deserts" continued unabated, while the thought of God's mercy faded almost completely from his tortured mind.

I write about this process as if it happened in the past, but since God did not create time, there is no time. Therefore, this second coming into being is happening right now. In every seeming instant, man makes a separate world and adjusts to what he makes. This self-deception is so powerful that nearly all memory of his first coming, of his true creation into being, is obliterated. In his mind, the second coming replaces the first coming, leaving barely a trace of the truth behind. The truth is this: nothing has happened. God's will for His creation has not been overthrown. God has not been defeated, nor has man lost the love of his Source. He merely sleeps in what Jesus calls in saying 28 a blind and empty state of drunkenness.

The effects of believing this dream, of confusing it with reality, are the same now as they were when Jesus spoke these words. Guilt is unavoidable when separation is taken seriously. It means that man has overthrown God. With guilt comes fear. From this presumption of guilt comes a fear of retribution so intense that man feels the impulse to blunt his pain by projecting guilt outward, beyond his mind, in the form of hostile forces. Such forces do not exist except in his imagination, where they serve a purpose. All of his problems could then be blamed on others or on forces beyond his control.

And so it goes. Life becomes a constant struggle in which pain, illness, and death are seen as proof that God is powerless and illusory. Only the ego-mind, the part of the mind that believes in separation, is considered reliable. Thus the dream becomes real, and the real becomes a dream. This is the second coming into being, not a true creation at all but the emergence of an alien identity made seemingly real in a dream of loss and limitation. The only escape from that dream is to wake up and remember God's love.

In the previous saying (18), Jesus urged his disciples to "know the beginning." By knowing the beginning, they will know the Kingdom and remember God's love. Likewise here in 19, by coming into being in the first and only creation, by letting go of all post-creation concepts of separation, the Kingdom is revisited and embraced. The world and its dream of separation vanish. The immense complexity of living in this illusion of a world is replaced in the mind by the utter simplicity of oneness. By seeking the stillness of God and by forgiving others as well as himself for his self-imposed guilt, man discovers his freedom and is truly blessed. The same Coptic word, translated here as "came to be" or sometimes "came into being," can also be found in saying 42: "Come into being as you pass away (Leipoldt/Schoedel translation)." In both sayings, it points to the same thing, the original and true creation. This is the first coming of this saying. It is this which Jesus urges the seeker to revisit and, by doing so, to know the Source from which he came.

The second coming, where the phrase "came to be" is repeated, is the coming of the ego within the mind of man. It is the coming of an idea and a new identity in the form of separation and violence that is based on nothing more than unjustified fear and guilt. How supremely ironic it would be, then, if from this saying in Thomas came the mistaken interpretation of this phrase, espoused by Christians for centuries, that Jesus would someday return to earth in physical form. This is what the Church has referred to as the "Second Coming." Clearly, however, this understanding is not consistent with the meaning of this saying in this gospel.

Jesus next speaks of the "stones" which will minister to those disciples who listen to his words. By listening to Jesus, they will learn that the world of stones, including all other manifestations of the world, is an illusion. They will learn that the world has no meaning or significance other than what they erroneously believe it has. If they closely listen to his words and apply them, they will be free to experience a world purified of hate and fear, and one which will softly relinquish its hold on their minds. Thus, they will have dominion over the world—the world as an idea, not as a fact. Unlike man's dominion of the world in Genesis 1:26 and 1:28, this dominion of the world is completely gentle and loving. Thus, before the dream is dismissed entirely from the mind, it becomes mild and pleasant.

Scholars have proposed endless theories about the meaning of the "five trees." I suspect that they simply allude to five characteristics of God's creation which, unlike anything in the world, are changeless and, therefore, dependable. *Perfection*, for example, might be one of them; *eternal truth* another. In the Kingdom, all is perfect and nothing changes. In Genesis, the tree of the knowledge of good and evil is God's concern but a dangerous thing for man. In Thomas, *knowledge* is a positive thing—not the dualistic knowledge of good and evil but the knowledge of God's love. *Love* itself might be included among the five, a love in which the rule of *sinlessness* is an essential feature. Thus we have five trees: perfection, eternal truth, knowledge, love, and sinlessness.[1] Jesus may have had others in mind, but these appear to fit the ideals of changelessness and spirit-centered awareness suggested by the last two lines.

Lastly, this Thomas version of Genesis claims that "whoever becomes acquainted with them (the five trees) will not taste death (not experience it as a meaningful loss)." That is to say, he will not experience loss. In contrast, when Adam and Eve become acquainted with the tree of the knowledge of good and evil in Genesis 3, they lose their immortality and become weak and vulnerable to death. God tells them, "You are dust and unto dust you shall return." The message of Jesus in this gospel is not that man is dust but that he is one with his creator, eternal in spirit and inseparable from His glory.

That is his reality, despite his efforts to hide from that glory in an alien and fabricated world.

---

1 These terms were borrowed from a section in *A Course in Miracles*, M-4.X.3:1-4 which refers to them as "the Son of God's inheritance." Their use seems appropriate here. Foundation For Inner Peace, *A Course in Miracles*, 2nd edn. (New York, Viking, 1996).

Saying 20

> **(20) The disciples said to Jesus, "Tell us what the Kingdom of Heaven is like."**
> **He replied to them, "It is like a mustard seed, the smallest of all seeds. But when it falls on tilled soil, it produces a great plant and becomes a shelter for birds of the sky."**

> *"This is what the Sovereign Lord says: I myself will take a shoot from the very top of a cedar and plant it; I will break off a tender sprig from its topmost shoots and plant it on a high and lofty mountain. On the mountain heights of Israel I will plant it; it will produce branches and bear fruit and become a splendid cedar. Birds of every kind will nest in it; they will find shelter in the shade of its branches." (Ezekiel 17:22-23)*

Here again in this saying, we have the same themes that we find in many of the others. Among these are the absurdity of the situation (in sayings 8, 9, 21a, 57, 64, 65, 76, 98, 107), the preference for the small (9, 76, 98, 107) or impractical (8), the generational power of the small (9, 96) and lastly, the need for prepared ground (9).

The mustard plant was chosen for this saying precisely because most farmers in ancient Palestine considered it a noxious weed. Evidence of the nature of this troublesome little plant comes from Pliny the Elder. Writing circa 78 CE, he states that it "grows entirely wild," and when sown "it is barely possible to get the place (the plot of land) free of it, as the seed, when it falls, germinates at once."[1] It would seem more likely that Jesus would have compared the "Kingdom of Heaven," referred elsewhere in Thomas as the "Kingdom of the Father," to the mighty cedar, which in Ezekiel (see above),

God plants from a small sprig of a tree on a high mountain. Indeed, Ezekiel says of this tree that in its branches "birds of every kind…find shelter." But instead, Jesus chooses the noxious mustard plant. It is, of course, completely unlike a cedar tree and grows only to the size of a small shrub. It would never be considered a "great" plant. Any informed, first-century Jew listening to these words of Jesus would have surely remembered the Ezekiel passage and wondered why the speaker did not compare the Kingdom to the cedar. But rather than choosing that useful and imposing tree, from the viewpoint of the world, Jesus settles upon a weed, which the farmers of that day would have shunned. It is a plant of little commercial value—an absurd choice.

The disciples say to Jesus, "Tell us what the Kingdom of Heaven is like." The "Kingdom" is the keystone of Jesus's teaching. The word appears between twenty-one and twenty-four times in the Coptic text, depending on how it is translated. In this gospel, the "Kingdom" is a realm completely unlike the finite realm of the world. It is important to understand this difference. In the world's realm, everything is separate from everything else. The value of everything is measured by the effect it has on the body, and knowledge is limited to what is experienced by the senses or conceptualized by the intellect. Such a realm is unstable and undependable. On the other hand, the Kingdom is a spiritual realm that is unchanging and beyond what the senses can perceive or the brain conceive. In this saying (20), it is the awareness of this spiritual realm that is compared to the mustard seed. This tiny seed of awareness is germinated by a single decision, a resolute commitment to find a path that truly satisfies the soul and not just the pleasure centers of the body. As it grows, serenity comes without effort to a quiet mind. This is what the Kingdom is *like.* The present moment expands as all interest in the past and future loses its fascination. Gradually, judgments are relaxed and dualities lose their edge. Concern about the body disappears, and like a mighty river, peace sweeps through the mind and softens the heart. The appreciation of God's love expands as if it were a towering tree. And while the ego sees this spiritual realm as a useless thing, like the lowly mustard plant, the spirit's eyes see a grandeur there that is beyond anything the world can offer. Awareness of God's Kingdom becomes like the cedar of Ezekiel's prophecy in which the birds of the sky find shelter. These birds, however, are not the nations or client states envisioned by Ezekiel. In this saying, they represent those who find shelter not in the world but in the awareness of the Kingdom.

The sayings of Jesus are often described by scholars as subversive. In this saying, his message is highly subversive. He says here that although the world has little regard for the spiritual, and may even see it as a useless thing, like the mustard plant, it is far more. When embraced by a willing and prepared mind, it becomes immensely valuable and fruitful. In short, these two realms of being are sharply contrasted. It is the spiritual realm, represented by the mustard plant, not the worldly realm represented by the cedar tree that is more highly valued.

Again, consider the words of Ezekiel 17:22-23. From something small, something immense grows. In its branches, "birds of every kind" find shelter. What a paradox it is that Jesus chose this particular passage on which to model his saying! For in Ezekiel, these words have clear metaphorical and prophetic connotations. They are words spoken by God through His prophet in Babylon. It is generally agreed by scholars that what is metaphorically described here is a vision of the emergence of a leader from the House of David. And like a sprig of cedar, God will plant him on the "mountain heights of Israel," suggestive of Mount Zion or, more familiarly, Jerusalem. The promise of this passage was irresistible to those who yearned for a strong and righteous leader. This was to be the Messiah, the long-awaited one, the savior of Israel. That Jesus would use these same words to describe his little mustard plant is extraordinary. It suggests that the idea of a special, messianic savior was something of no interest to him. By this substitution of the mighty cedar by the lowly mustard plant, he appears to reject the messianic concept outright. Instead, he favors the idea that the hope of not only Israel but humanity at large lies not in such a grand and powerful leader. It rests instead on the tiny seed of God's love that is planted firmly in the minds of every man and woman. He chooses the hardy mustard seed to represent that tiny germ of awareness which, when carefully tended, grows to encompass the fullness of the Kingdom. With this preference of metaphors, making what seems to be an absurd claim for this little plant, he again affirms his conviction that the seemingly small, the ostensibly impractical, the hidden yet compelling realm of the Kingdom is the true wellspring of God's power.

---

1 Pliny the Elder, *Natural History*, translated by Harris Rockham Loeb, 1950, Book XIX, Chapter LIV.

Saying 21

> **(21a) Mary asked Jesus, "Whom are your disciples like?" He replied, "They are like small children who have settled in a field that is not theirs. When the owners of the field come, they will say, 'Give us back our field.' They (will) undress in their presence so as to let them have their field back and they give it back to them.**
> **(21b) Therefore I say, if the owner of a house knows that the thief is coming, he will be on his guard before he comes and will not let him dig into his house of his domain (Kingdom) to carry away his things. You, then, be on your guard against the world. Gird your loins with great strength lest the robbers find a way to come to you, for the insufficiency which you anticipate, they will find.**
> **(21c) Let there be among you a man of understanding. When the grain ripened, he came quickly with his sickle in his hand and reaped it. Whoever has ears to hear, let him hear."**

There appear to be two separate sayings here with a concluding exhortation. However, as we shall see, the first saying prepares the reader to understand the second in a new light. Consequently, both segments work together to make an extraordinary claim, that the best defense is defenselessness. To demonstrate this point, Jesus constructs this logion very much as would a poet or an abstract painter. He explains nothing, but instead arrays ideas on the page like strokes of color on a canvas. He then asks the reader to step back to experience the effect of this image on his mind. What at first seems baffling and inconsistent eventually comes into focus and engages the observer as no simple statement of fact can. It is the reader's inner work to which Jesus appeals to complete his poem and message. By connecting the dots, the reader discovers the hidden meaning of the logion and thus shares, in a sense, in its birth.

There are two ways in which the first saying might be understood. Either the disciples are seen negatively as immature squatters or positively as the rightful followers of Jesus. How they are envisioned metaphorically will determine how this saying is interpreted. Here are the possibilities:

The disciples as immature squatters. In this scenario, the children (the disciples) are unwelcome outsiders. They are squatters who have settled in a field that is not their own. The owners, apparently concerned with developing the field for profit, order the squatters off their land. In shame, the children take off their clothes and leave the field with nothing. As a consequence of their unlawful and unruly behavior, they have lost everything. The owners are the winners in this scenario. They now justifiably have control of their field. One may conclude that it is they who are the worthy exemplars of this story and, metaphorically, the rightful followers of Jesus.

The problem with this interpretation is that it favors the "owners" of the field over his disciples, represented as children. It also ignores what Jesus says of his disciples elsewhere in this gospel. In saying 50, he describes them as "the chosen of the Living Father" and as coming "from the light." According to Jesus, then, this is their identity; this is who they are. It, therefore, seems peculiar that he would also describe them as squatters. The worst that can be said of them, looking at their behavior throughout this gospel, is that at times they seem confused. Some sayings begin with the disciples expressing fear and confusion. However, in the context of these particular sayings, this appears to be a rhetorical device used to dramatize the point of the dialogue. They give voice to the standard view of reality. However, such sayings are designed to reveal a message, not to expose the failings of his disciples. In short, his disciples are just that—his disciples; those who follow his teachings.

However, my main objection to perceiving the disciples in a negative light is that in saying 37, the removal of garments "like little children" is metaphorically equated with seeing "the Son of the Living One." In that saying, those who shed their clothes, in the sense of dropping their defenses and attachments, are clearly blessed and esteemed. This appears to be the underlying message in this saying as well.

The disciples as the rightful followers of Jesus. Here, and in Thomas as a whole, Jesus uses metaphors far more assiduously than is commonly recognized. The "field" stands for the world, the realm of separation. The children represent those earnest disciples who have settled in this world, though it is not their home. Like Jesus, they are "in it, but not of it." They are innocent, like little children, although the world is a place in which innocence is seen as a sign of weakness. Metaphorically, the "owners" (literally, "the lords of the field") are not external players. They represent those beliefs that support the belief structure of the ego. They are the personifications of fear and guilt. They rule a world of their own making, a world which reflects outwardly that which is experienced inwardly. The innocence of the children is a threat to these owners. Innocence is always a threat to fear and guilt. And so, the owners wish to own the field/world outright. They say, "Give us back our field." In response, the children paradoxically become utterly defenseless and remove their clothes. In Thomas, clothing is a metaphor for defensiveness, and in a later saying (36), Jesus suggests that in the Kingdom, God will provide such people their "cloak," by which he means their security. (See my commentary on the Greek version of saying 36, as well as sayings 37 and 112.) So they surrender their defenses, their few remaining fears to the world, trusting solely in God. They give back what belongs to the world and thus attain for themselves what the world cannot give—real security and peace. In the context of this gospel, they metaphorically return to their true home in the spiritual realm of the Kingdom. To those who carefully study this gospel, the story is a familiar one. The Kingdom of the Father is won by those willing to give back to the world what belongs to the world and, by doing so, discover the lightness of their being.

In 21b, "Mary," presumably Mary Magdalene, is no longer the person addressed, as she was in 21a. The plural pronoun "you" has taken her place, as it has in the concluding remarks. I see no problem here. The speaker simply turns to his wider audience for effect. In this second saying, the "owner" is a sympathetic character. He is no longer the personification of fear and guilt, but just a man. He is the owner of a "house." Again, this code word in Thomas nearly always refers to a structure of convictions essential for the comprehension of reality or, conversely, a structure of beliefs that prevents that comprehension. This can be observed by comparing how the word works in other sayings (16, 35, 48, 71, 97, and 98). The phrase used in this saying, "house of his domain," further narrows its meaning. There is no logical reason why this extra word "domain" should be added to the word "house" unless it has a special significance. It would seem superfluous. In fact, it is the same word commonly translated elsewhere in Thomas as "Kingdom." The implied phrase, "house of his Kingdom" suggests that there is a thought structure (house) required to welcome and give shelter to the Kingdom of the Father. It is this "house" that must be secured. This is what the "thief" is threatening to carry away. Metaphorically, Jesus is saying that a preventive measure is needed to safeguard the truth of the Kingdom. That measure is the comprehension of the non-dualistic nature of the Kingdom. This understanding must be fully accepted and secured so that the "robbers" cannot take it away.

Jesus then equates the "robbers" with the "world": "You, then, be on guard against the world." The world here represents the projections of the ego-mind. (See my introduction and saying 89 for this use of the word "projection.") The "robbers" represent the beliefs of the ego and have the same function here as the "owners" do in the first saying. He says, "Arm yourselves with great strength lest the robbers find a way to come to you." In a similar saying (103), Jesus says essentially the same thing, again urging the "man" to muster his "domain," which is the Kingdom, and allow this Kingdom to be his sole defense. Once more, the first saying (21a) informs the second (21b), suggesting a new definition for "bind up your loins." In the Kingdom, what is of value is defended by defenselessness. One defends best by abandoning all support of fear and guilt. Consequently, with nothing to struggle against, the ego-mind recognizes that it has no purpose for existing and quietly relinquishes its hold on the mind.

The next line says, "for the insufficiency which you anticipate, they will find." This phrase has been translated many different ways. The key word, "insufficiency," is translated from *chreia*, a Greek loanword which is the nominal form of the word for "need" or "lack." This additional line does not negate the saying as a whole but adds a twist to it. It seems to be saying that one should not only defend the truth against error, but one should do so fully and wholeheartedly. Anticipating or fearing the insufficiency of these defenses is an integral part of the error itself. The message seems to be that one must trust completely in the sufficiency of the Kingdom. Otherwise, the robbers will "find a way to come to you"; that is, the ego will discover one's doubts and exploit them. Metaphorically, one must shed one's clothes of defensiveness and stand wholly naked before God. Complete trust in the Kingdom is all the armor one needs. This is how the Kingdom is defended.

The final exhortation applies to both 21a and b. It refers to a passage in Joel 3:13:

> "Swing the sickle, for the harvest is ripe. Come trample the grapes, for the winepress is full and the vats overflow—so great is their wickedness!"

In this Old Testament passage, this is a call to arms from God for Israel to "prepare for war" against their enemies. He additionally urges them to "beat (their) plowshares into swords" (Joel 3: 9-10), the reverse of the well-known passages from Isaiah 2:4 and Micah 4:3, where the "swords" will be beaten into "plowshares." It apparently was chosen by Jesus to further clarify his message, a typical stratagem in Thomas. As in the previous saying (20), he compares an Old Testament passage to his own version to contrast his radically different message. Whereas Joel calls for violence as the appropriate response to external enemies, Jesus calls for surrender and defenselessness as the appropriate responses to internal enemies. Whereas Joel swings the sickle to destroy, Jesus urges the man of understanding to harvest his "grain," which is the awareness of God's Kingdom. The implication is that for Jesus this is the preferred girding of loins—to trust in God's love and to harvest His healing power. To drive home this point, he adds, "Whoever has ears to hear, let him hear." Wherever this line appears in Thomas, it always follows a difficult saying. It is as if Jesus is suggesting, "Take your time. Consider the saying as a whole. Weigh my words carefully."

Saying 22

> **(22) Jesus saw some infants being suckled. He said to his disciples, "These infants being suckled are like those who enter the Kingdom." They said to him, "Shall we then, be infants to enter the Kingdom?" Jesus replied to them, "When you make the two one, and when you make the inside like the outside and the outside like the inside, and the above like the below, and when you make the male and the female a single one, so that the male not be male nor the female female; and when you make eyes in the place of an eye, and a hand in place of a hand, and a foot in place of a foot, and a likeness in place of a likeness; then will you enter the Kingdom."**

There is no logion in Thomas that supports non-duality more directly and more convincingly than this one. One might even say that in this combination of affirmations, we have the very definition of non-duality. Consider the first assertion. Jesus compares the Kingdom of the Father to infants being suckled at their mothers' breasts. This brings to mind saying 4 in which a seven-day-old infant's wisdom is superior to that of an elderly man. It is because of that infant's state of purity and innocence that he most exemplifies the wisdom of the Kingdom. He has freshly emerged from the wonder of creation and has not yet learned about complexity and judgment. Likewise in this saying, the nursing infants represent the state of oneness with Source. In contrast with the world of countless identities and endless dichotomies, nursing infants are the perfect metaphor for union with God. The mothers and their children, in their love for each other, barely comprehend where child ends and mother begins. It is nearly seamless, and seamlessness reflects the true state of man's relationship with his creator. Moreover, infants are wholly dependent on their mothers. In this comparison with the Kingdom, it follows that this is the message—that man's intrinsic nature is to be wholly dependent on God. In short, it is because of the infants' purity and innocence, their oneness with and absolute dependence on their mothers, that they are "like those who enter the Kingdom." In Thomas, this is not *how* life should be; it is how life *is*. This is man's true nature, and it is by realizing this that man enters the Kingdom.

The disciples ask, "Shall we then, be infants to enter the Kingdom?" They, of course, cannot physically become infants again. But they can become *like* infants, and in the following lines, Jesus explains how this is achieved. His first requirement, making the "two one," encapsulates everything that follows. Making the "two one" is also mentioned in saying 106 as being the precondition for metaphorically moving mountains. Seeing everything as one has this power over the world because the world is a manifestation of dualistic thinking. Despite what the senses appear to report to the brain, the world is not a fact but a projection resulting from such thinking. Therefore, any significant change on the level of the mind will be reflected on the screen of consciousness. Oneness experienced on this level will be projected onto consciousness as harmony and peace. This is a key principle of non-dualism. It is difficult to grasp because the egocentric intellect rejects anything that seems to challenge its long-held belief in separation. But take that mode of thinking away and what remains is the oneness of the Kingdom. I will write again about this phenomenon later. However, this is not a theory; it can be experienced by anyone willing to test it for himself. It has a long tradition, having been called moksha, nirvana, self-realization, and many other names.

The oneness of the Kingdom cannot be described in words or comprehended by the ego-mind. It is a spiritual reality and thus incomparable with anything in space and time. Commentators often overlook the sweep of this saying, conceptualizing the making of two into one as an integration or fusion of the two. It is not fusion. It is the relinquishment of perception for vision, vision being the spiritual insight required to witness oneness. It is the willingness to comprehend, beyond the range of the senses, a unity that is experienced directly by the mind. It is the spiritual focus of the mystic and the sage—of Jesus, the Buddha, and Lao Tzu.

Jumping ahead a few lines, if we carefully ponder the words, "and when you make the male and the female a single one, so that the male not be male nor the female female," we will understand that this single one is not an androgynous being but one in whom neither maleness nor femaleness has any meaning. To see either a male or a female in this way is to suspend belief in bodies and see them both as spirit, at one with life and one with their Source. By "making the two one," an error is reconciled with the truth. The Kingdom of the Father, which has nothing to do with bodies, the world, or separation, is thus restored to its rightful place in the mind.

As an experiment, if we go back and attach the same explanatory phrase that applied to the male/female dichotomy, this time, to the outside/inside split, we get, "when you make the inside like the outside and the outside like the inside, *so that the inside not be inside nor the outside outside.*" With the application of that additional phrase to this dichotomy, we can see more clearly that envisioning such dualities as meaningless does not suggest a combination of the two, but the complete denial of duality itself. Likewise, the above/below duality is denied in the same way. From this understanding, we can conclude that in Thomas, wholeness of spirit is all that exists, and what is not of this wholeness is illusion. Essentially, there is only "one," not "two." All else is meaningless. When man "makes" this so, he confirms its reality by waking up from his dream of separation.

In the final phase of this logion, Jesus describes what happens when the illusion of "two" is released. You will enter the Kingdom "when you make eyes in place of an eye," that is to say—when spiritual vision replaces perception. The body's eyes perceive only what the mind projects, and the mind projects only what it accepts as true. As I previously mentioned, this reversal of what man has always believed to be true is admittedly a very difficult thing to accept. What Jesus is saying here is that when spiritual vision is made to replace the world's perception, man will witness the Kingdom of the Father's love, not the world of his own fearful projections. Once the truth of vision cuts through the heavy fog of projection, he will find his true home.

In the same manner, Jesus, in the remainder of this saying, compares physical features with their spiritual counterparts. He says that to enter the Kingdom, one must make "a hand in place of a hand, and a foot in place of a foot." The spiritual "hand" is the same "hand" as in saying 41. In that saying, it states, "Whoever has something in his hand will receive more." This is the hand that shares love, and by giving love away, the giver discovers that he has not lost anything but has gained more than he has lost. To "make" this hand is not to create anything new but simply to change one's mind and let go of what is not true. In this case, what is not true is the body's insatiable need for *more*, symbolized by the physical hand. That hand is a grasping tool and useful in serving the body. But man is not his body, and the giving "hand," the spiritual hand, is really his only hand. Likewise, the spiritual "foot" is the conviction on which man stands in the knowledge that the Kingdom is found in the here and now. It is not found through needless journeys or by chasing after magical remedies. It is found when restless roaming ends in the awareness of the present moment.

Finally, the Kingdom is found when you make "a likeness in place of a likeness." This asks the question: What is man's identity? Is he a product of the world, created by nature, or is he divine, created in the likeness of God? Does this not suggest that he cannot be both? He cannot be both like a body and also like a soul. To know the truth of the Kingdom, he must abandon dualistic thinking and identify not with his physical likeness but with his divine likeness, which is his true identity.

In this logion, Jesus not only explains the process of becoming like an infant, of experiencing the same sense of wonder and serenity as does the infant, he sets out for the reader his philosophy of non-dualism that informs and explains nearly every other saying in Thomas.

Saying 23

> **(23) Jesus said, "I will choose you, one out of a thousand, and two out of ten thousand, and they will stand as a single one."**

The image we have of Jesus choosing his apostles in the New Testament is memorable. Responding to his call were such future luminaries as Simon Peter, Matthew, James, and John. Such men as these were always held in high regard in the Christian church. They were recognized as saints and, even today, children are named in their honor, reminding us of their virtues and acts of faith. Furthermore, as the gospel writers had it, Jesus appeared to select his apostles mostly from among strangers, giving the impression that his choice was divinely inspired. From that tradition of specialness evolved the hierarchy of the church, of deacons, priests, bishops, and later, of popes, the spiritual heirs of the first bishop of Rome, Simon Peter. This saying in Thomas reminds us of those choices. However, there is more going on here than the mere selection of apostles.

Consider the preposterous range of this choice: "I shall choose you, one out of a thousand, and two out of ten thousand." In a work having many such instances of hyperbole, this saying appears to fit that pattern. Other examples in Thomas are sayings 4, 16, 32, and 107. In saying 9, the seed falling on good soil produces good fruit, "sixty per measure and a hundred and twenty per measure." In that saying, however, the claim of productivity is exaggerated but not absurdly so. It simply suggests that the "seeds" of God's love are enormously fruitful. In this saying (23), the numbers suggest something else—the extreme specialness of those apostles ultimately chosen. As we have seen in other sayings, when Jesus exaggerates anything, there is always a glimmer of humor about it. One can witness that humor in this saying. It is as if Jesus is saying, "Did I say one out of a thousand? Oh, it's much more than that—two out of ten thousand!" The numbers themselves have no particular significance. He is simply saying that his choice will have the effect of drawing from a huge group of people a very special few.

Now consider this: in this gospel, specialness is repeatedly denied. Man is not something separate and special; he is one with all of creation. As we saw in the previous logion (22), the Kingdom is entered when "you make the two one." Only when dualities of every kind are denied can the oneness of the Kingdom be experienced. How strange it is that this saying (23), with its claim of extreme specialness, should follow directly after saying 22, which so unconditionally rejects duality and thus specialness. The juxtaposition of these two positions is both intriguing and troubling.

The final phrase, however, pulls the saying back from the brink of inconsistency with this line: "and they shall stand as a single one." The literal translation is "and they will stand to their feet, they being one alone." Again, we see these two code expressions: "stand to their feet" and "one alone." In the context of Thomas, "stand to their feet" always gives rise to an experience of waking up to a profound realization. "One alone" is familiar too. In the previous saying (22), it describes, in the literal Coptic, the singularity of male and female. This line might be restated as, "and they will awaken to the fact that they are wholly one." An almost identical phrase can be found in the literal version of saying 16: "and they will stand to their feet, they being whole ones." In both 16 and 23, the phrase completely reverses the duality of the previous lines. In each case, the initial statement is one of extreme duality. Then at the very last moment, an idea is proposed that completely confounds and challenges the reader. It is as if one is snapped back from an easy and conventional understanding of the saying and reminded of the "hidden" meaning of this gospel.

So what is being said here? It seems to be saying initially that on the level of the world, Jesus is seeking and choosing those rare individuals who might be open to receive his message. But the irony is that those rare individuals will learn from Jesus that they are not rare at all, not unique, nor even individuals. There is, in fact, nothing that separates them from the one thousand or the ten thousand. They are oneness itself, the Kingdom itself. That is the insight to which they will awaken.

Again, Jesus contrasts the two realms or kingdoms of existence. The Kingdom of the Father is often portrayed in extreme or absurd terms. A fisherman throws a whole boatload of fish away. A shepherd abandons his flock of sheep. Here Jesus, in a sense, ignores almost ten thousand potential apostles. But, it is also true that from the viewpoint of the Kingdom, the world is a realm of absurdity. It is an absurd hallucination that has nothing to do with reality. Both realms seem utterly insane to each other. However, the realm in which Jesus stands and has his being is the oneness of God's Kingdom. That realm is real. Once allegiance to His Kingdom is chosen over allegiance to the absurdity of man's kingdom, no additional choice is possible or necessary. Where all is one, true choice is impossible. There are no dualities to choose between.

Saying 24

> **(24) His disciples said to him, "Show us the place where you are, for it is necessary for us to seek it."**
> **He said to them, "Whoever has ears, let him hear. There is light within a man of light, and he lights up the whole world. If he does not shine, he is darkness."**

The disciples say to Jesus, "Show us the place where you are." The word "place" is a code word in Thomas, not for a physical location but for the locus of spiritual freedom, or more precisely, the experience of ultimate freedom from the limitations of the world. It is a code word for the Kingdom. When this is understood, then it can be seen that the disciples are asking for the most profound revelation possible. The "place" where Jesus resides is beyond any worldly location, beyond any psychological state, and beyond any concept of which the mind can conceive. In an earlier saying (17), he says, "I will give you…what has never occurred to the human mind." This is the "place" that the disciples seek. (For a more thorough commentary on "place" as a code word, see my remarks on saying 67.)

In his reply, Jesus asks his disciples to truly listen. He says, "Whoever has ears, let him hear." In Thomas, this is always an invitation to deeply ponder his words and not allow an easy response to dismiss a profound question. He then invites them to consider a "man of light." This is presumably any man or woman who becomes aware of his or her inner light. "Light" is a word that appears repeatedly in Thomas. In saying 77, Jesus identifies himself as "light." In 50, he tells his disciples that they came from the "light," that it is their source. The "light" of the Father (God) is specifically mentioned in 83. In 61, to be whole, or not divided, is to be full of "light." In 11b, one comes to "dwell in the light," and finally, in 33, light must be shared for it to be of any value.

One may conclude from these examples that Jesus considers light a core quality which man and God share. Also, it can be seen from these examples that light represents both the brilliance of God's love and the knowledge of His Kingdom. One is an inseparable aspect of the other. When man extends this light to others, its radiance increases, as does his own awareness of it. If he does not extend it, or as our present saying expresses it, if he does not "shine," the fog of the world closes in on him, and "he is darkness."

Jesus expands on this idea when he says that when a man of light shines, his light "lights up the whole world." He shines on everything without exception. If separation is a lie, as this gospel suggests, then man's light cannot be confined to one individual. It touches every mind, because there is only one mind. For this reason, when one allows his light to shine, it fills the darkness. And though the awareness of it may be blocked, it is still received in every corner of the Kingdom. This is because the Kingdom is intrinsically open. There are no hiding places there.

Here, Jesus is saying that it takes only one person, a man or a woman who has found the light within, to extend that light to the entire universe. However, if he does not shine, "he is darkness." This final line reminds us of saying 3b, where it says that if one does not know himself, he dwells in poverty, and he is that poverty. The similarity of these two sayings suggests that Jesus equates the failure to shine with the failure to know one's true identity. Both result in either darkness or poverty of spirit, and. in truth, these consequences are the same.

In this saying, Jesus shows his disciples the "place" or key to his wisdom and spiritual power by pointing to the "place" within themselves where light abides. He urges them to let that light shine. Thus, he gives to his disciples by inviting them to give of themselves. By extending their light, they will know what he knows and thereby know what their divine Father knows as well.

Saying 25

(25) Jesus said, "Love your brother like your soul; protect him like the pupil of your eye."

In Leviticus 19:18, it reads:

> "Do not seek vengeance or bear a grudge against one of your people, but love your neighbor as yourself."

This quote from Leviticus is the source from which Jesus adapted the above saying. Though not one of the Ten Commandments, it is among the many "do not" proscriptions that God additionally revealed to Moses. Specifically, this rule was designed to codify how Israelites should treat other Israelites. One's neighbor was just that—"one of your people," not someone counted among Israel's enemies. In fact, later in Leviticus God is reported saying, "You will pursue your enemies, and they will be slain by the sword before you" (26:7). The author clearly had no soft spot in his heart for Israel's foes. However, aliens living among the Israelites were spared; they were exempted from this rule. But for the most part, "love" in Leviticus was confined to Israel's own people.

In contrast, Jesus uses the word "brother" instead of "neighbor." Some commentators have speculated that "brother" might refer to siblings or to friends within his community of followers. If this were so, then Jesus would be restricting love to an even narrower range of individuals than does Leviticus. That seems hardly likely for one who speaks of the power of making peace in saying 48, and who describes himself as "not a divider" in 72. If, on the other hand, his use of "brother" encompasses all of mankind in the generic and inclusive sense, both male and female, then he would be far surpassing Leviticus in the promotion of brotherly love.

Needless to say, all three of the synoptic gospels—Matthew 22:39; Mark 12:31, 33; Luke 10:27—have Jesus using the word "neighbor." In each case, reference is made to the "law"—that is to say, to this same quote from Leviticus. In Luke, the notion of what it means to love one's neighbor is further illustrated by the parable of the Good Samaritan (Luke 10:29-37) that immediately follows this saying in his gospel. Luke apparently recognized the necessity to understand love as applicable to all individuals, regardless of their ethnic or national identities. However, it seems to me that Luke's parable would have been stronger if it had used the word "brother" rather than "neighbor." The parable is not about neighborliness; it is about brotherly love.

In this saying, we have "Love your brother like your soul." In a gospel that consistently affirms the oneness of creation, there can be no limit or discrimination as to who is loved. This is a call to each of his listeners to love everyone, to literally love everyone as one would love one's own soul. Here again, Jesus exceeds the scope of the saying in Leviticus, where the object of the simile is "yourself." The word "soul" better describes the divine essence of every man and woman. In contrast, "yourself" applies more to what is separate and limited to each individual. For example, man defines himself in a variety of ways: ethnically, professionally, as a member of a particular religion, or as a male or female. He identifies with the world of diversity, and so a multitude of characteristics might define him. But beneath all such definitions is the soul, which in this non-dualistic gospel cannot be separate or dissimilar. Here, Jesus is saying that man should love his brother, not for any of his worldly characteristics but because he has a soul like his own, and in fact, these two souls are one. By using the word "soul," he declares that nothing should come between one soul and another in the wholeness they share—not ethnicity, not religion, or even nationality.

In the next line, we are told to "protect him like the pupil of your eye." Some have translated this as "protect him like the apple of your eye."[1] However, the literal translation has "pupil," not "apple." Using the English idiom "apple of your eye" needlessly complicates the message. It suggests that our brother has special and unique qualities that make him particularly valuable. However, Jesus suggests that we protect our brother, not because he is *special* to us but because he has a soul like ours. In fact, in compliance with non-dualistic principles, he *is* us, despite our false belief in separation. This saying is not about specialness but, again, about oneness.

We protect the pupil of our physical eye because it allows us to see. Without it, we would be blind. In the same way, we protect our brother because he also allows us to see. Loving him, as he truly is, opens our inner eye—the mind's eye—to the truth that creation is one. We need his inclusion in the whole of creation because without him, it is incomplete and meaningless. We protect him, whomever he may appear to be, and we protect the love we find in that relationship. Our brother is the pupil of our eye; therefore, we must not reject him for any reason. If we reject him, we reject ourselves and become blind to the wholeness of creation. It is through him, not in spite of him, that we find clarity and peace.

---

1 Wikipedia, *Apple of my eye*, https://en.wikipedia.org/wiki/Apple_of_my_eye. Although somewhat controversial, the most informed study of this phrase seems to suggest that it was originally a ninth-century English idiom. It later was employed as a translation of the literal Old Testament Hebrew "dark part of the eye" in English translations of the Bible. In any case, the best literal translation of the Coptic word in question is "pupil," and that seems to be the understanding of the author who loosely based this saying on Deuteronomy 32:10: "He found him in a desert place and in the howling waste of a wilderness; He led him about, He instructed him, He protected him like the pupil of His eye."

Saying 26

> **(26) Jesus said, "You see the mote in your brother's eye, but you do not see the beam in your own eye. When you remove the beam from your own eye, then you will see clearly to remove the mote from your brother's eye."**

The conventional interpretation of this saying is correct, but there is more that can be said about it. The standard reading is that before one can remove an impediment in the eye of another, one must first remove an even larger block in one's own sight. The larger block might be a psychological blind spot or a character fault. Lurking behind that simple explanation, however, is a familiar Thomasine and biblical ploy at work: something miniscule is compared to something huge. A mote (a speck of dust) is compared to a beam of timber. The speck of dust is understandable. The beam, however, is clearly an exaggeration. How can one have a huge beam in one's eye? It is impossible of course, so the "beam" represents an extraordinary obstacle, not just an ordinary character fault or blind spot.

The beam is a metaphor for what impedes the sight of the *inner* eye. Being so disproportionately large, it represents an immense bar to spiritual vision. In the context of this gospel, only the world of duality, the world of separation, can block vision so completely. More precisely, the impediment is the belief in such a world and the willingness to trust one's life to it. It is that which makes it impossible to "see" anything as it truly is.

Such a large impediment in the inner eye would make a person spiritually blind. And being blind, he cannot judge. He might imagine he sees a mote in his brother's eye—his "brother" being anyone, male or female,—but he is blind. The "mote," in fact, may be unreal, a projection of his own belief in limitation. And so, he cannot "remove" it until he deals with his own false belief in limitation. What is needed is a complete change in the way he thinks, holds grievances, and believes himself to be separate. It is not a physical beam, so all he needs to do is to change his mind. An essential part of that process is to love his brother like his own soul (25). He must practice true forgiveness, not only of others but especially of himself. He must trust his connection with divinity in the same way that the nursing infant of saying 22 trusts his mother. Only then will he see the truth of his own identity and, consequently, see the truth about his brother.

His accurate assessment of his brother hinges entirely on his accurate assessment of himself. These are not separate assessments. In the non-duality of the Kingdom, there is no separation, only oneness. If one's identity is that of a child of God, so is the identity of the other. Furthermore, if he sees clearly, he will understand that he *is* his brother. He will understand that his brother's soul is united with his own and innately perfect and free. Achieving that understanding is what Jesus means by "then you will see clearly to cast the mote from your brother's eye." It is not a matter of visibly doing anything. It is a matter of releasing the beam, the egoic beliefs that block one's own awareness of God's love. This is the primary theme of this gospel. All other themes spring from this one.

This awareness of oneness is a vision so compelling and lovely that a tiny "mote" in the spiritual eye of one's brother cannot prevent that brother from seeing its light and experiencing its beauty. When accomplished, this coming together of brothers unleashes such power that, metaphorically, it can move mountains (48). Two sights restored to the vision of perfect oneness can indeed cut through the illusions of a separate realm. This is how clarity is shared. This is how a brother helps a brother.

Saying 27

(27) <Jesus said,> "If you do not fast from the world, you will not find the Kingdom. If you do not observe the Sabbath as a Sabbath, you will not see the Father."

Patterns matter in Thomas. They matter in any work of literature, but particularly here. In this cryptic and challenging gospel, they serve as clues in helping us to understand who the author was and what he tried to communicate. This author, this man named Jesus, nevertheless remains an enigma, as does his New Testament counterpart. We cannot assume, however, that the Jesus of the New Testament and the Jesus of Thomas are the same man in all respects. Yes, their words are often similar; about half the Thomas sayings have biblical parallels. But we cannot take for granted that the questions posed by this gospel are necessarily answered in those other gospels. In particular, we cannot assume that the New Testament gospels were more authentic or written earlier than Thomas. Some eminent scholars question that claim of Thomas's dependence on these gospels. In any case, it appears doubtful that these two gospel traditions can be harmonized so that Thomas can be fully explained in terms of the Bible's better-known teachings.

In my commentaries, I have tried to avoid such assumptions. Instead, I have based my analysis on patterns and themes intrinsic to the work itself. This approach is not infallible, but it appears to be the best way of determining the author's intentions and what he considers important. Expanding on this foundation, I have focused on the implications of these patterns and what they might suggest about his frame of reference, his perspective, and fundamental philosophy.

In this saying (27), we can again detect a pattern. It is similar to saying 53. There, Jesus mocks the practice of circumcision but maintains that "circumcision in spirit has become highly profitable." What this is saying, in effect, is that the physical trimming of the foreskin has no value, but the trimming away of impediments to the awareness of God's Kingdom has significant value. Thus, a traditional practice is compared to a similar, but more spiritually beneficial, practice. In this saying (27), the traditional practices are not renounced, but the implication is that they are not enough.

Both fasting and observing the Sabbath, in the limited sense, are insufficient for entry into the Kingdom.

In sayings 6 and 14, the pious practice of fasting from food is scorned. It is hateful and something that will "give rise to sin." The implication is that such fasting—as a religious obligation—is counterproductive at best and, at worst, dishonest and manipulative. But in this saying, fasting "as regards the world" is a higher-level practice which stands in contrast to the lower-level fasting from food. The lower-level practice involves sacrifice as a means of getting something, of giving up one thing to get something else. On the other hand, when one fasts from the world, it need not be a sacrifice at all; it can be a mere adjustment in which the mind focuses only on the eternal qualities of peace, love, and joy. It can be a decision to look beyond the superficial to what resonates deep within the mind. When one learns that the world has nothing to give of lasting value, its passing pleasures are willingly exchanged for the enduring joy of the spirit.

On the heels of this comparison, one would expect a similar position on the Sabbath practice. Indeed, though the idea of a day of rest is not condemned anywhere in this gospel, there is the suggestion here that a higher-level Sabbath is being proposed. In his book *The Gospel of Thomas, The Hidden Sayings of Jesus*, Marvin Meyer suggested that the line "observe the Sabbath as a Sabbath" could be translated as, "observe the (whole) week as the Sabbath."[1] It is indeed true that the Greek word for Sabbath, *sabbaton*, can also be translated as "week." As a play on words, the line can then be translated as:

> "If you do not observe the week (sabbath) as a Sabbath, you will not see the Father."

Evidence of this alternate meaning of *sabbaton* can be found in the Greek translations of Luke 18:12, Mark 16:9, and 1 Corinthians 16:2. So, it appears that what Jesus is doing here is quite subtle. He is hinting that there is another way of thinking about the Sabbath. It can be limited to one day out of seven or extended to every day of the week in a continuous Sabbath. It is not about having a better Sabbath on one day of the week; it is about having a completely restful day, *every* day, continuously. Only with such a full commitment to personal peace can one "see (experience) the Father." As there is no mention anywhere in Thomas of following draconian rules, the practices of fasting from the world and resting continuously are mild ones. As Jesus confirms in saying 90, "Come unto me, for my yoke is easy and my lordship is mild, and you will find rest for yourselves."

1 Marvin Meyer, *The Gospel of Thomas, The Hidden Sayings of Jesus* (San Francisco: Harper, 1992), 82.

Saying 28

> **(28) Jesus said, "I stood in the midst of the world, and in the flesh I appeared to them.**
> **I found all of them drunk. None of them did I find thirsty.**
> **And my soul ached for the sons of men,**
> **because they are blind in their hearts, and they cannot see;**
> **for they came into the world empty,**
> **(and) they also seek to depart from the world empty.**
> **But now they are drunk.**
> **(But) when they shake off their wine, then they will change their minds." (Coptic version)**
>
> **(28) *Jesus said, "I became enlightened, though still in the world, and outwardly, I appeared to them as flesh.***
> ***I found all of them drunk. None of them did I find thirsty. And my soul ached for the sons of men,***
> ***because they are blind in their heart, and they cannot see;***
> ***for they came into the world empty,***
> ***and they also seek to depart from the world empty.***
> ***But now they are drunk.***
> ***But when they shake off their wine, then they will understand beyond their reasoning minds." (My restored version)***

Many commentators have taken the opening lines of this saying to represent what has come to be called the "Gnostic redeemer myth." This is the idea that a spiritual emissary, generally identified as Jesus, descended to earth to save humanity. The story has many versions and roots in so-called pre-Gnostic traditions. There are even similar examples in Philippians 2:5-11 and John 1:1-5, 9-14, and 16-18. The question then is this: Do these lines represent Jesus as incarnating into the world as a body from a higher realm, or do they suggest something else? Literally, this sentence may be translated as:

> "I stood to my feet in the midst of the world, and I appeared forth (or outwardly) to them in flesh."

Looking at the literal rendering of this key Coptic excerpt is particularly helpful for several reasons. As mentioned before, in Thomas, the phrase "stood to my feet," in various forms, always suggests a waking up to a radically new understanding. One stands to one's feet after sleeping. Thus it suggests an awakening to the experience of God's Kingdom, or more familiarly, the experience of enlightenment. (See also my commentaries on 16, 18, 23, and 50.) With this in mind, the line may be rephrased, "I became enlightened, though still in the world, and outwardly, I appeared to them as flesh."

This raises an additional question: Is Jesus saying that he is not a physical body (flesh) but only appears to be? Does he now understand himself to be wholly spirit? The phrase "stood to my feet" forcefully drives the meaning of this line in this direction. The word "appeared" does not necessarily mean that he incarnated or suddenly materialized. It could also mean that he *seemed* to be in flesh, to have a body, but in fact, has awakened to the truth that he is spirit. As I understand this saying, Jesus is not describing how he came to earth as a spiritual emissary but how he made the profound discovery of his spiritual identity. He no longer identified himself as a body. He had discovered his oneness with all of life, and after that life-changing revelation, he had a fresh perspective on and concern for his fellow man.

He found the "sons of men" drunk, but none of them thirsty. The word "drunk" conveys a more negative meaning here than it does in saying 13. It suggests that they were intoxicated with the world but not "thirsty" for spiritual nourishment. Additionally, they were "blind." They lacked the inner vision to see what is in their best interests. Because of this, they "came into the world empty, and they also seek to depart from the world empty." In Thomas, emptiness has a negative connotation, comparable to dwelling in spiritual poverty (saying 3b). Because they are not "thirsty" for spiritual nourishment, they have never acquired wisdom and the fruits of wisdom. They have lived all their lives this way, and it appears that unless they change this pattern, they will die this way.

Jesus refers to these people as the "sons of men" or "sons of mankind." The singular form of this expression is mentioned in saying 86. There, the foxes and the birds have safe shelters, but the "son of man has no place to lay his head and rest." In writing about this, I argue that in that saying, the "son of man" does not refer to Jesus but the part of man's mind that sleeps and has not awakened to its true identity, not as a son of man, but as a son of God. In this saying, these "sons of men" are those who have likewise identified with their egos. They are intoxicated with the world, and they languish in ignorance of their true identity.

As is typical of many other sayings in Thomas, this one concludes on an optimistic note: "When they shake off their wine, then they will change their minds." It is interesting that Jesus provides an answer to spiritual blindness here that does not involve supplication, making amends, prayer, sacrifice, or any other practices promoted by the early church. "Shaking off their wine" may be interpreted as becoming spiritually sober or as clearing the mind of what is not spiritual. What numbs the mind is shaken off, and what remains is clear and meaningful. The Greek loanword *metanoein*, used here to describe this change of mind, does not mean "repent," as it does in the New Testament. It alludes to a profound transformation in understanding. It derives from the Greek words *meta* (beyond) and *nous* (the reasoning mind).

This saying begins with a profound change of mind and ends with one. In an indirect way, Jesus urges his listeners to follow his example and release the world's grip on their minds. Shake off its hold, he seems to say. Get free of it, and then see how differently things begin to look.

Saying 29

> **(29) Jesus said, "If the flesh came into being because of spirit, it is amazing. But if spirit came into being because of the body, it is indeed amazing. As for me, I am amazed at how this great wealth has come to dwell in this poverty."**

The above version of this saying is an adaptation of Bentley Layton's translation in his book, *The Gnostic Scriptures.*[1] It is preferred because it translates the Coptic word that is commonly translated as "a wonder" or "a marvel" as "amazing." All of these options are acceptable from the translator's point of view, but the word "amazing" suggests an attitude of incredulity that is essential to the meaning of this saying. In contrast, "wonder" and "marvel" impart a sense of approval, as in the words "wonderful" and "marvelous." For that reason, they are inappropriate in this context. Here, three creation scenarios regarding spirit and flesh are presented, all of which seem amazing or incredulous to Jesus. Their status as marvels is not the point. They are simply incredulous and, therefore, amazing. These creation scenarios may be stated this way:

A. Spirit came first and produced flesh: "Flesh came into being because of spirit." For Jesus, this is amazing if true.

B. Flesh came first and produced spirit: "Spirit came into being because of the body." For Jesus, this is even more amazing if true. It is "indeed amazing."

C. "This great wealth (spirit) has come to dwell in this poverty (flesh)." For Jesus, this is truly amazing, clearly in the negative sense.

The first proposition (A) requires answers to the following questions: Can we conceive of spirit (understood as divine) without accepting its principal characteristic of perfection? There is no evidence in this gospel that we can. Surely, we cannot. Is the concept of spirit meaningful without it being perfect? Again, it is not. Remember that in this saying Jesus refers to spirit as "this great wealth," so he is not referring to anything impoverished or limited. Additionally, is not flesh (the body) imperfect, subject as it is to pain, decay, and death? Obviously, it is imperfect. What this first proposition (A) is basically saying is that perfection (spirit) produced imperfection (flesh). Jesus finds this an amazing statement. If perfection made imperfection, then perfection would not be perfect. Within it would be the seeds of imperfection, and therefore it would not be perfect. Yet this is the basic understanding of the dualistic religions of Judaism, Christianity, and Islam. In this gospel, however, non-dualism appears to be the operating philosophy. In non-dualism's purest expression, the world of matter, space, and time is an illusion; and therefore, spirit creates only spirit, and perfection creates only perfection. Man, being free to accept or deny his spiritual nature, may believe he is flesh. However, in accordance with this philosophy, he is not a body; he is spirit.

The second proposition (B) states the seemingly opposite idea that imperfection (flesh) produced perfection (spirit). Jesus is even more amazed by this premise. Of course, imperfection cannot create perfection. If it did, it would be perfect. Yet, this is the ego's position, that God was created in man's image, not the other way around. In this view, the ego is placed in the middle of its world, and God, if acknowledged at all, is exiled to near oblivion. The world is seen as creating itself. This option is also dualistic. In fact, options A and B are two sides of the same dualistic coin.

So here we have two fundamental questions essentially reduced to this: Did God create imperfection, or did imperfection create God? If either proposition is true, Jesus says, it is amazing. By wording it this way, he subtly hints at the inconsistencies in both and allows his audience to draw their own conclusions. This is what great spiritual teachers do; they point to the answer but resist wrapping it up in a neat little package. Man must find the truth for himself. The truth is that there is no imperfection, because anything less than perfect could not have been created by a perfect God. Only the Kingdom of the Father exists, and within that Kingdom is man in perfect oneness with his Source. But the full realization of this must come from within a peaceful mind.

In the final proposition (C), Jesus flatly states that he is also amazed "at how this great wealth has come to dwell in this poverty." Spirit is equated with "this great wealth," and flesh is equated with "this poverty." Of course, "poverty" is the word used in saying 3b for the consequence of not knowing one's true identity as a son of "the Living Father." To "dwell in this poverty," then, is to believe that flesh is one's identity. In truth, man's identity is spirit. That is the *hidden* premise of this saying. The word "wealth" not only describes spirit but describes the man himself who discovers that he is spirit. So when Jesus says that he is amazed "at how this great wealth (spirit) has come to dwell in this poverty (flesh)," he is saying that he is amazed at how man can believe he is a body when spirit is his true identity and wealth. As Jesus repeatedly reveals in this gospel, only spirit truly exists. The world is a corpse (saying 56) and "Whoever has known the world, has (also) found the body" (80). The body, therefore, is a corpse. It lives only in the mind of one who sleeps and believes he is a body.

1 Bentley Layton, *The Gnostic Scriptures, Ancient Wisdom for the New Age* (New York: Doubleday, 1995), 385.

Saying 30

> **(30) Jesus said, "Where there are three gods, they are gods. Where there are two or one, I am with him." (Coptic version)**
>
> **(30)** Jesus said, "Where there are three, they are without God. And where there is only one, I say, I am with him. Lift the stone and there you will find me. Split the wood and there I am." (Greek Oxyrhynchus version)
>
> *"Again, I say unto you that if two of you on earth agree about anything you ask for, it will be done for you by my Father in heaven. For where two or three are gathered together in my name, I am there with them." (Matthew 18:19-20)*
>
> **(30)** ***Jesus said, "Where there are two or three, they (representing pluralism) are without God. And where there is only one, I say that I am with him. Lift the stone and there you will find me. Split the wood and there I am." (My restored version)***

This was a difficult saying, even before ancient scribes, as we shall see, managed to make it yet more difficult. Commentators generally agree that the Coptic version is corrupt and meaningless. Therefore, a certain amount of judicious restoration is necessary to reveal the original intention of its author. What follows is my best judgment about that intention and how it was misunderstood.

In contrast to the Coptic version, the earlier Greek version appears familiar. It has an abstract quality about it that reminds the reader of sayings

22 and 106. We have a choice in this saying to understand the numbers mentioned as referring to individuals, divine figures, or, abstractly, to the numbers themselves. In Koine or Biblical Greek, pronouns assume the case, number, and gender of the words to which they refer. In this saying, "him" and "they" have the grammatical characteristics of the words they represent. The word "him" is properly masculine because the word it refers to, "one," is masculine. So, this word "him" does not necessarily refer to a person. The same can be said for the word "they." In fact, the alert reader of Greek would understand that he has a choice to see the numbers "one" and "three" as referring to people or as mere numbers standing alone.

In this Greek version, the choice is to accept the idea that God would abandon three people but support each as individuals, or that He would deny the number three in favor of the number one. Of course, the idea that God would forsake those who gather together in groups is preposterous. Therefore, this interpretation of the saying must be wrong. The second choice is the correct one; God does not recognize the number three because oneness is His creation and separation is not. That idea is consistent with the teachings of Jesus in this gospel.

A clearly visible theme in Thomas is the promotion of oneness over duality. In sayings 22 and 106, making the "two one" is the key to the Kingdom and a source of spiritual power. In contrast to oneness, dichotomies such as inside and outside, above and below, male and female are all sense impressions and, therefore, unreliable. The mind does not simply report what it sees through the eyes. It projects what it takes to be true, and the results can be highly variable. If the mind believes in separation, it will tend to see separation everywhere. If the mind is in a state of great anxiety and chaos, it will tend to see chaos everywhere. Of course, the reverse is also true. If the mind embraces unconditional love and forgiveness, it will not experience chaos but see evidence of harmony everywhere. A quiet mind is a mind that has learned to mistrust its sense impressions and, instead, finds rest and confidence in its vision of oneness with all that lives. The Greek version of this saying appears to agree with this idea.

The concept of acosmic monism is roughly equivalent to our understanding of non-dualism. Monism is the metaphysical theory that there is only one basic principle or substance that is real. This gospel's monism is acosmic because it denies the existence of a physical world. Therefore, acosmic monism describes reality as empty of form and characterized by oneness. The antithesis of monism is pluralism—the theory that, in reality, there are two or more independent elements. In this understanding, the world of form is real, and so too are its limitations.

The Greek version says, "Where there are three (representing pluralism) they are without God." According to the non-dualistic principles, and for those who additionally accept the reality of God, anything experienced apart from perfect oneness is without God, because God knows only oneness. He does not know separation because He did not create separation. Another way of saying this is that God knows only love, and therefore, anything that is unloving, and consequently separate, is not recognized by God. In the context of this saying then, there is no "three." There is only one. God created oneness, and what is not one is illusory. Jesus further says in the Greek version, "And where there is only one, I say, I am with him." He is speaking abstractly; the word "one" represents the oneness of everything, joined in spirit. Jesus is with that oneness, which means there is no separation between him and the insect living under the "stone" or the creature that has burrowed into the "wood."

In the Matthew (18:19-20) parallel, "if two of you" come together to appeal for God's help, it will be granted. It then says that if "two or three are gathered together in my name, I am there with them." It is interesting that the phrase "two or three" is used in this connection and not "two," the single number that appears in the preceding line. One would expect these numbers to be the same. I suspect that the "two or three" phrase in Matthew survived from the earliest composition of this saying. It expresses a sense of pluralism without focusing on any particular number. On the other hand, in the Greek version of this saying, the number "two" was apparently thought extraneous and dropped. If we restore it to this saying, we have what I believe is more likely a closer representation of the original version:

(30) Jesus said, "Where there are two or three, they (representing pluralism) are without God. And where there is only one, I say that I am with him. Lift the stone and there you will find me. Split the wood and I am there." (My restored version)

Many explanations have been proposed for the odd and seemingly meaningless Coptic version of this saying. Both the Coptic and the Greek versions focus on the number three. The "two" had apparently been dropped from the saying sometime earlier. The question then becomes, what is significant about the number three? That indeed must have concerned the translator of the Greek into Coptic or possibly a later copyist. At precisely the time when this question was being asked (late third century to early fourth century), the number three had strong connotations. It represented the emerging doctrine of the Trinity—the Father, the Son, and the Holy Spirit. The First Council of Nicaea (325 CE) was assembled primarily to decide the issue of Jesus's relationship to the Father and hence the character of the Trinity. It was, in fact, an unresolved controversy for many years.

In a saying about the Trinity, however, one would expect its description to be positive rather than negative. The Greek version says that the three are "without God." This presented a problem for the Coptic scribe. How can the Trinity be without God? Surely, Jesus would not have said this. Consequently, he modified the line to affirm the Trinity rather than to attack it: "Where there are three gods, they are Gods." This is not the only instance in this gospel where a scribe has injected his own biases into the text. Such intrusions always appear to defend some orthodox belief about the teachings or status of Jesus, sometimes by changing only a single word. The final line of this Coptic version, "Where there are two (gods) or one (god), I am with him," is a further defense of the Trinity. Inadvertently, the scribe left evidence of his trespass by not changing the final "him" to "them." The word "him" would only make sense if it referred to "one" only, not "two or one."

Either this Coptic scribe or a later scribe did something else. He apparently saw no connection between the Trinity and the lines in the Greek version about splitting the wood and lifting the stone. Consequently, he either moved these lines to the end of saying 77 or deleted them here and allowed 77, which might have also ended with these lines, to remain as we find it. In either case, these final lines appear to be consistent with both 77 and my restored version of this saying. The life within the "wood" or under the "stone" is not a separate life. The true condition of life, as explained by the philosophy of non-dualism, is oneness. Look to that oneness, Jesus says, and "you will find me." Indeed, you will find everyone.

If we compare the four versions quoted above, it can be seen that my restored version is nearly identical to the Greek. It salvages the "two or three" phrase from Matthew and retains the final lines about lifting the stone and splitting the wood. It is also the version most consistent with the Gospel of Thomas as a whole.

Saying 31

> **(31) Jesus said, "No prophet is accepted in his own village; no physician heals those who know him." (Coptic version)**

> **(31)** Jesus said, "A prophet is not acceptable in his own homeland. Nor does a physician do healings for those who know him." (Greek Oxyrhynchus version)

This saying is commonly classified as a proverb. A proverb is defined as a short, pithy saying in general use that states a commonplace truth or useful thought. In this case, that commonplace truth appears to be that familiarity breeds mistrust. In this connection, the similar proverb that familiarity breeds contempt is not quite right. It is the villagers' mistrust of the prophets and physicians that is the issue, not necessarily their contempt of them.

In the New Testament, only the "prophet" part of this saying is mentioned. The "physician" clause is not included but intimated in Mark 6:4-6 and Luke 4:23-24. In both of these gospels, this allusion to Jesus as a rejected prophet is used as a literary device rather than as a wisdom saying. It merely explains the lack of support Jesus encounters in his hometown. I suspect that the evangelists did not understand this saying. But seeing how well it foreshadowed the rejection of Jesus by the jeering crowds on his way to the cross, they decided to weave it into the narrative about his hometown.

There are additional problems here. It is a proverb on its surface only, and its truth is anything but commonplace. First, it is simply not true that every prophet is rejected in his own village; nor is it true that every physician fails to relieve the suffering of those who know him. Certainly, either part of this saying may be partially true, but as a general rule, it is absurd.

Second, Jesus is not speaking of himself in this saying. There is no evidence in this gospel that he ever sees himself as either a prophet or a physician. The word "prophet" appears three times in Thomas—here and in sayings 52 and 88. In 52, Jesus refers to the prophets as "the dead." He suggests to his disciples that for guidance they should consult "the one living in your presence," rather than the dead prophets. In my commentary on that saying, I demonstrate that this "one" is more likely a reference to the Father than it is to Jesus. In 88, the word "prophets" appears in tandem with the word "angels." In that saying, both terms are used abstractly to represent anyone bestowing love and inspiration. No allusions to actual prophets are suggested. As for the word "physicians," it appears only here in this saying. However, the word "heal" appears in saying 14, where the disciples are urged to heal, presumably on a spiritual level, but not to become physicians.

From this, we can infer that the roles of "prophet" and "physician" do not apply to Jesus, nor do they even have his approval. He appears to have little regard for either practice. In the realm of the Kingdom, spiritual truth emanates from inner guidance, not from living or dead prophets. The Jesus of this gospel is not such a prophet but one who points to the source of guidance within (see 44 and 52). The statement "No prophet is accepted in his own village" is only conditionally true in the eyes of the world. But from the viewpoint of the Kingdom, it is always true. It is always true because, in that realm, guidance is recognized as coming from spirit, not from any external source or prophet. From this perspective, the statement may be understood as: no external prophet is accepted by those who know the true source of wisdom. No prophet is accepted as a prophet in his true "village," which is the Kingdom.

Likewise, those who abide in the realm of the Kingdom will never accept a physician as a true healer. From that viewpoint, physicians treat symptoms, sometimes quite successfully, but they do not heal in the strict sense of that word. As non-dualism affirms, true healing is of the mind, not of the body. True healing restores the Kingdom to man's awareness. In Thomas, the body is "this poverty" (29), and like the world, it is a "corpse" (29 and 80). The body is not man's identity; his identity is undivided spirit.

Here again, Jesus is expressing his distaste for external obligations and traditions. As with fasting, giving alms, supplication, and circumcision, he casts doubt on the value of prophets and physicians. All such revered traditions focus their attention on the body. As Jesus locates reality on the level of spirit, the body is seen as a manifestation of a mind in ignorance of its true identity. The body is not evil; it is simply nothing, a projection of the belief in separation.

So when he says that no prophet is ever accepted in his own village and that no physician ever heals those who know him, he is articulating his profound skepticism of their ability to make meaningful change. They may be the finest of men, but those who truly know them know that, for all their qualities, they cannot of themselves put right what is truly amiss. No prophet or physician can truly guide or heal. They only temporarily alleviate the symptoms of a much deeper problem, the problem of separation. In this saying, Jesus is not the "prophet" or the "healer/physician," as he is in the New Testament. He is merely one who points to the real prophet and the real physician within.

Saying 32

> **(32) Jesus said, "A city built on a high mountain and fortified cannot fall, nor can it be hidden." (Coptic version)**

> **(32)** Jesus said, "A city, having been built and established on the summit of a high mountain, can neither fall nor can it be hidden." (Greek Oxyrhynchus version)

Two prominent features of this gospel are its use of hyperbole, the literary device of deliberate exaggeration, and whimsy, the use of fanciful images. In saying 107, a shepherd speaks to a sheep and tells him that he wants him more than he does the other ninety-nine sheep. In 4, an old man asks an infant about the place of life. Preposterous situations are presented as if they were completely normal. In the Greek version of this saying, a whole city is built on the summit of a high mountain—literally, "the high point of a high mountain." This obviously is a fanciful and hyperbolic image. Yet, the Coptic version blunts this description somewhat, leading some commentators to compare the mountain to the mounds or tells on which many towns and cities in ancient Israel were built.

Of course, no city would be built on the summit of a high mountain, and that is the point. In the realm of the world, this would be impossible. However, in the realm of the Kingdom, the summit represents ultimate freedom and grandeur. Those who manage to escape the limits of the world and wake up to their true Selves live in this city. They share it with all of their brothers and sisters who have realized their oneness with each other and with God. To reach this height, they must, like mountain climbers, scale with great courage the sheer cliffs of doubt and fear. Yet, having reached the city, all seeking comes to an end. Fortified by their love for each other and for God, this city cannot "fall." It is indeed the only secure place in existence. However, it is not a place in the usual sense. It is anywhere where ordinary people discover their true nature.

The point is made that the Kingdom is like a city built on the top of a mountain. But what is possible for the Kingdom is impossible for the world. There is no place in the world where safety is guaranteed. There are no soaring heights, no matter how well fortified, that will not in time fall into ruin. Only fools seek refuge in the world. Why would anyone seek shelter in a place of death and division?

And just as the Kingdom cannot fall, it cannot be "hidden." Such splendor cannot be contained in a mind that is one with all other minds. Like a beacon in a vast space, it will call to every living soul to abandon its futile struggle to find freedom where there is no freedom, meaning where there is no meaning. As saying 60 affirms, "You too, look for a place for yourselves within rest, lest you become a corpse and be eaten." That "place" is the summit of what man as spirit is capable of. It is his ultimate refuge and home.

Saying 33

> **(33) Jesus said, "What you will hear in your ear, in the other ear, proclaim from your rooftops. After all, no one lights a lamp to put it under a bushel, nor does one put it in a hidden place. Rather, one puts it on a lampstand so that all who come and go will see its light." (Coptic version)**

(33) Jesus said, "What you hear in your one ear..." (Greek Oxyrhynchus fragment)

Two sayings are linked together here to form one. Each focuses on a different sense organ—the ear and the eye. We know, of course, that in Thomas such allusions to hearing and seeing refer not just to the body's ears and eyes. They suggest a hearing and seeing that is an attribute of the mind. For example, six times in Thomas we encounter some form of this advice: "Whoever has ears to hear, let him hear." It is always attached to a saying that is particularly challenging. It is not advising the listener to clean his ears but to think deeply on what is being said and listen with his whole mind and heart. This is listening with the mind's ear. It is having both an open mind to appreciate other possibilities and an open heart to respond to what resonates with peace on a deeper level.

Only a fragment of the Greek version has survived. Fortunately, it contains a clue that in the Coptic version is absent or unclear. It refers to hearing with "your one ear." This suggests that the ear in question is not one of the two ears of the body but the one inner ear, the mind's ear. In the Coptic version, the literal translation of this phrase is "ear, in the other ear," an awkward phrase that most scholars believe is a scribal error that only obscures the point. It appears, then, that this saying is about experiencing truth on the level of awareness rather than on the level of sense perception.

This reference to listening with the inner ear is open-ended. It may refer to listening deeply to the sayings of Jesus with an open mind, or it may refer to listening within for inner guidance. Yet, because the second part of this saying alludes to light, and because light in Thomas always refers to an inner light, it would seem that what is heard here is likewise nonconceptual, something felt rather than believed.

From the earliest recorded times, people of every religion and of no religion have claimed to have received guidance from a source within their minds or seemingly out of thin air. The range of such guidance extends from intuition to the most extraordinary revelations. Apart from this saying, there is little mention of inner guidance in Thomas. There are hints that such guidance is required to solve the dilemmas described in sayings such as 34, 52, and 69, but this is not directly stated. In saying 44, the Holy

Spirit is esteemed, apparently as an inner guide or bridge between man and God, but otherwise, His function is not explained. In this saying, all it states about what is heard is that it should not be bottled up but shared openly. It should flow. In a metaphorical sense, it should be "proclaimed from your rooftops."

There is a similarity here between guidance and the city on the high mountain in the previous saying (32). It cannot be "hidden." Such divine assistance indeed is a Kingdom experience, not a worldly one. As such, it cannot be contained by the limitations of the world. The non-dual nature of the Kingdom would prevent it from being limited to one individual. Like unconditional love, to remain in the mind it must be extended. Extension is a feature of what it is. And so, inner guidance is not just for the individual but for everyone. To be clear, I am not referring here to preaching or proselytizing. Extension is not about changing anyone's mind. "Proclaiming," in this case, suggests simply being a conduit of God's love and wisdom, expressed by example, flowing naturally and peacefully from one mind to all minds.

The next part of this dual saying rephrases this same idea that was applied to the inner ear. Now, it is applied to light. In Thomas, light is what exists "within a man of light," and "if he does not shine, he is darkness" (24). Light is both what a man is and what he extends. Light is also his Source (50). It is the totality of the Kingdom. Again, it is not something that can be contained and remain what it is. For that, it must shine. It cannot be limited to words. Words point only to where it can be found. It cannot be "hidden." It must be put on a "lampstand" for all to see. The truth of who and what a person is can be temporarily obscured by fear and guilt, but inevitably that person must allow his nature to express itself. Until he does that, until he extends that nature and lets his inner light shine, he will remain in darkness.

Saying 34

> **(34) Jesus said, "If a blind man leads a blind man, they will both fall down into a pit."**

Under the guise of physical blindness, it is reasonably clear that this saying is referring to another kind of blindness. The word "blind" also appears in saying 28. There, the sons of men are said to be "blind in their hearts" and "empty." "Blind in their hearts" suggests spiritual blindness, and "empty" suggests a life that lacks meaning or significance. Indeed, it appears that spiritual blindness is the condition addressed in both of these sayings.

"Leaders" do not fare well in this gospel. In saying 3, "those who lead you" are ridiculed for confusing the Kingdom with the world. Likewise, "prophets," who might be thought of as leaders, do not fare well. In this saying, we have a leader who is blind. The underlying message appears to be that if a spiritually blind person leads another spiritually blind person, both will suffer the consequences. The follower will suffer because his trust will be betrayed, and as long as he remains ignorant of his leader's blindness, he will never find the truth. The leader will suffer because his assumptions about spirituality are confirmed when the follower agrees with him, thus supporting him in his ignorance. He too will never find the truth as long as he mistakenly trusts in his own ability to see. Consequently, both will fall into the metaphorical pit.

This is a fine saying, and it certainly works on the level described above. But there is more here than is seen at first glance. Consistent with this gospel, there is a layer of meaning beneath its surface. Just as saying 7 describes the relationship between the true man and his inner lion or ego, this saying describes that same relationship from the viewpoint of guidance. In that earlier saying, the man and his lion/ego side vie for dominance. To survive, one either consumes the other or is consumed himself. This saying portrays what happens when someone blindly trusts his ego self and, consequently, is consumed.

If a man follows the guidance of his ego, he will fall into a pit. The ego is not this person's true Self; it is not who he is. It is who he thinks he is. The ego is simply the idea of separation, which when embraced by the mind, assumes control of the mind and claims authority over it. It draws power from it and appears to become its identity. All of this, of course, is freely granted by a fearful mind. Being unstable, the ego will project, as if on a vast screen, an unstable world, and while the man accepts this idea of separation, he will accept as fact everything his ego shows him. He will see a world at war with itself. He will experience guilt and, consequently, see himself condemned by God's wrath. He will lose his way. He will wander aimlessly toward the pit of despondency and self-hate. Both he and his ego guide will fall into that pit because both are blind to God's love.

To escape that fate, a man or woman must have a different guide, a guide who is not blind. In the context of this gospel, that guide would appear to be the Holy Spirit (44), although in saying 52, the Father is suggested. In 44, the Holy Spirit is considered so revered that He must not be blasphemed. In early Christianity, as well as in the Dead Sea Scrolls, it is the Holy Spirit who represented the bridge between man and God. Sometimes referred to as the "still small voice," the Holy Spirit has been described as the presence of God's truth within man's mind. If a man is "blind in his heart," he must have guidance on that level. It is the Holy Spirit who has the spiritual vision to gently lead him back to his home in God.

Saying 35

> **(35) Jesus said, "It is not possible for one to enter the house of the strong man and take him by force unless he binds his hands; then he will move him out of his house."**

The key to this saying is the metaphorical meaning of the phrase, "strong man." In a similar saying, Mark 3:27 suggests that the strong man is Satan, the implication being that before the "house" can be entered, the devil must be bound. In Thomas, there is no narrative or context to explain these lines other than the context of the other logia. Indeed, looking at these other sayings, we find hints for the metaphorical meaning of both "strong" and "house." While there are no other instances in the text of the Coptic word for "strong," there is a clue as to *who* is strong in saying 7. In that saying, the lion, the universal symbol of strength, is locked in mortal combat with the ostensibly weaker man. As both sayings appear to be allegorical, representing internal confrontations rather than external clashes, I propose that the strong man in this saying represents the ego, as does the lion in saying 7. Remember that the concept of the lion (ego) nature of man goes back to Plato and long before that in India.

A person cannot confront his ego directly as long as he believes he *is* his ego. If direct confrontation were possible, he would be perpetually at war with himself. But remember, the ego is merely the belief in separation. As long as that belief is cherished in the mind, it cannot be dismissed. Clashing beliefs result only in conflict and anxiety. The ego-mind, the part of man's mind that believes the ego's lies, assumes the identity of the whole man. In truth, it is not the whole man, but it will not give up this identity easily. The peaceful way and the only possible way to resolve the dilemma of the ego is to clearly see it as an artifice, a set of beliefs enshrined in a belief structure, fashioned in reaction to a single erroneous thought. That thought is that man is separate from his Source.

The ego's belief structure is represented in this saying by the word "house." The "house" shelters and protects whatever belief or conviction is established there. It serves the same function in sayings 16, 21, 48, 71, 97, and 98. The only way that this structure might be breached is by the use of insight into how it operates. Only that remedy can bind the hands of the strong man/ego and permanently deflate his power. This is what these sayings do. When understood, they penetrate the internal structure that protects the ego. The long-held assumptions, attachments, and defense mechanisms of the ego are exposed to the light of inquiry. This reveals the "strong man" to be an illusion, an illusion built on baseless fears. This is how the "strong man" is bound.

If we understand this raid on a house as the action of the mind against an error in its thinking, we can then see it as an act of purification rather than an act of plunder, or looting. The literal translation of the word generally rendered as "ransack," "plunder" or "loot" is either "move" or "carry." In the two other sayings where this word appears (48 and 106), it is translated unambiguously as "move." Nothing is looted from this "house." The "strong man" or ego is simply moved out, rooted out, or extracted from its belief structure. The part of the mind that previously believed in separation and alienation has been *reclaimed.* Awareness has rendered the ego powerless. It is cut off from its source of power and structure. The mind is now wholly unencumbered and able to experience its freedom in the knowledge of its oneness with God.

The final phrase, "Then he will move him out of his house," is similar in form and function to the phrase in 98: "Then he slew the powerful man." Both employ the Greek loanword *tote* for "then," and *tote* has a double meaning. It can mean that the moving of the "strong man" here in 35 and the slaying of the "powerful man" in 98 are subsequent actions, actions that follow from previous ones. But *tote* can also mean "at that moment," just as "then" does in English. In 98, the slaying of the powerful man (the ego) happens the moment the ego's structure (the house) is pierced by the sword of inquiry. In this saying (35), the strong man (also the ego) is extracted from the mind the moment his hands are bound. These two sayings essentially imply the same thing. To bind the hands of the ego is the same as piercing its defenses with the sword of inquiry. By this, the ego is disabled by the light of truth, its power is contained, and its influence over the mind is ended.

Saying 36

> **(36) Jesus said, "Do not worry from morning until evening and from evening until morning about what you will wear." (Coptic version)**

> **(36)** Jesus said, "Do not worry from morning until late nor from evening until morning. Worry neither for your food, what you will eat, nor for your clothes, what you will wear. You are much greater than the lilies which neither card nor spin. As for you, when you have no clothing, what will you wear? Who can add to your time of life? He it is who will give you your cloak." (Greek Oxyrhynchus version)

As you can see, the Greek version is more extensive than the Coptic. This is not to say that either should be considered more original. No one can be certain of that. Nevertheless, it is the Greek version on which I will base my comments. Unlike the Coptic, it mentions two worries instead of one. The worry about food is joined with the concern about clothes. It focuses, however, on the clothes issue as an example of why worry of any kind is never justified.

This saying suggests that the extent to which freedom from care and worry is experienced by anyone is determined by how much he values himself. It says, "You are much greater than the lilies which neither card nor spin." Lilies are what lilies do. They are true to their nature, which is to grow and produce beautiful flowers. Man, too, must be true to his nature.

He must be himself as he was created. And like the lily, he was not made to suffer but to bloom and be happy. If he truly values himself, he will see himself as blessed by God. He will trust that connection and ignore his ego's fixation on guilt and fear. If he would accept that he was made perfect in the likeness of God, he would not need an elaborate system of defenses to protect his illusions.

In this gospel, clothes represent defenses. Thomas does not advocate nudity; it uses clothing as a metaphor. In saying 21a, the disciples remove their clothes in order to give back the field (the world) to its owners (thoughts of guilt and fear). By doing so, they trust entirely in the protection of God. In 37, Jesus suggests to his disciples that they will see the "Son of the Living One" when they disrobe, drop their defenses entirely, and trust wholly in God. When they tread on their clothes like little children, they "will not be afraid." In this saying (36), such trust is advocated in regard to food and clothing. This implies that for one who truly understands his value as a child of God, insufficiency is impossible.

Jesus then asks the question, "When you have no garment, what will you wear?" Again, he is speaking metaphorically. In essence, he is asking what will replace your ego defenses when they have been abandoned. What will protect you? Characteristically, he does not answer this question directly. Instead, he asks another question: "Who might add to your time of life?" Commentators have labored much over this response, attempting to make sense of it. It abruptly moves the question of "what" to "who," as if to say that what is to be eaten or worn is not as important a question as who would provide these things. The suggestion is that the Father, the Source of all love and protection, is that one. The Father represents true protection, in contrast to the ego that feeds on fear and guilt and, therefore, denies that man is worthy of protection.

The Greek word for "time of life" is sometimes translated as "stature" and also as "lifespan." The problem with the English word "stature" is that it implies relative importance. One has stature in comparison to something or someone else. However, in this gospel, man is one with all of creation. There is no man deserving of less protection than another. Oneness with one's brothers and with God is a guarantee of perfect safety. As for the word "lifespan," what value can a longer life have for a person who no longer fears death? Such a person lives in the present and has no interest in the future.

Rather, this question seems to be asking, "Who might sustain you throughout your life?" The question is then answered: "He it is who will give you your cloak." In other words, when man finally learns that his ego defenses, based as they are on fear, only increase his fears, he becomes aware of another cloak that surrounds him and protects him in every situation. Thus, his safety has always been guaranteed. Who is the guarantor of this protection? The Father is. His "cloak" represents the pledge of His unqualified love for his Son. It is His assurance that man, as spirit, is still as he was created—incapable of being harmed, just as He Himself is incapable of being harmed. The message of this saying is that worry is never justified, nor are defenses ever needed. Defenselessness is a virtue because it affirms the truth that man is at home in God's Kingdom and has never left his home, except in his imagination.

Saying 37

> **(37) His disciples said, "When will you become revealed to us and when shall we see you?"**
> **Jesus said, "When you disrobe without being ashamed and take up your clothes and place them under your feet like little children and trample on them, then [you will see] the Son of the Living One and you will not be afraid."**

When I read this, I am reminded of the William Butler Yeats poem, "A Coat":

> I made my song a coat
> Covered with embroideries
> Out of old mythologies
> From heel to throat;
> But the fools caught it,Wore it in the world's eyes
> As though they'd wrought it.
> Song, let them take it,
> For there's more enterprise
> In walking naked.[1]

There is more enterprise in walking naked. In this poem, Yeats uses the metaphor of "walking naked" to describe the freedom of defiantly rejecting what to others might be an experience of vulnerability and loss. Having his writing style plagiarized, the poet decides that there is more value in dropping his defenses and letting the issue pass. He says of the metaphorical coat, "Let them take it." This is expressed with a boldness and finality similar to the trampling underfoot of the clothes in this saying. But here, Jesus goes further. He says that only when his disciples "disrobe without being ashamed" and "trample" on their clothes like children will they *see* the Son of the Living Father. He is saying that not only is such a bold rejection of psychological defenses and attachments liberating, it is essential for spiritual vision.

In a world experienced as limited and divided, clothes protect man from cold and exposure. But in the Kingdom of the Father, in the realm of non-duality, defenses have no value. They undermine man's trust in his perfection as created by God. Defenses deny that a perfect God must create a perfect creation. If His creation is not perfect, then neither is He. (See my commentary on saying 29.) There is no idea more alien to the core principles of this gospel than the idea that man has been excluded from the perfection of God's Kingdom. Using the metaphor of clothing to represent defenses, Jesus is saying here that man is fundamentally blind until he boldly rejects his belief in limitation. To do this, he must refuse to see himself as a body in a hostile world and refuse to see himself excluded from God's love.

The disciples ask Jesus when they might see him. The question presupposes that his identity, his true Self, is presently beyond their limited vision. It is an innocent question, but Jesus pounces on it with a shocking response. As if to awaken them from their stupor, he abruptly tells them that to understand him they must disrobe and tread on their clothes like little children. Then he says that if they do that, they will see the "Son of the Living One," and they will not be afraid. Notice what Jesus does not say. He does not unambiguously say that, as a consequence of this, they will see *him*. It says that they will see the "Son of the Living One." So here again is this question of identity. Who is this "Son?" Is it Jesus, or is it the wholeness of God's one Son of whom the man, Jesus, is a manifestation? Is Jesus saying that to see him truly, they must experience the wholeness of creation?

Saying 3b unequivocally provides the answer. It says, "When you come to know yourselves, then you will become known, and you will realize that it is *you* (plural) who are the Sons of the Living Father." The "Son of the Living One" in this saying (37) is not Jesus in isolation but everyone, the totality of God's creation. This "Son" must be seen if Jesus is to be truly seen. If the disciples do not see this oneness, it is because they have aligned themselves with their ego's defenses and not with God's perfection. They have clothed themselves in their ego's message of limitation and have not accepted God's cloak of protection. In short, they must resolutely strip themselves of their belief in separation before they can see anyone as he really is. This is the vision Jesus wants for his disciples.

Paradox is at the center of this saying. By letting go, man gains. By abandoning his fears, his eyes are opened. There is really nothing to fear. Man made fear; it is not God's creation, and man can let it go. By discarding their defenses, the disciples will open their hearts and minds to the truth that they were always safe in God's embrace, and that they were always one with their Source. And in the realization of that union, they will see as God sees, loving His one creation unconditionally as He does.

Some commentators have theorized that the word "clothes" represents the body, and that removing clothes is like the shedding of the body. However, there is nothing in Thomas that supports the idea that freedom is found only after death. Certainly, a mind free of all concerns of the body will experience less fear. But while true, this analogy is too limited. There are other defense lines that man erects against the Truth besides the body, such as guilt and the fear of love. These are the very defenses that separate brother from brother and man from God. Complete trust in the power and benevolence of God will make all such defenses pointless. Additionally, it will reveal that fear is impossible to an enlightened mind.

---

1 William Butler Yeats, *Responsibilities and Other Poems* (New York: MacMillan, 1916).

Saying 38

> **(38) Jesus said, "Many times did you desire to hear these words which I speak to you, and you have no one else to hear them from. There will be days when you will look for me and will not find me."**

In what appears to be intentional, the Coptic text of this saying uses the Greek loanword for "desired" or "craved" instead of the common Coptic word for "wanted." The fact that a stronger loanword was selected gives weight to the idea that a specific shade of meaning was considered worth preserving. The implication is that his disciples are dependent on Jesus and strongly *desire* his guidance. They might even be compared to drug addicts whose only supplier is Jesus. The question is: What are they going to do when their supplier can no longer be found?

Desiring the truth is not sufficient for finding the truth. It may launch the quest, but only attentiveness to the present will complete it. Desire dismisses the present in favor of the future. If his disciples looked for Jesus in the future, the present moment would go unread. In saying 91, Jesus states, "You do not know how to read the moment." He is likewise saying here (38) that truth is found only in the present. Those who cling to the past or look to the future for fulfillment are actively avoiding the truth. They will not find Jesus in the future, because the truth of Jesus cannot be found there. They must surrender to it in the present moment and not delay any longer their release from egoic thinking.

This is a theme found throughout Thomas. In 51, his disciples ask him when the new world will come. He responds, "What you look forward to has already come, but you do not recognize it." Likewise in 113, his disciples ask him, "When will the Kingdom come?" He responds that "it will not come by waiting for it...(it is) spread out upon the earth, and men do not see it." The Kingdom, which is the truth of Jesus, is here and now.

An additional theme in Thomas is self-responsibility. The search for meaning must begin at home. The words which Jesus speaks may point to it, but then the work begins. The disciples need to understand that the obstacles to truth are hidden within their own minds. They must confront them squarely and surrender them to spirit. Neither Jesus nor anyone else can do this for them. His disciples have become dependent on him. He warns them, "There will be days when you will seek me and you will not find me." They look outwardly and crave the truth they see in Jesus. However, seeking truth is an inside job. Dependence of this sort cannot play any part in it. Jesus is, in effect, saying, "Don't be a Jesus junkie." The search for truth must be both free of dependence on the world and free of any desire to look for it outside the present moment. Only by depending on God, which requires independence from the world, can the treasure of freedom be found.

Saying 39

> **(39) Jesus said, "The Pharisees and the scribes have taken the keys of knowledge and hidden them. They have not entered, nor have they allowed those who wish to enter to do so. You, however, be as wise as serpents and as innocent as doves."**

For the Pharisees and their scribes of the first century, the practice of their religion was largely focused on the legalistic promotion of rules and rituals. The mystical traditions of their faith, though not completely absent, were given a lower priority. Because of this focus on the protocol of religion rather than on the heart of spirituality, they had lost sight of what Jesus considered essential. In a sense, they had "taken" what should have been a natural blossoming of their spiritual practice and suppressed or hidden it deep within their minds, unaware of its value. As an analogy, when someone hides a key to a room that he has never entered, that usually means that he is afraid of what he might find there. Likewise, the Pharisees and the scribes of this saying appear to be afraid of what they might find buried within their minds.

What lies hidden within their minds is the awareness of the Kingdom, which only the keys to the Kingdom can open. Being unaware of the value of this realm and apparently afraid of it, they hide these keys and refuse to share them with those who wish to enter. Thus, as long as it remains locked up and hidden, this knowledge is worthless.

Notice once again the theme of that which is hidden. For the Pharisees and the scribes, their own spiritual liberation is at stake. Yet, their freedom is wholly dependent on finding what they have hidden from themselves. There is probably nothing more elusive than this. It is uncovering the truth within one's mind when part of that mind wants it to remain hidden. In response to this situation, Jesus offers this advice to his listeners:

> "As for you, be as wise as serpents and innocent as doves."

Uncovering the truth requires wisdom and innocence. In this saying, Jesus shows metaphorically how one might avoid making the same mistake as did the Pharisees and the scribes. As metaphors for wisdom and innocence, Jesus chooses serpents and doves to represent qualities that the Pharisees and scribes apparently lack. Here, serpents are said to be "wise." The Greek loanword in question, *phronimos*, may be translated as "wise" or "shrewd." As might be expected, the serpent of Genesis 3:1 is sometimes mentioned as the model for this creature. There, it is described as "crafty" or "shrewd." It is shrewd, yes, but in its dialogue with Eve, it is certainly not wise. It is more likely that Jesus had in mind a meaning closer to the Greek idea, which is that the serpent represents not a shallow shrewdness but practical wisdom.

In nature, the serpent is in full contact with the earth. For this reason, it appears that Jesus apparently chose the serpent as a metaphor for groundedness. Let me be clear, however; groundedness has no value in the Kingdom. The Kingdom of the Father, as described in this gospel, is a realm of oneness in which separation is impossible. The world is an illusion; therefore, there is no ground or earth that in any way is a part of this realm. Nevertheless, groundedness represents a willingness to recognize the illusion as an illusion before allowing it to pass. It is the necessary and honest assessment of the world without avoidance.

The serpent, being in full contact with the earth, represents the quality of accepting the experience of limitation by acknowledging it rather than by denying what seems obvious. One's experience of the world cannot be denied. Whereas the world can be denied and should be denied, one's *experience* of it cannot be. Man must be honest with himself and not pretend to be free of the world when he is not. From that honest appraisal of his situation, he then may inquire as to how he might see his situation differently and rise above it. However, it is important not to see a difficult situation as something that must be dodged. Evading anything is a subterfuge that ultimately accomplishes nothing and only strengthens the ego. The way of the serpent, metaphorically speaking, is to observe the world and all of its supposed problems dispassionately. The serpent is a quiet animal, and in that quiet, no elaborate defenses, judgments, or mental gymnastics come between it and its experience of the world. Here again are lines from a poem by William Butler Yeats entitled "The Circus Animal's Desertion":

> "Now that my ladder's gone,
> I must lie down where all the ladders start
> In the foul rag and bone shop of the heart."[1]

To "lie down where all the ladders start" is what man must do before he is free of the world. He cannot say to himself that it is all an illusion, and pretend that these mere words will make it so. Though it is true that the world is an illusion, it must be questioned and exposed to penetrating inquiry before the illusion can yield to the truth. The process must start at ground level, and every rock and hard place must be honestly appraised without fear. To do this is to look with utter defenselessness at whatever is causing pain, to spend time with it meditatively, and thus experience its emptiness. This is the ground on which "the ladders start," the necessary recognition before the upward climb can begin. This is the wisdom of the serpent.

The dove represents innocence and purity. The Greek loanword here, *araioske*, meaning "purity," is sometimes used to describe metals, as in pure gold. It is innocence that knows nothing of guilt. It is innocence untouched by the world. To be innocent as doves is to know one's identity as spirit and to keep that knowledge foremost in the mind. It is to realize the beautiful and precious purity of one's being.

In his essential purity and innocence, man was born to soar. This is what he was created for. As he grows in wisdom—first as a serpent, then as a dove—he will increasingly experience the lightness of his being and the immensity of his freedom. To be as wise as serpents and innocent as doves is to boldly claim ownership of the keys of the Kingdom. Once the door is open to the religious leaders, those who follow in their footsteps will learn by their example and enter as well.

---

1 William Butler Yeats, *Last Poems and Two Plays* (New York: MacMillan, 1940). Yeats was referring specifically in this poem to his desire to rise to the poetic heights accomplished in his earlier works. This is what his "ladders" were intended for. Nevertheless, I think that he also had in mind a more general image of going to ground, of returning back to his roots, and resolving issues there. It seems to me that his language, so beautiful and evocative, can be applied, as well, to this idea of groundedness.

Saying 40

(40) Jesus said, "A grapevine has been planted outside of the Father, but being unsupported, it will be pulled up by its roots and destroyed."

The question might be asked: Is it likely that the Jesus of this gospel, having so consistently promoted the supremacy of oneness over division (sayings 22, 23, 48, 72, 106, and 108), should understand God as existing in a separate place, separate from His creation? The answer is no; it is not likely. He cannot be inside or outside of anything while, at the same time, he is one with everything. In regard to this saying, the question then becomes, what is there that can be planted outside of the Father while remaining inside the oneness of the Father? The answer must be nothing. If the separation of the Creator from His creation is an illusion, then anything planted outside the Father must also be an illusion.

What is an illusion? My dictionary defines it as something that deceives by producing a false impression. Non-dualism asserts that an illusion is anything that is not infinite and perfect. This latter definition, of course, goes way beyond the usual meaning of the word. Nevertheless, it logically follows from what this philosophy has to say about permanence. In short, the world of matter is not permanent; it constantly changes, comes and goes, and, on the quantum level, seems tied to what is observed or not observed. Even space and time are extremely elusive concepts that physicists and mathematicians have strived for centuries to understand. One exception to this phenomenon appears to be awareness, also known as consciousness. Pure awareness resists change. It is always present. Some traditions refer to this as the soul, but it is not an object, and it cannot be stained or altered or be anything it is not.

A third question might be asked: Who is it that planted this "grapevine" outside of the Father? Who but man in his drunken, blind, and empty stupor (saying 28) could have been so unconscious of reality that he would have attempted such a thing? The grapevine represents the world of separation. It is an idea that is not "supported" by the Father; therefore, it is an illusion. It appears vast and solid, and so it is within the dream. It is the nature of dreams to be fantastic yet nevertheless convincing. This dream world has its own rules that naturally conform to the nature of the dream. These rules are likewise unreal. In short, nothing within the dream is real. Even the river of time is unreal, being an essential part of this incredible fantasy of separation.

The crucial point of this saying is that the grapevine is not "supported." The Jesus of this gospel does not toy with words. When he states in saying 56 that the world is a "corpse," that is what he means; there is no life in this realm of the world. There are only dream figures here, a projection of man that is endlessly fragmented. And all these figures believe that their natural lot is to suffer, struggle for survival, and die. But, no matter how lush this dream/grapevine may appear to be, its fruit cannot sustain the Son of God. It is ultimately empty of meaning. It can only last as long as the maker of the illusion believes in his separate existence. When he finally tires of this illusion and all of its separating thoughts and concepts, then by this awareness, will he wake up to reality. Then, like the father of the Prodigal Son, God will welcome His child, who is neither male nor female, back to where he truly belongs.

In the Hebrew Bible or Old Testament, the grapevine was used as a metaphor for the land of Israel. Consistent with what we know of the Jesus of this gospel, it appears that he chose this word deliberately, despite the fact that many of his listeners would have surely been outraged. Here, he seems to be saying that Israel has been planted outside the Father, and, consequently, it will be destroyed. To understand why he would do this, one must remember that this iconoclastic subversive always tackles misplaced loyalties head-on. He, of course, uses the word "grapevine" as a metaphor for not only Israel but for the entire illusion of a separate world. That would include not only what is disagreeable about the world but also what is most cherished. Jesus is saying here (40) that even what is most loved and treasured by man will fall. Being not of spirit, it is an illusion. It is unsupported. It is an idea that was "planted outside the Father," and ultimately it will cease to be taken seriously. In truth, it will be rooted out and returned in man's awareness to the nothingness it always was.

As I mentioned in the introduction, all of the sayings in this gospel, except for one inauthentic saying (12), either support or allow the premise that the world of space, time, and matter is an illusion. They further support the idea that man's true reality is his oneness in spirit with God. A few sayings, such as this one, appear to do this more pointedly. Sayings 11, 22, 29, and 111, when properly understood, point to this same conclusion, that anything not of spirit, being unreal, is unsupported. Because it is an idea solely in the mind of man, this "grapevine" will be destroyed—not by violence but by the gentle light of truth.

Saying 41

> **(41) Jesus said, "Whoever has something in his hand will be given more, and whoever has nothing, even the little he has will be taken from him."**

This is a challenging saying, as it appears to be expressing a sentiment that is quite out of accord with the values of this gospel. It seems to be saying that the rich get richer and the poor get poorer, and that this is simply the way of things. On the level of our everyday world, this is true. The world is a place of immense unfairness. The evidence is strong, however, that the Jesus of this gospel is not particularly interested in the way of the world. He appears to be more concerned about how an enlightened soul might overcome the idea of a separate world. In saying 111, he alludes to the "one who lives from the Living One" that "the heavens and the earth will be rolled up in your presence." In 10, he metaphorically sets fire to the world. It is clear that this gospel attaches little value to the world. In this saying, therefore, having "something" of value in the hand should not be equated with having more of the things of this world. The world possesses nothing of value. Rather, under the guise of worldly values, Jesus is speaking here of spiritual values.

This saying is about giving or sharing love. The "hand" is a metaphor for that spiritual capacity to give magnanimously from the heart. It contrasts with the physical hand, which was made to grasp or take for one's own. (See my commentary on the "hand" in saying 22.) To give unconditionally is to share love with others in a way that acknowledges that, in truth, there is no "other." In the awareness of oneness, one always gives to oneself. That is why it is more blessed to give than to receive. That is why when one fully gives of himself, he experiences more love, not less. The awareness of that love increases as it flows unimpeded through God's undivided Son. (See also my commentary on 88.)

If one does not extend love from his hand in giving, the flow of love from God to man is blocked. Where love is not expressed, there is no acknowledgment of oneness. Unawareness of this oneness is like having nothing. It is like not knowing one's true Self and experiencing spiritual poverty (3b). It is like owning a grapevine planted outside the Father (40). Therefore, if a man refuses to share love, he will feel deprived of even the little love of which he previously was aware.

The meaning of the word "gospel" is "good news," and in this gospel, we come face-to-face with the highest expression of good news. This news is the revelation that the price of salvation is simply the awareness of God's love and nothing else. It is this gospel's core message. When man wakes up to the truth, he will realize that all of God's children are one with their Father and that separation never occurred. This awareness will unblock love and allow it to flow unimpeded through the entirety of God's Kingdom. His love is generative. That means that the more one becomes aware of God's love, the more it expands. The more he allows it to flood his mind and spill over onto his fellow brothers and sisters, the more will he realize how great and inexhaustible this gift is.

Saying 42

> **(42) Jesus said, "Become passers-by."**

> **(42)** *Jesus said, "Come into being as you pass away." (Leipoldt/Schoedel translation)*

Of the two translations of this saying from the Coptic text, I prefer the latter version, "Come into being as you pass away," first postulated by Johannes Leipoldt in a German translation in 1958. Subsequently, William Schoedel adopted Leipoldt's idea for his own English translation in 1965. Most commentators, however, prefer what has more or less become the standard translation, "Become passers-by."

Supporting this standard version is the distinguished Thomas scholar Stephen J. Patterson, author of the book, *The Gospel of Thomas and Jesus.* While admitting that Schoedel's translation is "certainly defensible in terms of the Coptic grammar," it seems to him that it is inconsistent with the theology of the Gospel of Thomas. He argues that in this gospel, "it is the world (Thom 56), the cosmos, (Thom 11:1, 111:1) that passes away, not the Thomas Christian, who is immortal (Thom 1; 11:2; 18:3; 19:4; 85:2 111:2). Furthermore, neither does the Thomas Christian come into being; paradoxically he or she exists already before coming into being (Thom 19:1). Such a translation, while grammatically possible, is therefore to be rejected."[1] Consequently, he prefers the "Become passers-by" version.

Patterson, however, appears to assume in this context that to "pass away" means literally to die, and to "come into being" means to be born as a body. If that is so, then indeed the Schoedel translation is inconsistent with the theology of the Gospel of Thomas. However, there is another way of looking at this. I would argue that to "pass away" means to allow one's habitual and illusory self-image to *pass* from the mind, and to "come into being" means to awaken to a new realization of one's true nature. In saying 11, the Greek loanword for "pass away" is employed but so is the Coptic word for "die." If the two words were understood as synonyms by the author or translator, he would not have used two different words here but one, the word for "die." In Thomas, to "pass away" means something else; it means to die to a limited idea of self and be reborn to one's true Self as unlimited awareness. In a sense, one discovers that he is not a child of the world but, as saying 3b asserts, a child of the Living Father. In this process of abandoning what is false and making room for what is true, a profoundly richer and clearer understanding of reality emerges in consciousness.

When the world of separation is recognized as an illusion, the veil of ignorance drops from the mind, and the ineffable truth is experienced. What was always there, but hidden, can now be seen. It should be understood that the realm of the ego and that of the Kingdom cannot share the same consciousness at the same time. They are inconsistent with each other and unknowable to each other. This is so because each seems absurd to the other. Therefore, if one is convinced that his ego can be trusted to represent the truth, the Kingdom of the Father will be hidden from his awareness. He will not see it, although evidence of its presence is everywhere (113). He will not recognize it as long as he clings to the idea of separation. The Gospel of Thomas testifies to this idea in many of its sayings. Consider for example:

(5) Jesus said, "Recognize what is in front of your face, and that which is hidden from you will become plain to you. For there is nothing hidden which will not become manifest."

It is a matter of recognizing what is there already and allowing the awareness of that truth to come into being in the mind as the false passes away. It is not about acquiring anything new. What is there is what has always been there. In saying 19, the same Coptic word for "come into being" or "came to be" is used to describe the true creation followed by the false creation or emergence of the ego:

> "Blessed is he who came to be before he came to be."

By allowing the false ego identification to dissolve or pass away, the awareness of the true Self, the original Self, comes forward, as if for the first time.

For a fuller examination of the weaknesses of the "Become passers-by" translation, see Charles W. Hedrick's book, *Unlocking the Secrets of the Gospel According to Thomas.*[2]

---

1 Stephen J. Patterson, *The Gospel of Thomas And Jesus* (Polebridge Press: Sonoma, 1993), 129.

2 Charles W. Hedrick, *Unlocking the Secrets of the Gospel According to Thomas* (Cascade Books: Eugene, 2010), 87.

Saying 43

> **(43) His disciples said to him, "Who are you to say these things to us?"**
> **"Do you not recognize who I am from what I say to you?**
> **Rather, you have become like the Judeans, for they love the tree but hate its fruit, or they love the fruit but hate the tree."**

In this saying, his disciples ask Jesus, "Who are you to say these things to us?" The suggestion is that he is not like other men. He speaks with authority on matters currently beyond their understanding. He proposes ideas that threaten to overturn everything in which they believe. Who is this man? They are bewildered. Their attention is focused primarily on the man, not on his teachings. In his reply, Jesus suggests that they do not understand him because they do not understand his message: "Do you not recognize who I am from what I say to you?"

What Jesus is proposing here is that in him, the tree and its fruit are one. The man and his message cannot be set apart. He personifies his teaching. And just as there is no separation between the tree and its fruit, there is also no separation between the speaker of truth and truth. To know the truth of which he speaks is to know Jesus. His words flow naturally from who he is. He teaches oneness because he experiences oneness. To explain this point, he compares the dualistic thinking of his disciples to the dualistic state of religious observance in Judea.

The Greek loanword for "Judeans," *ioudaios*, is sometimes translated as "Jews." However, since his audience would have been Jews, it is hardly likely that he would have compared them to themselves. Rather, he appears to be referring to the sectarian situation in Judea. At that time, except for a few minor sects such as the Essenes, there were primarily two religious parties in Judea, the Sadducees and the Pharisees. The Sadducees were aristocratic, allied to the Roman occupiers, and guardians of the Temple. The Temple was "God's house," where sacred sacrifices were performed. Their religious function was primarily to cultivate the worship of God as prescribed in the Torah. The worship of God was the "tree" of their faith and their sacred duty.

The Pharisees, on the other hand, were more gregarious; they were the people's party. As such, their concern was primarily for the "fruits" of their religion as it applied to the common man. As a reward for living a righteous life and adhering to strict rules and guidelines, their followers were promised a pure and honorable existence in this life and an afterlife of joy and serenity. The Sadducees did not ascribe to the idea of an afterlife and, therefore, could not offer this assurance—this fruit, if you will—to their followers.

These two factions cooperated in some respects, yet deep divisions kept them apart. Thus, Judaism became unfocused and sectarian. Here in

43, Jesus says of the people of Judea that, "they love the tree but hate its fruit, or they love the fruit but hate the tree." Their religious loyalties were divided. Their spiritual life was splintered and complicated. In contrast, Jesus presented himself as simple and uncomplicated. In him, there were no warring parts. His words expressed the philosophy of non-dualism in which oneness was both the tree and its fruit. His words were a declaration of that oneness, consistent in their exaltation of both the Father and His creation.

The Father is also like a tree, and his undivided Son is the fruit of that tree. One is incomplete without the other. One fulfills the other, and each, in their joining with the other, intensifies their mutual love. Like the Judeans, the disciples tended to be drawn to one side or the other, the tree or the fruit of that tree. In this saying, they consequently fail to understand the oneness that unites both the Father and his Son.

Saying 44

> **(44) Jesus said, "Whoever blasphemes against the Father will be forgiven. Whoever blasphemes against the Son will be forgiven. But whoever blasphemes against the Holy Spirit will not be forgiven either on earth or in heaven."**

Many commentators have maintained that this saying reflects the Trinitarian formula of God the Father, God the Son (Jesus), and God the Holy Spirit. If this is so, it would then seem reasonable to date it to a time well after the death of Jesus, when this concept was being debated in the emerging Christian church. Therefore, they say, it could not have been an authentic Jesus saying. Nevertheless, before making this judgment, additional considerations should be examined. While it is clear that the "Father" refers to God, it is not at all clear that the "Son" refers to Jesus alone. Nowhere in Thomas does Jesus explicitly state that he is the one and only Son of God. The closest he comes to admitting this is in saying 37, where the phrase "Son of the Living One" appears to refer to Jesus exclusively. However, in my commentary on that saying, I point out that it is more likely that this is a reference to the Sonship—that is to say, to the totality of God's creation. This would be consistent with the "Sons of the Living Father" phrase in 3b, as well as with the theme of non-duality found throughout this gospel. In other words, the "Son" in this saying is not one person among many but one indivisible Son, who as spirit, is God's one creation. Only in man's dream of separation does he appear to be many.

Looking now at another part of this trinity, we cannot be certain precisely how the Jesus of this gospel understood the function of the Holy Spirit. He (or it, if you will) is only mentioned here in this saying and not again. In the Old Testament, angelic beings appear as guides and emissaries from God. In Exodus 23:20-23, Moses is given a spirit guide as God's representative to lead him through the desert to the Promised Land. The term "Holy Spirit" is repeatedly used in the Dead Sea Scrolls. There, He is sometimes called the "spirit of truth." He is given by God to a man for the entirety of his life, not just after being saved, as in the Gospel of John (7:37-39). In the *Thanksgiving Hymns*, a Dead Sea Scroll text, He is given to man to guide him in wisdom and offset the evil forces present in his mind. He is given to man to "draw him near to understand of thee (God)" (XIV 21). In other words, understanding God is not a prerequisite for receiving the Holy Spirit but a consequence.

It should not be forgotten, as well, that Greek and Roman culture had thoroughly influenced the entire Mediterranean area by this time. The ancient Greek religion had supernatural beings called eudaemons. These were good and benevolent spirits who served and guided individuals for their benefit. They were not the evil and malicious demons of the Judeo-Christian scriptures, although that term was derived from the same root word. The philosopher Socrates was said to have had such a eudaemon who spoke to him and warned him of danger. Likewise, the Romans had genii, the plural of the word genius. A genius was believed to be the indwelling guardian of a person or inanimate object. They were often viewed as protective spirits and, in fact, were thought essential for the well-being of the individuals in which they dwelt.

So in the culture of first-century Palestine, the idea of an inner guide or spirit was well-established. In this saying, Jesus suggests that the "Holy Spirit" is such a guide. He might be compared to the angel that guided Moses through the Sinai to the Promised Land. Like this angel, He guides man as long as he *needs* guidance. He is a temporary reminder of man's oneness with the Father, a bridge between God and His Son as long as His Son *believes* himself to be separate.

Although we cannot unerringly know the function of the Holy Spirit as the Jesus of this gospel understood it, we can hypothesize a meaning consistent with the non-dualistic character of the text. Man is lost in a dream, but if he should attack (blaspheme) his Father within the dream, no harm is done. It is just a dream. If he blasphemes the whole or any part of the Sonship, still no harm is done. It is just a dream. However, if he attacks or ignores the Holy Spirit, he attacks what may be his only hope of waking up from his dream of separation.

As Jesus apparently envisioned Him, the Holy Spirit was expressly given the task of leading man out of the wilderness of separation, to gently whisper in his inner ear that his nightmare of a separate life makes no sense. So important is this function, Jesus says, that "whoever blasphemes against the Holy Spirit will not be forgiven." He will be denied enlightenment—not by God, but by his own pride and arrogance. As long as this arrogance continues, he will suffer. When he finally learns to trust the Holy Spirit more than he does his dream world, then he will find peace. There is no forgiveness for such pride, either on earth or in heaven, until man himself accepts the Holy Spirit's love and guidance. When that is accomplished, forgiveness is no longer needed, since within the Kingdom, guilt and innocence cannot coexist.

Saying 45

> **(45) Jesus said, "Grapes are not harvested from thorns, nor are figs plucked from thistles, for they do not produce fruit. A good man brings forth good from his treasury; an evil man brings forth evil things from his evil treasury, which is in his mind, and says evil things. For out of the abundance of the mind he brings forth evil things."**

A major theme in Thomas is the promotion of the Kingdom of the Father over the world. One superior realm of being is compared to an inferior and, ultimately, nonexistent realm of being. Examples are found in the next two sayings, 46 and 47. In saying 46, those who "come to be a child," who identify with their spirit nature, are superior to those who are "born of women," who identify with their bodies. In 47, these two realms, spirit and world, are shown to be utterly inconsistent with each other, so that metaphorically, one cannot "mount two horses" or "stretch two bows." The Kingdom is not like the world in any respect, and attempting to straddle both must always end in frustration and failure.

Here in 45, we have the contrast of grapes and figs with thorns and thistles. Some say that Jesus is simply stating here that nothing positive can come from a negative mind. This is true, but throughout this gospel, his focus is consistently much broader than that. His aim is to destroy the world as an idea (10), to encourage fasting from the world (27), and to teach that, basically, the world is already dead (56). His delineation of these two realms—spirit from flesh, God's realm from man's realm—is cloaked in allegory and metaphor. Nevertheless, this type of contrast, found throughout Thomas, is unrelenting.

So in this saying, the world is again contrasted with the spirit. Like thorns and thistles, it is incapable of producing "fruit." "Fruit" is used here as a metaphor for anything of lasting value to man. Hence, the world is incapable of producing anything of lasting value. This is an idea that continually arises in Thomas. Examples are sayings 27, 56, 63, 76, 80, 110, and 111. From such evidence, the overall impression is that the world is neither alive nor capable of sustaining life. It is an illusion, a dream. It is nothing. Expecting something from nothing is futile. Expecting lasting fulfillment from the thorns and thistles of this barren realm of separation is irrational. There is no "fruit" here to be harvested. This is the first point that Jesus makes.

We have seen from saying 22 that, for Jesus, dichotomies of any kind are meaningless. They are blocks to the awareness of the Kingdom. So when he speaks here of "good" and "evil," he is explaining what these words mean in the context of his teachings. Some commentators have rendered the Coptic word *exo* as "storehouse;" others prefer "treasure." The fusion of these two meanings suggests a treasury in which the owner stores that which he considers most valuable.

A "good" man is defined as one who "brings forth good from his treasury." An "evil" man is one who "brings forth evil things from his evil treasury." Consistent with Thomas, the good man's treasury is his awareness of the Kingdom, from which he draws spiritual strength. Making this choice is like harvesting grapes from grapevines and figs from fig trees. If, on the other hand, a man does not value awareness of the Kingdom but looks to the world for fulfillment, he will "bring forth evil from his evil treasury." This is like trying to harvest grapes from thorns and figs from thistles. This is what the "evil man" does to earn the label of "evil." He has made a fundamental error, yet Jesus does not condemn him for making such a choice. In other words, the preference is not expressed in moral terms but in practical terms. In the context of this gospel, the first choice is for the fullness of the Kingdom; the second is for the emptiness of the world. The "evil man" chooses the latter and, therefore, chooses poverty over spiritual wealth.

It should be emphasized again that in the context of the Gospel of Thomas, the conflict between good and evil is nonexistent. Good versus evil is a dualistic concept that only appears to make sense in a world of separation. In the Kingdom, there is only oneness. Thus, the real choice is not between good and evil but between wholeness and nothing. This is not to say that the Kingdom is amoral. It is a realm in which love binds everything together and in which competing interests do not exist.

Man is not intrinsically evil, although what he calls "evil" may loom large in his dream of separation. In this dream, the "evil treasury" is the place within his mind where idols are stored. There they are conceived as substitutes for God and God's gifts to man. Only within a dream can man conceive of idols as his treasure. And yet, that is precisely what he does when he looks to the thorns and thistles of this world for sustenance. He makes idols of these things—things like worldly power, fleeting pleasures, and materialistic wealth—and calls them his treasure. However, it is not such things that are his true idols but the guilt and fear that lie behind them. That is what seems to justify and enhance the value of such empty things. His "evil treasury" is his egoic belief structure, wherein is stored every belief that denies God's love for His child.

Since there is no world, from the non-dualistic perspective, man's idols are inventions. To make this point, Jesus tellingly states that the "evil treasury" is "in his mind" and, presumably, nowhere else. Out of his mind come "evil things" and so he "says evil things." In other words, it is not the world that is evil; it is man's attachment to idols, to the nonexistent things of his dream world, from which evil appears to spring. Only in a mind that sleeps (102) and dreams a dream of separation, do idols exist. From this "abundance" of idols within the mind, from this busy preoccupation with meaningless things, does evil appear to manifest in the world. In the last line, Jesus suggests that evil is not a force directed against man or God. It is simply that which results from storing up an abundance of meaningless thoughts and fears within the mind.

Saying 46

> **(46) Jesus said, "From Adam to John the Baptist, among those born of women, there is no one so superior to John the Baptist that his eyes should not be lowered. Yet I have said, whichever one of you comes to be an infant will know the kingdom and will become superior to John."**

It should be evident to anyone familiar with this gospel or with the New Testament gospels, that the man known as Jesus was unabashedly iconoclastic. That is to say, he challenged some of the most revered religious practices and beliefs of his day. Indeed, here in Thomas he confronts traditions with an almost gleeful abandon. He pokes fun at the practice of circumcision (53) and warns of the dangers of prayer, of giving alms, and of observing the dietary laws (14). Even the blasphemy of God the Father is downgraded to a forgivable offense (44). In this saying, John the Baptist is at first praised above all men but then lowered below the level of anyone willing to be an "infant." This is a reference to saying 22a where the nursing infant enjoys a state of egoless dependence on its mother. The suggestion is that by being like an infant, by being empty of all worldly concerns and wholly dependent on God's love and guidance, one rises above even John.

The nursing infant is perhaps the closest metaphor found in Thomas for the Kingdom of the Father. It represents a total trust in Source and a state of absolute innocence and union. In this saying, the one who "comes to be an infant" is contrasted with those who are "born of woman"—that is to say, those who identify with their physical bodies. For them, it is impossible to return to a *physical* state of infancy, but it is quite possible for them to return to their *spiritual* state of innocence and trust, which is their true identity. Returning to that state is achievable, provided they have the willingness to release their hold on the world. (See other allusions to "born of woman" in sayings 15 and 79.)

In the first line, Jesus again reveals his fondness for iconoclastic concepts. He includes Adam among those born of women. Thus, he denies an important feature of the creation story in Genesis. Of course, he knew the story perfectly well. Adam, the Biblical first man, was born in God's image and also of dust, not of woman. Nevertheless, Jesus groups Adam together with his descendants to make a point: Neither cherished tradition nor sacred scripture can alter his vision of man's creation. For Jesus, God created man as spirit in His own image, not as a body. Only in man's dream of separation did God create man as a body. Yet despite their great stature, neither Adam, as portrayed in the story, nor John the Baptist could grasp this principle. Their stature was perhaps the problem. They could not make themselves little enough or humble enough to understand. They were attached to the idea, as all of Adam's descendants are, that they were bodies born of woman, not spirit born of Spirit. Nevertheless, those who realize their dependence on God as "infants," who look to their Source, not to the world, for meaning and sustenance, will know the Kingdom and recognize their true grandeur as spirit, as John apparently did not.

Saying 47

> **(47) Jesus said, "It is impossible for a person to ride two horses or to stretch two bows. And it is impossible for a servant to serve two masters; otherwise, he will honor the one and dishonor the other. No man drinks vintage wine and immediately desires to drink new wine. And new wine is not poured into old wineskins lest they burst; nor is vintage wine poured into new wineskins, lest it spoil. An old patch is not sewn onto a new garment because a split would result."**

Here, a string of analogies and metaphors come together in one saying to compare two perspectives. Seemingly unconnected activities are contrasted but with no clarification as to how we should understand what links them together. Instead, the reader is left to ponder this saying's meaning and look to the gospel as a whole for clues. A careful study of the text will show that such unexplained perspectives are compared, not just here, but throughout its length.

Jesus has a unique vision that he wants his listeners to understand. It is a radical vision, yet it is simple. It only asks that a choice be made between two diametrically opposed frames of reference. Below, I describe what these frames of reference are, focusing on their most elemental features. In the context of these perspectives, Jesus asserts in this saying that there can be no compromise between truth and error. In effect, he says that the first perspective or frame of reference is true, and the second is false.

The first of these is that man's supposed separation from God never happened. It is a vast illusion or dream from which man has not awakened. This is not overtly stated but strongly suggested in sayings such as 84, where man's true likeness will "neither die nor become manifest." He is spirit, and as such, he is free of the world and immortal. (See also my commentaries on sayings 29 and 80.) Opposed to this view is the conviction that separation is real and that all forms of death, or loss of any kind, is inevitable. Outside of these two choices, there are no other options. These two frames of reference, the Kingdom and the world, are what Jesus labors to define in this saying and throughout this gospel. For the one who chooses, it is a crucial choice, either to accept God's will for his Son or invent a world that is in opposition to God's will. These two paths lie before him.

Nothing in Thomas is spelled out succinctly, but there are many clues as to what this Jesus taught and what these teachings suggest. If we fail to follow these suggestions in the direction they seem to lead us, nothing in this gospel will make any sense. I have outlined the following perspectives with a broad brush, but with one that is consistent with all of the sayings. It is also consistent with the key proposals of non-dualism, the philosophy with which this gospel seems to agree.

Perspective # 1. God, who may also be called "Source" or "limitless consciousness," created man in His own image, as spirit. As spirit, he neither dies nor manifests as a body (84). He exists only in the mind of God. There is nothing outside of God's mind (40). Separation is an illusion. Neither space nor time exists, having no function. Man is neither male nor female, as all dualities are meaningless (22). We might think of the relationship between God and man as one of father and son, not in the biological sense, but as a metaphor for God's love for his creation. The Father shares everything that He has with His Son. Love binds them together, and there is no way to distinguish where one ends and the other begins (22a). Loss is impossible.

Perspective # 2. Man made God in *his* (man's) image, envisioning Him as having form and personality. He conceives of this God as a larger version of himself, with all the ego traits of man. As portrayed in the Old Testament and other ancient scriptures, these traits include anger, jealousy, vindictiveness, and pride. This God is thought to be living in a far-off heaven, remote and separate from worldly life. As for man, he is "born of woman" (15 and 46) into a world where everything is separate from everything else. In that world, all that is alive struggles for existence. It prospers briefly, descends into decay, suffers pain, and finally dies. Man is many, not one. He is a victim, both individually and collectively, of the world he perceives. There are limits to everything. Nothing lasts.

In this saying, the metaphors of horses, bows, servants, wines, and patches are not explained. One needs to understand their significance in the context of the other sayings. However, they only work consistently with each other if we accept that Jesus is referring to two fundamentally different perspectives. One cannot straddle these perspectives, but faithfully serve one or the other. One cannot mix one with the other; they are incompatible. In the case of the wine and cloth analogies, the old and stable, representing God's Kingdom, is valuable. The new and unstable, representing man's kingdom, has no value. With that in mind, this is my interpretation of each:

"It is impossible for a person to ride two horses or to stretch two bows." It is impossible to make the jump to perspective # 1, represented by the first horse and bow, without completely abandoning all investment in perspective # 2, represented by the second horse and bow. The choice of truth over illusion must be decisive. Compromise of any kind denies that truth is all-encompassing. As such, it can have no meaningful opposite. For that reason, straddling both perspectives will leave the rider without a horse and the archer without a working bow.

"It is impossible for a servant to serve two masters; otherwise, he will honor the one and dishonor the other." It is impossible to serve both God and the ego. Divided loyalties result only in confusion and frustration. Honoring equally both perspectives is a game that no one can win. Only one is true. The first perspective reflects God's love; the second is enshrouded in fear and guilt. Therefore, choosing to serve God with all of one's heart, mind, and soul is the only choice possible if lasting happiness is to be experienced. In this way, one honors both God and oneself.

"No man drinks vintage wine and immediately desires to drink new wine." Once a man tastes the Kingdom of the Father (vintage wine), he will never go back to drinking from that big ego jug in the corner (new wine). The ego offers novelties and distractions, but the Kingdom offers unsurpassable freedom. The ego offers empty promises, while the Kingdom, as represented by the first perspective, offers real peace and joy. The new wine of the ego is ultimately nothing, while the vintage wine of the Kingdom is everything.

"New wine is not poured into old wineskins lest they burst; nor is vintage wine poured into new wineskins, lest it spoil." In ancient times, new wine was sometimes placed in new wineskins while the fermentation process was not yet complete. These skins, being new, were able to expand to accommodate the resulting gas. Old wineskins, being less flexible, were not used for this purpose, as they would burst. Old wineskins, however, were perfect for holding vintage wine. Such wine was stable, and its finished richness was secure within a pure and seasoned wineskin. A treasured wine would never be placed in a new wineskin. That skin, having too recently been the hide of a goat, and hence impure, would spoil the vintage wine and taint its fine qualities. Therefore, old seasoned wineskins were treasured and never wasted on new wine.

Minds are like wineskins; they work best when both the container and its contents work in harmony on the highest level. Access to the Kingdom requires purification, which is the shedding of all unloving and fearful thoughts. Allowing the ego, represented by the "new wine," entry into such minds, represented by the "old wineskins," would undo all efforts to join with God and chaos would be the result. Likewise, the "vintage wine" of the Kingdom cannot remain pure and true in minds that have not been seasoned and prepared like old wineskins. In short, like fine vintage wine, the experience of the Kingdom of the Father is without equal. But only in minds made ready by unqualified love and forgiveness will the fullness of that experience be known. This is true for the Kingdom but not for the ego. For the prepared mind, the "new wine" of the ego had best be left on the shelf. Again, this is equivalent to saying that perspectives # 1 and # 2 are wholly inconsistent.

"An old patch is not sewn onto a new garment because a split would result." Notice that contrary to similar New Testament sayings in Mark (2:21), Matthew (9:16), and Luke (5:36), the new fabric, not the old fabric, is the weak fabric. In those gospels, it is the old garment that needs the patch. Thus in Thomas, the new/old scheme of the wine analogy is preserved in this analogy as well. In both, "new" equates with weak, unstable, and valueless; "old" with strong, stable, and valuable.

The "new garment," representing the second perspective or ego perspective, has a gap or weak point. Whoever made this garment did shoddy work. What value is there in keeping it? It would be better just to toss it out. Should it be patched with an old and presumably firmer cloth, a split would occur between the two incompatible fabrics. Both, when washed, would stretch at different rates. Perspective # 1, represented by the old patch, is incompatible with perspective # 2, represented by the new garment. Conclusion: Make your garments of strong and sensible fabrics. Rather than trying to fix a weak perspective (# 2) that promises fulfillment but consistently fails, toss it out. Temporary fixes (patches) do not work. There is a better cloak, a stronger cloak, waiting for you to try. It is perspective # 1.

What all of these metaphors and analogies have in common is the way they dramatize in this logion the utter incompatibility of fundamentally different perspectives. Valuing one over the other will result either in waking up to the Kingdom or remaining in the mire of the ego. Throughout the Gospel of Thomas, we find many allusions to this incompatibility of perspectives, the inherent antithesis between the Kingdom of the Father and the realm of man, between truth and illusion. Such examples are sayings 87, 93, 101, and 112.

Saying 48

> **(48) Jesus said, "If two make peace with one another in this single house, they will say to the mountain, 'Move away,' and it will move away."**

The key to understanding this saying is to recognize that the phrase "this single house" refers to the Kingdom, the realm of oneness, which is the central focus of this gospel. The literal translation of this Coptic phrase is "this house alone" or "this single house," which suggests that it is only within this "house," the Kingdom of the Father, that true peace can be found. The saying further suggests that this peace generates such power that it can "move mountains." Compare this saying to saying 106:

> Jesus said, "When you make the two one, you will become the sons of man, and when you say, 'Mountain, move away,' it will move away."

The meaning of these two sayings is essentially the same. In 106, making "the two one" corresponds to this saying (48) and its allusion to making "peace with one another in this single house." Making "the two one" also appears in saying 22 where it alludes to adjusting one's mind to the idea that all dualities are meaningless. Likewise, here in this saying (48), making peace in this "one house," which is the Kingdom, is like making the "two one" in the sense that within the realm of this "house" or Kingdom there is only one life without separation. What formerly was perceived as two or more is now seen as spiritually one. Recognizing this oneness is what this saying means by the phrase to "make peace." In other words, man is not a multitude of separate bodies with separate interests. As spirit, he is free of all manifestations of separation, whether mountains, bodies, or specks of dust. Therefore, by his awareness of oneness, man is free of all perceived sources of conflict.

Such manifestations were made in the mind of man, and when he awakens to the reality of his spirit nature, he will cease to believe in these illusions of separation. And so, with his growing awareness that spirit is his reality, the world will begin to fade from his consciousness. Yet, as long as he believes himself to be limited in any way, he will see himself confined to this world, at least partially, and experience himself as a victim of its phantom "laws" of pain and loss.

The significance of the word "house" in Thomas has been debated by scholars for many years. In at least one saying (64), it seems to refer simply to a dwelling. But in the other appearances of the word (16, 21, 35, 48, 71, 97, and 98), its meaning is less apparent. In the culture of ancient Israel, the term was used to designate a family or lineage to which one belonged. For example, Jesus was said to belong to the house of David. However, in the New Testament and particularly here in the Gospel of Thomas, Jesus dismisses the importance of family ties repeatedly (55, 99, and 101). Therefore, it is unlikely that Jesus, in these "house" sayings, would be appealing to family loyalty.

In 71, we find another use of the word "house." Jesus says, "I will [destroy this] house, and no one will be able to build it [up again]." In my commentary on that saying, I explain how unlikely it is that he is referring to a physical structure, the Temple in Jerusalem, or even to his body. Another possibility is that he is referring negatively to Judaism. This would suggest that Jesus wishes to destroy the house or teachings of Judaism. However, if the overthrow of Judaism is the intent in 71, how could Jesus approve of it here in 48, where the "house" is one of peace? The solution to this conundrum seems to be that "house" should be understood as a metaphor for a belief system or structure of convictions. This structure either shelters and supports truth, as here in 48, or shelters the distortions of the ego, as in 71. This "house" is not an outer structure but an inner structure within the mind.

By excluding these other possibilities for the meaning of "house," we see that what apparently matters to Jesus is the *truth*—not his body, the Temple, or family loyalty. It follows from this, then, that his only loyalty is to that which upholds the truth, gives shelter to truth, or, if you will, supports a "house" of truth, which is the Kingdom.

Likewise, whatever supports illusion or gives shelter to illusion, Jesus opposes. What gives shelter to illusion is, of course, the ego. It is itself an illusion, a complex of beliefs that draws its power and seeming reality from a mind that believes its distortions. This house or belief structure of the ego harbors and protects the beliefs of separation and fear. This is the "house" that Jesus proposes to destroy in 71. In our present saying, the alternative thought structure is presented. It has, as its central characteristic, oneness. Like the ego, it exists in the mind. Unlike the ego, it does not struggle or obstruct; it simply surrenders all thoughts of defensiveness or fear and joins with others in the spirit of oneness.

Outside of this oneness, there is no other frame of mind in which two can truly make peace with one another. If they attempt union while still ensnared in the ego's belief system, they might form an alliance, a negotiated peace, but they will not fully join with each other in unqualified love. They will not give up their illusions of separate interests.

If two make peace with each other in the way this saying suggests, they will then realize that the world is merely a projection of their beliefs in separation. And as these beliefs fade, mountains of resistance will shift and fade, and what seemed difficult before will now appear easy. The complete acknowledgement of man's wholeness in God is thus brought closer, waiting only for all of God's children to find shelter within this "single house" of the Kingdom.

Saying 49

> **(49) Jesus said, "Blessed are the solitary and elect, for you will find the kingdom. For you are from it, and there you will return."**

> **(49) *Jesus said, "Blessed are the whole ones and the chosen, for you will find the kingdom. For you are from it, and there you will return." (My restored version based on a translation by Jean-Yves Leloup)*[1]**

This saying appears to be claiming that in its use of two powerful words, there is a special group of people who, by their isolation, have earned the exclusive right to return to the Kingdom. If this is what it actually says, it would completely contradict what Jesus says elsewhere in Thomas. The words in question, of course, are "solitary" and "elect." They appear to suggest that the route to spiritual salvation is through separation, and that only those favored by God, his "elect," can achieve this ultimate goal.

However, in saying 72 Jesus asks the rhetorical question, "I am not a divider, am I?" It would be inconsistent, judging from this response, to think of this Jesus as someone who would elevate one person above another. His reputation, as implied in these sayings, was not as a divider but as someone who taught oneness. In the previous saying (48), the act of joining with someone else in peace was so powerful that it could move mountains. It is not the power of remaining solitary that moves mountains but the realization that man is one with all of creation. So it seems odd that in this saying (49) Jesus would use the words "solitary" and "elect," as most translators have proposed. Nevertheless, with some Greek and Coptic words, a broader range of interpretations is possible, and that appears to be the case here. My version of this saying (above) is based on a translation by Jean-Yves Leloup.

Leloup translates the Greek loanword *monachos* as "the whole ones," although the literal meaning is "the single one" or "the solitary one." The word "single" may certainly suggest the meaning of being alone and isolated. But it also could allude to the focus of those who become aware of the connectedness of everything they see. They are singular not by their isolation from others but by their singularity of vision. In 22, those who make the "two one" see themselves as one with everything. Such people are whole, not isolated or separate. Such awareness is precisely the goal of the Gospel of Thomas. It is not about seeking oneness while at the same time avoiding others. It is about realizing the hidden wholeness of creation that underlies and gives value to everything. I have likewise emphasized this alternate understanding of "the whole one" where the same word appears elsewhere in Thomas (16 and 75).

The word that is literally translated as "chosen" is sometimes translated as "elect." However, the word "elect" is problematic, as it suggests a God who is limited in His capacity to love. He has favorites. He loves some but not others. This brings to mind references in Isaiah to the "chosen ones" which are the elect of God. However, the question must be asked: Can the idea of a separate elect exist in the mind of a loving and perfect God? Indeed, dividing His creation into two camps, the elect and the non-elect, demonstrates a belief in duality. But in 22, Jesus makes it clear that one cannot enter the Kingdom unless all such dualistic concepts are seen as meaningless. So, according to the Jesus of this gospel, in taking the concepts of elect and non-elect seriously, God would not be able to enter His own Kingdom. That, of course, would be impossible.

Those who are "chosen" in this saying (49) are also those who choose. In saying 3b, there are those who "know" and are "known," beyond duality. In that saying, to "know" in the active voice is also to "be known" in the passive voice. In the realm of the Kingdom, there is no distinction between the active and the passive, between "know" and be "known" or "choose" and be "chosen." An example of this fusion of active and passive voice can be found in the Gospel of Luke (15:11-32) in the story of the Prodigal Son. When the son returns to his father's home, the father rejoices. And despite the son's protests that he is not worthy of such an honor, the father calls for a celebration and proclaims his joy to everyone present. He says, "This son of mine was dead and is alive again; he was lost and is *found*." Strictly speaking, the son was not found by the father. The word "found" is used to suggest that the son was lost to himself, and in finding himself, he returned to the awareness of his father's unconditional love. In the same way, those who choose to embrace the Kingdom are the chosen ones. They choose their true selves. God does not choose, as He knows only the truth. For Him, there is nothing to choose *between*. To God, being the essence of non-duality, both choice and rejection are meaningless terms. It is different for man. He is lost in this dream of a world. So, he must choose between nothing (the world of the ego) and everything (the Kingdom). In the non-dualistic realm of the Kingdom, he chooses and is chosen, finds and is found, loves and is loved. There is no distinction between the active and the passive. When oneness is realized, all such distinctions become meaningless.

The meaning of this saying is that those who are whole and chosen are "blessed." They will find the Kingdom, because they are "whole" by their own awareness of it and "chosen" by their own choice. By their choice of truth, they will be welcomed home to a place (the Kingdom), which in truth they never left. They are "from it," and by realizing that the Father and the Son can never be separate, they "will return" to it or, more accurately, awaken to it.

It is at this point that Jesus switches in mid-sentence from the third person of "the whole ones" to the second person of "you." It is as if he were saying, "It is you of whom I am speaking. It is you who are the whole ones. It is you who are the chosen. You are the blessed ones to whom this will happen."

---

1 Jean-Yves Leloup, *The Gospel of Thomas: The Gnostic Wisdom of Jesus* (Rochester, Vt: Inner Traditions, 2005), 31.

Saying 50

(50a) Jesus said, "If they say to you, 'Where do you come from?' say to them, 'We have come from the light, the place where the light has come into being of itself and established itself and became manifest through their image.'"
(50b) "If they say to you, 'Is it you?' say, 'We are its children, we are the chosen of the Living Father.' If they ask you, 'What is the sign of your Father in you?' say to them, 'It is movement with rest.'" (Standard Coptic version)

(50a) *Said Jesus this: "If they say it to you this, 'Did you become forth from where?' say it to them this, 'We come forth from in the light, the place that did the light become there. We have come out of the light, the place which the light came to be there. Outward by his hand as a single one, he stood to his feet, and he appeared forth in their image.'"*
(50b) *"If they say it to you this: 'Who are you?' say, 'We (are) the sons and we (are) the chosen ones of the Father who is living.' If they ask you this: 'What is the sign of your Father, which (is) in you?' say it to them this: 'A movement it is with a rest." (Literal translation of the Coptic version by Thomas Paterson Brown with minor changes for readability)*

(50a) ***Jesus said, "If they say to you, 'Where do you come from?' say to them, 'We have come out of the light, from the place (the Kingdom) where the light has come into being. (Extending it) outward by our hands as one, we stood to our feet (awakened) and appeared forth in our (true) likeness.'"***
(50b) ***"If they say to you, 'Who are you to say this?' say, 'We are His sons; we are the chosen of the Living Father.' If they ask you, 'What is the sign of your Father in you?' say to them, 'It is movement with rest.'" (My restored version)***

The phrasing of this saying seems to have been somewhat corrupted in its long passage through copyists and translators. Indeed, several commentators have maintained that this saying is impossible to understand and quite impenetrable. This is particularly true of 50a. It has been translated many different ways, all to no avail. Nothing seems to work to make it intelligible. My approach to this problem is to examine the literal translation first. In some ways, that version is even stranger than the usual standard translation. But despite the differences in word order and syntax between Coptic and English, the literal version begins essentially the same way:

> (50a) Said Jesus this: "If they say it to you this, 'Did you become forth from where?' say it to them this, 'Did we come forth from in the light, the place that did the light become there. We have come out of the light, the place which the light came to be there.'"

In English, this is a strange arrangement of words, but its meaning is reasonably clear. It roughly matches the standard translation. But then, in the sentence that follows the words, "came to be there," an outside figure, indicated by the pronoun "he," suddenly appears:

> "Outward by his hand as a single one, he stood to his feet, and he appeared forth in their image."

Who is this "he?" He does not appear in the standard translation. This question may be answered by recalling that in Coptic, there is no "it" pronoun. What would be considered the neutral pronoun would be written as either masculine or feminine, depending on the object to which it refers. So in this instance, the "he" can be translated as an "it," avoiding what seems to be the awkward intrusion of someone into this saying. Thus, translators have rendered "outward by his hand as a single one, he stood to his feet" as "of itself and established itself." They then rendered the next phrase, "and he appeared forth in their image" as "and (it) became manifest through their image." Accordingly, the pronoun in English is identified as "it," referring not to a person but to the "light." In this interpretation, it is the "light" that establishes itself or stands to its feet, not an unidentified person. The standard translation of this phrase, referring to light, thus becomes:

> "of itself and established itself and (it) became manifest through their image."

The problem, however, is that if we restore "he" to this line instead of the standard "it," the resulting sentence makes no more sense than it did before. It is still impossible and impenetrable. Consider what Jesus is saying. He is telling his disciples that if they are asked where they come from, they should reply that they "have come from the light, where the light has come into being." One would expect them to explain further what they did with this "light" after coming from it. That is precisely what happens when the pronoun in question is seen as originally neither "he" nor "it" but "we." The literal "he" does not belong in this saying. Its presence is evidence of deliberate scribal alteration. The logical concluding phrase in 50a would then be a reference to what "we" did, rather than an obscure allusion to what the "light" did or what the mysterious "he" did. Consider my restored version of this portion of the saying:

> (50a) Jesus said, "If they say to you, 'Where did you come from?' say to them, 'We have come out of the light, from the place (the Kingdom) where the light has come into being. (Extending it) outward by our own hands as one, we stood to our feet (awakened) and appeared forth in our (true) likeness.'"

Notice that where the literal translation has "Outward by his hand as a single one, he stood to his feet, and he appeared forth in their image," I have restored the words "we" and "our" to this phrase to indicate that it is the disciples who logically would be referring to themselves.

Deliberate scribal alteration appears to be the explanation for the confusion encountered here. Scribal alteration occurs when someone acts as an editor to correct and improve the original text. My contention is that the original pronoun in question was the plural "we," not the singular "he," and certainly not an "it." In the literal translation of this saying, Jesus is telling his disciples what they should say in answer to the question, "Where did you come from?" In answering this question, they should have consistently used the words "we" and "our." Their reply should have continued uninterrupted without a "he" or "it" being injected into the middle of the saying. The disciples would have followed their statement about coming out of the light with a line that further develops this idea. However, at some point in its transmission, an ancient scribe apparently decided that a reference to Jesus belonged in that answer.

This is what seems to have happened: The original phrase in the final sentence of 50a that would have read, "We stood to our feet and appeared forth in our likeness," reminded this scribe of an almost identical line spoken by Jesus in saying 28. The literal translation of that line is, "I stood to my feet in the midst of the world, and I appeared forth (or outward) to them in flesh." Because the scribe did not understand this saying (50) as written, and because saying 28 uses these same words in regard to Jesus, he assumed that Jesus was likewise referring to himself in this line. He consequently changed the latter instances of "we" to "he," and "our" to "his" and "their," making all the proper grammatical changes to accommodate this correction. Additionally, the phrase "outward by his hand" was originally "outward by our hands," a reference to the light being extended further by the disciples, not a self-reference to Jesus.

In my restored rendition, the disciples are consistently identified as the subjects of the reply. In the context of the saying, this would be a sensible statement for them to make. The scribe changed the latter instances of "we" and "our" to "he" and "their" to reflect his understanding that only Jesus could both "stand to his feet" and "appear forth" as he did in saying 28. In effect, the scribe's tinkering with this saying made it seem that the disciples could not have "come out of the light" without the help of Jesus. He "appeared forth in their image" to temporarily take their place and do something that they were unable to do for themselves. This brings to mind the "sacrifice" of Jesus on the cross and what came to be called "substitutionary atonement." This emerging belief in the early Jesus movement might have been what this scribe had in mind.

Looking at the entirety of this gospel, there is ample evidence to suspect that a scribe or multiple scribes had altered some words and phrases at some point in its transmission. There is additional evidence that in each case this was done to make a saying consistent with what the scribe knew about Jesus or thought he knew. Such alterations seem always to revolve around the identity of Jesus. However, the level of mistrust they seemed to have for this gospel, as they received it, should not surprise anyone. Its author espoused radically unfamiliar ideas in a gospel that in the second and third centuries was increasingly compared to the more commonly accepted gospels of Matthew, Mark, Luke, and John.

My restored version of this saying is grammatical, straightforward, and relatively clear. It reestablishes the disciples as the focus of Jesus's attention. It also leaves intact two code expressions seen here and in other Thomas sayings. The first of these is the word "place," which in many of the sayings is a code word for the Kingdom. So in this saying, the "place" or Kingdom is where the "light came into being." The other code expression is the phrase, "stood to (one's) feet." It appears in the literal version of this saying and in four other Thomas sayings that refer to either Jesus or to humans in general (16, 18, 23, and 28). In all of these sayings, the phrase implies a spiritual awakening, evoking the representation of a man standing to his feet after being asleep. As for the word "image," the Greek loanword in question can be translated as "likeness." "Likeness" is the preferable translation in this saying, as it implies identity. It is the identity or likeness of the disciples that is the object of this inquiry.

Here is my restored version of the remaining section of this saying:

(50b) "If they say to you, 'Who are you to say this?' say, 'We are His sons; we are the chosen of the Living Father.' If they ask you, 'What is the sign of your Father in you?' say to them, 'It is movement with rest.'"

This saying presents what Jesus believes about his disciples. In 50a they are from the light and from the "place" or Kingdom where the light originates. By not keeping this light for themselves but extending it outward in love, they "stand up" or awaken and become aware of their true identity. The Father is the Source of light, but by extending His light, they demonstrate that they are His sons. In 50b, it reads, "We are the chosen of the Living Father." The phrase "Living Father" also appears in 3b and clearly refers to God. In that saying, those who know themselves will realize that they are "the sons of the Living Father." Being sons of the Father, therefore, is their true identity. In the literal version, these sons of the Father are described as the "chosen," a word that better fits their relationship with God than does the word "elect," which has a ring of exclusiveness about it. They are "chosen" in the same non-dualistic sense that the "chosen" were in the previous saying (49).

The sign of the Father in them is "movement with rest." It is "movement" because the Father creates by extending His love, represented in this saying as "light." The disciples discover their wholeness and identity as children of God by further extending this light to others. This "sign" in them is also "rest" because, by experiencing this wholeness and oneness with God, they can *rest* in the knowledge that they are complete. There is nothing more for them to obtain. Like their Father, they continue to extend His love from this place of completion.

The final line has been translated as "movement *and* rest" but also "movement *with* rest." Since this first translation, employing the word "and," suggests duality, the alternative "movement with rest" is preferred.

Saying 51

> **(51) His disciples said to him, "On what day will the repose of the dead come about, and on what day will the new world come?" He said to them, "That which you look outward for has already come, but you do not recognize it."**

The disciples ask Jesus about end times and future rewards. Their question reminds the reader of similar concerns found in the New Testament. In Thomas, however, there is no particular interest in these things. For this Jesus, salvation is something given in creation, always present and needing only to be recognized.

Two expectations of first-century Jews living in Palestine are presented here. The first is that the dead in Sheol, the Jewish equivalent of Hades, restlessly wait for the resurrection of the dead, an event that presumably would happen at some future time. Some religious leaders thought this entailed a physical resurrection, others a resurrection in spirit only. The second expectation is that a new world order would come about in an end-times scenario. By this restoration, justice would be done and the world, at last, would be put right. But Jesus states here that the outcome of these expectations, in both cases, has already come: "That which you look outward for has already come, but you do not recognize it." In other words, there is nothing to do. It is merely a matter of recognizing what exists in the present moment. Everything is given; nothing is withheld. The problem with looking outward for all of these things in the future is that, in non-duality, all questions are already answered, all problems are already solved, and all resolutions are already present within the mind.

In theology, a system of beliefs concerning end times is called "eschatology." Scholars have attempted, with mixed results, to pin down the specific type of eschatology found in Thomas. Clearly, the old "apocalyptic eschatology"—the eschatology of the book of Revelation—is wholly incompatible with this gospel's focus on the present moment. What is called "realized eschatology" dismisses the notion of end times altogether but suggests that some prophecies of the Old Testament point specifically to the ministry of Jesus and his lasting legacy. It is this legacy that is the target of these prophecies. Perhaps closer to the mark is what New Testament scholar John Dominic Crossan calls "sapiential eschatology." He compares it to apocalyptic eschatology in this way:

> "Apocalyptic eschatology is world-negation stressing imminent divine intervention: we wait for God to act; sapiential eschatology is world-negation emphasizing immediate divine imitation: God waits for us to act."

The word "sapiential" means "characterized by wisdom" and the Gospel of Thomas is clearly that. However, what Crossan means by "world-negation" seems closer to the idea of world-rejection. In Crossan's understanding of this eschatological vision, the world of form exists but is rejected as something radically trivial and undesirable. But in these sayings, the world is not negated in this limited way; in physical terms, it is utterly denied. In saying 56, it is called a "corpse." It is dead. In 18, time itself is denied. There, Jesus says, "He who will take his place in the beginning will know the end." This describes an awareness of reality that displaces all concepts of separation, including space and time. The beginning and the end are seen as the same. He who achieves this awareness does not "imitate" God but surrenders to God's wholly spiritual vision of oneness. God, then, does not "wait for us to act" since, in this awareness, there is no time in which to wait. More accurately, man discovers that he and the Father are one—one without a past and one without a future. They are one in the eternal present.

What Jesus tells his disciples in this saying is that there is no need for them to "look outward" for anything. In 113, he says that the Kingdom "will not come by watching for it." Rather, it is "spread out upon the earth, and men do not see it." The "new world" is here in the spiritual sense, but it is not a physical manifestation; it is not of space and time. It is not "here" or "there," (113) either spatially or temporally. Being wholly free, God cannot be subject to space and time. As for man, he needs only to understand that God created him whole and perfect like Himself. There is nothing he needs to do except to be aware of this perfection. Time, being a dualistic concept and an expression of limitation, is meaningless. In short, there is no eschatology in Thomas. This Jesus exhibits no particular interest in end times or even in time itself.

Saying 52

> **(52) His disciples said to him, "Twenty-four prophets spoke in Israel, and they all spoke of you." He said to them, "You have omitted He who lives in your presence and have spoken of those who are dead."**
>
> **(52) *His disciples said to him, "Twenty-four prophets spoke in Israel, and they all spoke to us." He said to them, "You have omitted He who lives in your presence and have spoken (only) of those who are dead." (My restored version)***

Besides the challenge these sayings present to those unfamiliar with non-dualistic principles, there is an additional obstacle to understanding their original meaning. It is the problem of ancient scribes changing a word here or a phrase there, often rendering the text incomprehensible. Where such doctoring arises in Thomas, it seems to do so in a particular way. It appears to follow a discernible pattern. Frequently, a saying is altered when its message appears to conflict with the scribe's understanding of the historical Jesus.

When in a saying it seems that Jesus is undervalued or overlooked in some way, someone will attempt to "correct" that supposed error. The work of such a scribe or scribes can indeed be detected in this saying.

Here, the disciples make a statement, and Jesus responds. The problem is that his response does not match their statement. They say to Jesus, "Twenty-four prophets spoke in Israel, and they all spoke of you." This appears to be a messianic declaration, asserting that Jesus is the long-awaited Messiah. Furthermore, they say that as many as twenty-four prophets spoke of him. That number is more than twice the number claimed by the New Testament evangelists (assuming multiple prophecies for some). Indeed, most Biblical scholars would agree that such a statement is an absurd exaggeration. In any case, as it is written, it appears to be a statement about Jesus, of *his* significance, not about the prophets. In his response, however, Jesus does not address the issue of his messianic identity at all. Nor does he clearly acknowledge that they are referring to him. He says instead that they have "omitted He who lives in your presence" and have spoken only of the dead. In point of fact, if "the one living in your presence" is Jesus, then they are not omitting him at all. Rather, he seems to be the focus of their attention. Furthermore, the evidence from the other sayings in this collection is that "He who lives" or the "Living One" is a reference to the "Father," not to Jesus. In fact, the "Living Father" is specifically mentioned in sayings 3b and 50. (See also my commentaries on the prologue and saying 59.)

Some commentators have suggested that "twenty-four prophets" may refer to the twenty-four Hebrew books mentioned in the apocryphal 2 Esdras (14:45). The implication is that each of these books would have been written by a prophet, hence "twenty-four prophets." I think it is more likely that this was a somewhat random reference to the sum of all the major and minor prophets mentioned in the Old Testament. In any case, the number was probably chosen to magnify the disciples' interest in the prophets.

There is another way of understanding this saying. Jesus tells his disciples that instead of seeking wisdom from ancient scrolls written long ago by now-dead prophets, they would do better to seek guidance from "He who lives," the Father, who lives in the present moment. For Jesus, the "Living One" is not a remote deity but an ever-present guide. If this is so, this is what the original saying would probably look like:

(52) His disciples said to him, "Twenty-four prophets spoke in Israel, and they all spoke to us." He said to them, "You have omitted He who lives in your presence and have spoken (only) of those who are dead."

By merely changing two small words, "of you" to "to us," the saying is restored to what I believe was its original design. The statement of the disciples now matches perfectly with what Jesus says in his response. The disciples are speaking of their personal relationship with the prophets of Israel and of the guidance these spiritual masters brought to their lives. Jesus tells them that they have omitted the Source of wisdom, the Father, who forever lives in their presence. An ancient scribe, however, could not resist the temptation to turn this into a statement affirming Jesus as the Messiah. Likewise, he could not accept what seemed to him to be a depreciation of the ancient scriptures. To "correct" this saying, therefore, all he had to do is change two little words, from "to us" to "of you."

There is no evidence in Thomas that Jesus ever thought of himself as the one and only Messiah. His disciples obviously held him in high esteem, but no mention is made in this gospel of this exalted designation. In saying 13, he tells Thomas that he is not his "master" but merely one who "measured out" something—presumably truth—from the "bubbling spring." In several sayings, he speaks of some people having a superior understanding of the truth. But there is no mention of any one person being special and, for that reason, separate. In other words, in this gospel, no man rises above the oneness of God's Kingdom. (See also my commentary on 61.)

Saying 53

(53) His disciples said to him, "Is circumcision beneficial or not?" He said to them, "If it were beneficial, their father would beget them from their mother (already) circumcised. Rather, the true circumcision in spirit has proved completely profitable."

In this saying, Jesus mockingly dismisses the idea of physical circumcision but states that "true circumcision in spirit has proved completely profitable." For Jesus to say this, at a time when circumcision was still considered a sacred rite, was astonishingly courageous. It might be helpful to examine how circumcision achieved its revered place in the culture of first-century Palestine.

It was an ancient practice. The Canaanites and the Egyptians both practiced a form of circumcision that marked for young men their coming of age. In Genesis 17:10-14, Abraham is told by God that, as a sign of the covenant between Him and Abraham's descendants, all men should be circumcised. This was to occur for infants on their 8th day of life. Similar forms of this procedure have been practiced in a range of cultures for a variety of reasons. For those who did so for religious reasons, a man's penis was considered a symbol of human desires and urges. Therefore, circumcision symbolically represented submission to God's will. In the first century, Paul, of course, was the most outspoken advocate of removing the requirement of circumcision for the admission of Gentiles into the Jesus movement. But even before Paul's time, the rite was challenged and considered barbaric by many in the prevailing Greco-Roman culture.

Jesus makes the distinction between unbeneficial and beneficial circumcision to make a point about spirit. For him, the spirit, not the body, is the level on which anything meaningful is accomplished. He makes this point repeatedly throughout this gospel. For him, the ultimate submission to God's will is the abandonment in the mind of anything that is not natural to it. This symbolic circumcision is the paring away of all unloving and untrue thoughts that come between God and His creation. Without this act of spiritual purification, man is blind and adrift, as on an ocean without a compass. So in saying 26, one must remove the beam from one's inner eye before spiritual vision is possible. In 89, one is admonished to clean the inside of the cup, representing the mind or soul. In this saying, this cleaning is called "circumcision in spirit."

The centrality of spirit in everything man is and does is a major theme of this gospel. It explains how the tiny mustard seed, which is the awareness of God's love, can grow to represent the glory of the Kingdom (20). It explains how the leaven of love can be "hidden" within the mind to make the "bread" that nourishes the soul (96). Without this focus on spirit, only division, spiritual poverty, and meaningless rites are left to take its place.

Saying 54

(54) Jesus said, "Blessed are the poor, for yours is the Kingdom of Heaven."

There is no intrinsic value in being poor, of being homeless, or of having little to eat. Nor is there any value in being hated or persecuted, as one might mistakenly conclude from saying 68. This saying (54) does not promote poverty as a way of life, although that is what it seems to say. Nor does it promote spiritual poverty; quite the contrary. The experience of the Kingdom, as described elsewhere in this gospel, is one of fullness and completion.

I am indebted to Jean-Yves Leloup, author of the book, *The Gospel of Thomas, the Gnostic Wisdom of Jesus*, for advancing an interesting insight into poverty. In his commentary on this saying, he refers to the sermons of the 14th-century mystic, Meister Eckhart. Eckhart examined the meaning of poverty as represented in the Matthew (5:3) version of this saying: "Blessed are the poor in spirit, for theirs is the Kingdom of Heaven." In this context, he proposed that "a poor man is one who wills nothing, knows nothing and has nothing." Further, he maintained that although an outward and voluntary practice of poverty might be commendable, Jesus, in this verse from Matthew, was speaking not of physical poverty, not of spiritual poverty, but of interior poverty.

Expanding on what Eckhart wrote concerning these interior poverties, and using the generic "man" and "he" to represent both male and female, the man who *wills nothing* is he who is content in his oneness with God. He desires nothing more. His experience of God's presence is so acute that the world ceases to draw his attention. This is what it means to take one's "place in the beginning" (saying 18). Here, in this timeless state, nothing of this world can disturb his awareness of God's love.

The one who *knows nothing* is he who is certain that he knows nothing. For him, the lightness of his being is a merciful discovery. He no longer must bear the weight of the world. By surrendering his egoic will to God's will, all concepts ever learned, whether attached to intellectual beliefs or group identifications, can be questioned and abandoned. By doing this, he becomes poor in relative knowledge but immensely rich in the knowledge of his wholeness. He is free from his enslavement to egocentric thinking in a way that he could never be before. (See 17, 56, and 67.)

Lastly, a man who *has nothing* is he who maintains no place within his mind in which to harbor anything. He needs nothing but the awareness of who he is. His wealth is nothing more and nothing less than the union he enjoys with the Father (50). Yet, as long as he sees himself as a body in a world of limitation, he will hunger for fulfillment. As long as he identifies with his body, he will continue to experience an unquenchable sense of emptiness. But, by choosing peace in every situation and choosing to release everything that binds him to this world, he convinces the mind that peace is what it truly hungers for. Likewise, choosing to live a simple life need not be a sacrifice. It is a way to keep distractions to a minimum. Neither austerity nor extravagance will do this, but a middle way, a gentler way, will best serve the needs of one on a spiritual path.

The paradox of this saying is as sharp as anything found in Thomas: emptiness is the path to fullness. The world teaches that emptiness leads only to more emptiness. Paradoxically, however, the absence from the mind of all worldly distractions makes it possible to experience the harmony and fullness of the Kingdom. This is the "treasure" of which Jesus speaks. This is the spiritual wealth that, in comparison, makes all worldly wealth seem paltry and meaningless. With this awareness, it becomes clear that nothing in this world is worth endless struggle and pain. Only this awareness will ultimately satisfy. A life of willing nothing, knowing nothing, and having nothing, in the sense that Eckhart described, is the only life worth living. What is surrendered is more than made up for by what is gained. Or, as Jesus teaches in the Leipoldt/ Schoedel translation of 42, "Come into being as you pass away."

Saying 55

> **(55) Jesus said, "Whoever does not hate his father and his mother cannot become a disciple of mine. And whoever does not hate his brothers and sisters and bear his cross in my way will not be worthy of me."**

There is a well-known Zen koan that reads, "If you meet the Buddha on the road, kill him." This is a shocking statement, but murder is not what this koan proposes. The word "Buddha" is used here as a metaphor for either the expectation of enlightenment or the understanding of enlightenment as a concept. It is the concept, the expectation, the idea of enlightenment that must be extinguished from the mind before that which is utterly ineffable can be experienced. Likewise, Jesus often uses such provocative metaphors to stun his audience and to challenge them to consider a fundamentally new way of looking at life. In this saying, he is not proposing that one's family should be hated. It is the idea of specialness, that some people are special, some less and some more, that must be utterly expunged from the mind. Specialness is another word for separation, and in the Kingdom, separation does not exist. Therefore, it is the illusion of specialness that should be "hated." As for love, it is the appropriate response, not to illusion but to what is real.

What then is real? It is oneness. In saying 25, Jesus says, "Love your brother like your soul." How is it possible to love your brother like your soul? It is possible because your brother is your soul. He is everyone, as well as you. There is no other. There are no families, no clans, no sexes, no countries, no races, no dualities, or divisions of any kind. There is only God and what is forever a part of God, inseparable from God. Only in the dream of separation do any of these manifestations seem real. This is a theme that runs through all of Thomas, though hidden in metaphor and allegory.

Some scholars say that the original Aramaic word for "hate" also means "put aside," and since Jesus spoke Aramaic, this must have been the meaning he intended. While this is possible, I tend to think that such provocative language, found indeed throughout all of the gospels, was intended here. If you say that the author of this gospel intended a softer meaning for the word "hate," then you might also say that the author of the koan quoted above intended a softer word than "kill." But in both cases, I believe the harder, more provocative, word, was intended. See the pattern; the pattern is there. In saying 10, Jesus boldly announces that he wants to set the world on fire. Again, it is not the literal world but the idea of a separate world that he wishes to put a torch to. In 16, he says that although men think of him as peaceful, what he really wants to cast upon the world is fire, sword, and war. Such shocking words from a man of "peace"! Of course, the hidden message is the same. He wishes to kill the cause of the problem, not its effects. He wants to root out and destroy the poisonous idea of separation that sets man against man and man against God.

In Buddhism, the aim is to achieve oneness with all of life, not just with the part defined as the Buddha or indeed as Buddhism itself. Likewise, in Thomas, the aim is to embrace all of life unconditionally, not just the part that calls itself "family." Love cannot be parceled out—a little here, a little there—without one taking sides. Love that is conditional inevitably turns to fear. Conditional love is really a strategy for establishing alliances in an effort to defend the ego against a hostile world. If the world were not hostile, one would have no need for alliances and no need for conditional love. A man who makes peace with the world, who holds no resentments against anyone or anything, will consequently experience no hostility coming back at him from such a world. This is so because the world is not a separate entity, separate from the mind. In non-dualism, it is a projection of the mind. It is an illusion that mirrors the thoughts and beliefs of the mind. If he finds that hidden treasure of peace within the mind that Jesus talks about in this gospel, he will project that peace outward and experience it not only inwardly but outwardly as well. In effect, there is no difference between inside and outside, that being a duality (22). The man who experiences this peace of non-duality will have no need for conditional relationships. On the other hand, he who limits himself to conditional love and refuses to open his heart to unconditional love, will, in fact, strengthen his belief that he has enemies and thus confirm that he needs allies for protection.

Jesus did not hate his family. He loved his family, as he did every living soul without exception and without judgment. That was the power of his love. That is what he taught, that there could be no distinctions or exceptions. To be itself, love must remain whole and intact.

It appears that the phrase "and bear his cross in my way" was appended to this saying by an ancient scribe who did not understand the author's subtlety. That Jesus would "hate" his family seemed preposterous and, from what he knew of his reputation, totally out of character. He decided to soften the saying's rhetoric and explain this hate in terms of *sacrifice*. The "cross" phrase proposes that Jesus sacrificed his love for his family for a higher purpose, just as he sacrificed his life for a higher purpose on the cross. However, such a notion is quite alien to the Gospel of Thomas. What higher purpose can there be than to love all of God's children equally and unconditionally? Moreover, this late addition reflects an interest in the crucifixion and in sacrifice, an interest that is not shared by any of the other sayings in this collection.

Saying 56

> **(56) Jesus said, "Whoever has known the world has found a corpse, and whoever has found (this) corpse, of him the world is not worthy."**

This saying proposes a thoroughly radical and unequivocal idea: Whoever has known the world, as it is, has found a corpse. Furthermore, the world is not worthy of he who has "found" or made this discovery. Presumably, anyone seeking to understand the world must first perceive it as something living, or at least as harboring life. But after further scrutiny, he discovers that, in fact, it is not alive nor does it harbor anything. It is dead. It is not partially dead but completely and categorically dead.

Notice what the saying does not say. It does not say that anyone has ever truly understood the world otherwise. In its ultimate essence, it is dead. It has always been so. Seekers of wisdom have long succeeded in making this discovery, that sometimes after a lifetime of searching for clarity and certainty in the world of space and time, the quest falls apart in total frustration. The egoic mind succumbs to what is hidden within. And there, in a world without a world, they find everything. This is the Kingdom, another realm entirely, the Kingdom of the Father.

If the world is not worthy of the one who discovers the truth, then what *is* worthy of him? This saying does not answer that question, but consistent with the rest of Thomas, the answer is the Kingdom. What is the Kingdom of the Father? It is the peace, love, and joy that call to us beyond the pain and petty pleasures of this world, a realm beyond the body's senses and concepts of the intellect. The Kingdom of the Father is the true home of man, despite his belief that he lives elsewhere in darkness while clinging to a corpse. The world is the false belief that man can permanently hide from God as long as he believes that he is separate from Him. However, he is not separate from Him and never has been, and when he comes to see at last that the world indeed is just a phantom of his imagination, he will let it go.

This discovery is not unlike the discovery in saying 2, where the seeker is astonished by what he finds and consequently rules over "the all." This is not a mere adjustment in thinking. To arrive at such a breakthrough, the seeker must dig deeper, beyond everything he has been taught and beyond everything his eyes and ears have seemed to witness. He must, in fact, trust nothing that the world has ever taught and follow the implications of these sayings to the silent and peaceful restoration of oneness to which they point. What he finds, then, will be truly astonishing.

This saying (56) is quite an important one, as it defines this gospel's view of man's relationship with the world. The world is not just the earth but the world of form, of space and time, and of everything that changes and evolves. If this world is dead, then he who knows and claims this truth must be alive. He must not only be alive; he must in no way be a product of the world. *He must be spirit.* Man *is* spirit. (See also 111.) That is his identity. This is why the world is not worthy of him. He is worthy of much more. Man is not confined by limitations; he does not change or evolve but lives beyond space and time, surrounded by love, within the mind of God.

Saying 57

> **(57) Jesus said, "The Kingdom of the Father is like a man who had good seed. His enemy came in the night and sowed weeds among the good seed. The man did not allow them to pull up the weeds. He said to them, 'I am afraid that you will go intending to pull up the weeds and pull up the wheat along with them.' For on the day of the harvest, the weeds will be plainly visible, and they will be pulled up and burned."**

Here again, we encounter a perplexing situation involving the planting of seeds. At first glance, the man's decision to ignore the weeds seems appropriate. But is it? In his book *The Gospel of Thomas, Annotated & Explained*, Stevan Davies comments on this parable. He points out that for a farmer to allow the young weeds to mature, to fail to pull them out before they have done their damage to the good plants, shows his incompetence.

No farmer in his right mind would do this. Left alone, the weeds would rob the domesticated plants of moisture, nutrition, and sunlight throughout the whole growing season. "By the time of harvest," he says, "weeds are irrelevant, for they have done their damage already, and cutting them down and burning them will no longer serve any purpose."[1] Coming from rural Galilee, Jesus would have been aware of standard farming practices, as would his listeners. They would have surely recognized the absurdity of this scenario.

But is this story any more absurd than the story in saying 8 of the fisherman who throws a large catch of small fish overboard to keep one large, unprofitable one? Is it any more ridiculous for the shepherd in 107 to abandon ninety-nine sheep to save just one sheep? More examples can be found in sayings 64, 66, 76, and 95. In the region in which Jesus taught his gospel, farming, fishing, and raising sheep were the mainstays of the economy. Therefore, there must have been few among these people who did not understand the absurdity of these situations. On the level of the world, these sayings present a logic that is foolish and unprofitable, but in the realm of the Kingdom, there is another set of rules to which these parables point.

There is an underlying message in this gospel, which is this: The laws of this world are not the laws of the Kingdom. What makes sense in one realm makes no sense in the other. From the viewpoint of each, the other is absurd. Throughout the text, we see this message repeated again and again. In this parable, we see a farmer acting foolishly from the viewpoint of the world. From this worldview perspective, his course should be clear. As soon as the weeds and wheat emerge from the ground, he should instruct his servants to pluck out the weeds, even if it means that some of the wheat is sacrificed in the process. In this way, at least some of his crop would be saved. This follows from the rules of the world. This makes sense to the ego-mind. Its rule is: Focus on the apparent problem, and destroy it before it destroys you.

However, in the realm of spirit, which is the Kingdom, there are no problems. Problems are projections of a mind that believes in separation. In the Kingdom of the Father, there is no separation, no separate interests, and nothing that requires correction, sacrifice, or even the least bit of concern. This is the Kingdom that Jesus experiences and wishes to share with his disciples. The ego and its seeds, represented by the weeds in this parable, have no power here. The enlightened mind knows that in this realm of existence, the ego is simply a structure of beliefs that is based on fear and guilt. It is a phantom image that disappears when exposed to the light of truth. It is this understanding that is metaphorically demonstrated in this saying. The presence of the weeds in his field does not worry this farmer.

Under the cover of darkness, the ego plants within the mind its thoughts of fear and guilt. These seeds are still small, so at this stage their nascent qualities appear almost normal. The farmer, however, representing the one who "seeks" in saying 2, recognizes the young plants as weeds. He sees them as a threat to his good seeds, which are metaphors for his budding awareness of God's love. He now is faced with a dilemma. Should he pluck out from within his mind the emerging weeds, which at this stage are barely recognizable from the wheat, or should he allow both to grow to maturity?

He chooses the latter path, which is the path of patience and trust. He knows that the part of his mind that responds with fear, the part that mindlessly reacts to what it does not understand, is also his "enemy," the ego-mind. The ego always reacts and is never patient. So instead of employing his ego to attack its own manifestations, the seeds of fear and guilt, he ignores them and allows the truth, represented by the good seeds, to mature and unfold. The truth needs no help in this. The weeds of fear and guilt, on the other hand, will shrink and die without constant attention. They thrive when taken seriously. This concern justifies their existence and strengthens the ego. If both plants are left alone, the wheat of truth will grow straight and tall, while the weeds of the ego will wither and die. Without the meddlesomeness of the ego, the awareness of God's love will blossom. In contrast, the manifestations of the ego will be "plainly visible." Their neglected and malnourished leaves can then be easily pulled up and banished forever from the mind.

---

1 Stevan Davies, *The Gospel of Thomas, Annotated & Explained* (Woodstock, VT: Skylight Paths, 2003), 76.

Saying 58

(58) Jesus said, "Blessed is the man who has toiled. He has found life."

Of the ten sayings in Thomas that mention the word "blessed," four may be grouped together as representing a particular kind of beatitude. These sayings are 54, 58, 68, and 69. What these beatitudes have in common is that they bestow blessings on a man in difficult situations. A man may be poor, but he is blessed. A man may be hungry, but he is blessed. It might seem that in this group of sayings, a man is blessed merely because he is poor, hungry, or stressed in some way. All have this surface meaning. In Thomas, however, virtually nothing is as it seems. In this gospel, one always finds an emphasis on internal states of mind and internal rewards. Knowing this, one would expect to find this true of these beatitudes as well. In fact, all of these beatitudes focus on internal or psychological conditions rather than on bodily or external states. Likewise, their rewards are internal. Such rewards have nothing to do with enhancing a physical experience but everything to do with intensifying the awareness of the Kingdom.

There are four ways that beatitudes, in general, may be understood or structured:

1. An external condition is experienced. He who suffers or embraces this experience is rewarded by God.
2. An external condition is experienced. The reward is an intrinsic outcome of that experience.
3. An internal condition is experienced. He who suffers or embraces this experience is rewarded by God.
4. An internal condition is experienced. The reward is an intrinsic outcome of that experience.

Most people are familiar with the beatitudes found in Matthew (5:1-10) and Luke (6:20-23). They are included among a set of wisdom sayings called, in Matthew, the *Sermon on the Mount* and, in Luke, the *Sermon on the Plain*. In both gospels, they are specifically presented to the disciples to prepare them for difficulties, similar to what the ancient prophets experienced in their day. The suggestion is that just as the prophets were persecuted for their beliefs and practices, the same challenges will face the disciples. Jesus assures them, however, that they will be rewarded for their suffering in heaven. Luke follows his list of beatitudes with this line: "Be glad in that day and rejoice, because your reward in heaven is great" (Luke 6:23). The implication is that poverty, hunger, or any suffering experienced in the service of God will be rewarded in heaven. And although such biblical beatitudes may be adapted to apply in a range of situations, it appears that in Luke, Jesus had classification number 1 in mind: an external condition is experienced—hunger, for example—but he who suffers for his service to God, will find his reward in heaven.

In Matthew, unlike Luke, both external and internal preconditions are mentioned. For example, a man is blessed if he is "pure of heart" but also blessed if he is a "peacemaker." He is blessed if he "mourns" but also blessed if he is "merciful." In other words, in Matthew, a man is blessed not only for internal conditions that result from his service to God but also for his overt acts of virtue. Such acts include being a peacemaker and being merciful. Also in Matthew, the list of beatitudes is longer and more nuanced. Yet, immediately following the beatitudes, Jesus links the suffering of his disciples to the suffering of the prophets, just as in Luke. He says as well, "Their reward in heaven is great" (Matthew 5:12). Such rewards in heaven appear to be what Jesus has in mind in all of the beatitudes in both gospels. So in Matthew, the beatitudes may be understood as conforming to classifications 1 and 3. What makes the beatitudes in Thomas unique is that although they appear to conform to 1 or 3, on closer inspection, they all conform to number 4.

Classification number 4 maintains that all conditions referred to in the Thomas beatitudes are internal conditions existing on the level of the mind. As I have argued before, all significant actions in Thomas happen on this level. They do not happen on the level of the external world because, in Thomas, there is no world. The world is a "corpse," as is the body (80), and he who discovers this fact must be alive and not of this world (56). It is in the mind where the belief structure of the ego is encountered. It is there where its belief in a separate world must be understood as false and consequently abandoned. When that is accomplished, the mind wakes up to its true identity.

In none of the Thomas beatitudes is a reward held by God for a later time. In none are the disciples compared to the suffering prophets. Where the word "persecution" appears, it is either linked to the inner pursuit of fulfillment (69) or resolved in the inner "place" or Kingdom that serves as a refuge from false beliefs (68).

As I explained in my commentary on saying 54, there is no intrinsic value in being poor, homeless, hungry, or persecuted. Neither is there any inherent value in toiling simply for the sake of toiling. If nothing meaningful is accomplished by it, then it becomes a meaningless struggle that benefits no one. However, effort spent on removing the obstacles to the awareness of the Kingdom is always meaningful and worthwhile. There is no higher use of toil than this. For this commentary, I have adapted the "Scholars Version" of this saying (Patterson and Meyer) that translates the critical word here as "toiled." This choice seems a better fit in the context of this gospel, one that stresses both meaningful effort and the mildness of such effort.

In saying 90, Jesus insists that his "yoke is mild," and so it is. In the Gospel of Thomas, preparing the soil of the mind for the seeds of awareness is exactly what "toil" means. Tending to that awareness and trusting that all power comes from this awareness of the Kingdom is a meaningful effort. It is mild compared to the struggles of the ego-mind that toils for meaningless rewards. But devotion to such a path involves great courage and a willingness to face one's fears and doubts. Finally, when the way is clear, when the Kingdom is restored to the mind, this toil can be set aside. As in saying 2, the seeker will then be astonished by what he finds. He will experience true "rest" and discover what it means to find "life."

Saying 59

> **(59) Jesus said, "Look for the Living One while you are alive, lest you die and seek to behold Him and be unable to do so."**

Sometimes readers suggest the idea that some sayings in Thomas can best be understood if they are seen as conveying not one meaning, but more than one. Some argue that a saying that has not one but many interpretations is consequently more carefully crafted and more honestly representative of a complex world. Such a world, they propose, cannot, and perhaps should not, be reduced to one comprehensive explanation. This approach to difficult or complex sayings is called "multivalence." It is akin to ambivalence, but unlike ambivalence, it can be seen as a positive characteristic. There are problems with this mode of interpretation, however. It suggests that the commentator writes from confusion rather than from conviction. It suggests that he detects no overriding themes in the work or hints that might reveal the intentions of the author. It suggests that he believes that the work is too complex to understand, and consequently, he may sometimes present a smorgasbord of explanations, referring to each as "equally valid." Thus, the commentator may portray the author as either indecisive or, worse, interested only in the play of ideas.

This is a saying that, once again, can be read on a superficial level or on a deeper, hidden level. Yet, there is only one meaning here. The Jesus of this gospel does not play with ideas but focuses his attention on basically two human needs: the need to be fully aware of God's love, and the need to confront those beliefs that deny that love. To be fully aware of God's love is the same as truly knowing oneself and knowing that one is God's child. In saying 3, this knowledge is equated with spiritual wealth. So in this saying, looking for the "Living One" is not about searching the world for some external presence but becoming aware of the divine presence within, which is the awareness of God's love. Only when that awareness is established can one know what it means to be alive. Anything outside of this experience is poverty and death—not physical poverty or death but spiritual poverty and spiritual death.

Before we go further, we should confirm the identification of the "Living One." Only in the prologue do we find the expression, "living Jesus." Some commentators have accepted this phrase as evidence that all occurrences of the "Living One" in the text refer to Jesus. However, the prologue is an introduction to the sayings and not a saying itself. No claim has been made for its function as a saying. Although the writer of the prologue may have considered Jesus to be the "Living One" of these sayings, this does not mean that its author intended such a connection. Indeed, the evidence is quite strong that the "Father" is the "Living One." In two sayings, 3b and 50, the "Living Father" is specifically identified.

In 37, there is mention of "the Son of the Living One," the "Living One" being the Father. And finally, in 52, "He who lives," seems at first glance to refer to Jesus, but on closer inspection is seen as referring to the "Father." The "Father," of course, is God the Father.

In this saying, Jesus presents a situation that, by his own logic, cannot exist. He says that one should look to God, presumably in the world of space and time, while one is physically alive, because after life, when one is dead, God may not be found. This presumes that the world of dualities, the duality of life and death being among the principal ones, is meaningful. Yet, Jesus tells us in saying 22 that belief in all such dualities bars one from entering the Kingdom. In Thomas, there is only life, and death is a condition of the mind as when man denies the awareness of God's love. Consider my alternate reading of this saying:

> (59) Jesus said, "Look to the Living One while you are alive to His loving presence, lest you die to this awareness and seek to see Him and are unable to do so."

This is the hidden meaning of this saying. It has nothing to do with the death of the body. The body, like the world in Thomas, is a corpse (80). It has no life and was never born. The reason that the Living Father cannot be found in death is because, like the world and the body, death is an illusion and God cannot be found in illusions. But He can be denied, and this is what man does when he dies to His awareness.

There is only life. It has no opposite, just as God has no opposite. If God had created anything in opposition to Himself, it would have been akin to creating lies to vie forever with the truth. This makes no sense. God did not create death, and if God did not create it, it does not exist. Therefore, there is no afterlife, only life. Whether it is death, evil, separation, or anything that opposes the love of God, in the estimation of this Jesus it does not exist.

Man has free will to the extent that he can remember God's bounty or choose to forget it. He can embrace it or submerge it in egoic thinking. But the truth remains that the Father loves His child, is one with His child, and nothing outside of this oneness exists. That is the hidden, but discernible, teaching of this gospel.

Saying 60

> **(60) <They> saw a Samaritan taking with him a lamb on his way to Judea. He said to his disciples, "<Why is> that man carrying the lamb?"**
> **They said to him, "So that he may kill it and eat it."**
> **He said to them, "While it is alive, he will not eat it, but only when he has killed it and it has become a corpse."**
> **They said to him, "He cannot do it otherwise."**
> **He said to them, "You as well, look for a place for yourself within rest, lest you become a corpse and be eaten."**

A missing word at the beginning of this saying was caused by a scribal error. This means that instead of "They saw" being the opening phrase, the preferred choice of most translators, it is possible for the saying to begin with "He saw." If that is the case, there is the further possibility that it is Jesus who is "on his way to Judea," not the Samaritan. This is unlikely, however, as it is uncharacteristic of Thomas to include in these sayings extraneous information. In this situation, Jesus recognizes the metaphorical potential of the Samaritan's walk to Judea and makes it a central feature of the story. It contributes allegorically to a theme first encountered in saying 7, that of the man and the lion.

Jesus asks, "Why is that man carrying the lamb?" The implied question, however, is, "Why is that Samaritan carrying the lamb to Judea?" If the Samaritan intended to sell the lamb, he would have done so among his own people in Samaria. He would not have been so foolish as to think he could get a better deal among the sometimes hostile Judeans. Apparently then, he was not traveling to Judea to sell his lamb. Moreover, in Judea, the sight of a man carrying a single lamb on a road leading to Jerusalem would have most likely meant one thing: he was on his way to the Temple to offer the lamb in sacrifice. However, this is a Samaritan, not a Judean, and Samaritans did not recognize the Temple in Jerusalem as legitimate. He would not have traveled to Judea for that purpose. As is often the case in Thomas, we encounter here a quality of unreality. Once again, a somewhat absurd scenario is presented to the reader. In this case, it is an actual event that Jesus adapts for its allegorical possibilities.

In their reply to his question, the disciples conclude that the Samaritan is simply looking for a place to kill his lamb and eat it. Jesus acknowledges that this is so, but at this point in the dialogue, he cunningly directs the conversation away from the simple scene of a man and his lamb to examine its metaphorical potential. As he often does in these sayings, Jesus takes a familiar figure from everyday life to represent an idea or theme that goes to the heart of his teachings. In this case, the relationship between the Samaritan and his lamb is reminiscent of the relationship between the "lion" and the "man" in saying 7. In these two sayings, the Samaritan and the lion can be seen as metaphors for the ego, while the lamb and the man represent the true Self. If the reader can overlook these slightly mixed metaphors, he might appreciate how appropriately and powerfully they work in their respective sayings.

As the ego often does, the Samaritan appears to have good intentions. In our mind's eye, we see him carrying the lamb around his neck. Short of walking him, this was the preferred method of conveying a lamb over long distances. It represents the iconic image of a man intent on sacrificing to God a creature that he genuinely values. If he did not value it, he would not consider it a worthy sacrifice. However, nothing can be further from the truth. This Samaritan is not what he seems. He is not on a spiritual mission to Jerusalem. He has no regard for the lamb. He just wants to kill it and eat it. Likewise, the ego has no regard for the true Self. Born of guilt and fear, it seeks only to prove that separation is real and that God is powerless. What better proof of this could there be than the death of God's creation? This is what it secretly wants. This is the ego's hidden agenda. Indeed, the belief structure we call the ego exists for no other purpose than to annihilate the true Self and win this battle at any cost.

As for the true Self, metaphorically represented by the lamb, it is wholly innocent and pure. In a world governed by sacrifice and struggle, it values neither of these things. In the words of saying 50, the sign of the Father is "movement with rest." It is in the movement of love with the silence of rest that it recognizes its being. But as long as it shares the mind with the ego, it will not yet realize its own immense value.

Jesus says that before the lamb can be eaten, the Samaritan must kill it. "He cannot do it otherwise." This is another way of saying that before the true and innocent identity of man can be consumed by the ego, the ego must kill it. In actuality, the true Self can never die, but it can be so lost in the darkness of the ego that its presence is all but forgotten. Jesus compares this to becoming a "corpse," a nonentity. However, the true Self is not a helpless victim of the ego. It can still be saved from this fate by its own will to prevail.

Jesus says to his followers, "You too, look for a place for yourself within rest, lest you become a corpse and be eaten." As we have previously seen, the word "place" is a code word in Thomas for the Kingdom. This is the place within the mind where safety is found. It is a wholly different place than the place to which the Samaritan goes to kill his lamb. It is not something found after death or in death but in life, within rest. Into this rest, the ego cannot go since the ego's existence depends on turmoil. The Kingdom of the Father is a fortress and a refuge. The ego represented by the Samaritan cannot penetrate this holy place. Here, man will find refuge and not "become a corpse and be eaten." (See my commentary on 68.)

Saying 61

> **(61a) Jesus said, "Two will rest on a bed: the one will die, and the other will live."**
> **(61b) Salome said, "Who are you, man? From whom have you come forth that you should come up on my couch and eat from my table?" Jesus said to her, "I am he who exists from He who is equal. I was given some of the things of my Father."**
> **<Salome said,> "I am your disciple."**
> **(61c) <Jesus said,> "Therefore I say, if one is destroyed (comes to be equal), he will be filled with light, but if he comes to be divided (unequal), he will be filled with darkness."**

As it sometimes happens, there is not one saying here but two. It is important to remember that in Thomas the system of assigning numbers to sayings is a modern invention. In the original Coptic codex, there are no line or paragraph breaks to indicate where one saying ends and the other begins. Furthermore, in antiquity, this gospel was organized somewhat artificially by linking together those sayings that contained the same catchword. For example, the Coptic word for "bed" here in 61a is linked with the same word translated as "couch" in 61b. Thus, the original editor joined these two sayings together based on the presence of the same word in each. Nevertheless, the differences between 61a and 61b/c, although not contradictory, are substantial.

Looking first at 61a, a similar saying is 42: "Come into being as you pass away." It urges the reader to allow his true identity to rise to consciousness by abandoning his false identity. One identity is nurtured while the other shrinks from inattention. This happens entirely within the mind. Likewise, the two who recline on a couch are, metaphorically, not two people, but one person with two conflicting identities. In the world of separation, all individuals have two selves. There is the person a man thinks he is and the person he truly is. Jesus refers to this dichotomy in saying 7, where he portrays the internal relationship between the lion self and the true Self. In the context of non-dualism, it may be described as the relationship in the dream of separation between the ego and the divine Self.

The word to focus on in this saying is "rest." When the individual is at rest or in full repose, the ego identity is weakened; it cannot sustain its hold on the mind. The reason for this is that the ego represents the antithesis of rest. A mind in turmoil is blind and deaf to its divine nature. Only when the incessant chatter of the mind is still can the light of God's love penetrate its darkness. With the discovery of one's true identity in peace and oneness, the ego's belief structure collapses. In that blissful moment, the true-Self rises to awareness while the ego-self dies in the glare of truth. As 61a says, "Two will rest on a bed: the one will die, and the other will live."

Now turning to 61b, we find quite a distinct saying. Here, Jesus has been described as an intruder at a dinner party. His appearance at Salome's table can indeed be interpreted this way. However, there is another way of understanding this dialogue between Jesus and Salome. This other way not only clarifies its meaning but also identifies the theme that connects 61b to 61c. That theme is the idea that Jesus is not special but the equal of Salome, and that this fundamental equality is a feature of God's Kingdom.

As frequently interpreted, Salome's initial question to Jesus seems indignant, bold, and even imperious. "Who are you?" she asks, as if she were a wealthy woman and Jesus was intruding on her privacy. This, of course, was not the Salome of Christian tradition who danced for the head of John the Baptist. This Salome was a follower of Jesus, often mentioned in the canonical gospels. There is no evidence, here or elsewhere, that she ever was a wealthy or powerful woman. In any case, her behavior in this saying is quite out of keeping with what we know about the subordinate position of women in first-century Palestine.

However, what Salome says can be seen in another light. Suppose the stress of her question is on the word "are" rather than on the word "you": "Who *are* you?" In essence, Salome is asking Jesus this question: What sort of man are you that you would descend to my humble level, share my lowly couch, and eat at my modest table? It is all about what emphasis one puts on which words. So, it is not an indignant tone that Salome expresses but a self-deprecating one, and it is this to which Jesus responds.

Most scholars believe that the words of this saying have been garbled in transmission. For example, immediately following Salome's question, "Who are you, man?" is the line translated literally as "while out of one." To make sense of this strange phrase, translators have proposed several possible restorations. These include, "From whom have you come forth?" and "as if you are from someone." Additional choices are, "like somebody important" or even "Whose son (are you?)." These translations suggest that Salome thinks of Jesus as someone special or unique. So what we have here is a woman immensely awed by the presence of Jesus in her home.

In response, Jesus says, "I am he who exists from He who is equal. I was given some of the things of my Father's." Here again, the translators have submitted several versions of this line. However, this rendering appears to come closest to the literal translation while best advancing the theme of the saying. Many times in Thomas, Jesus makes the point that God's creation is whole and indivisible, not two but one—beyond all seeming divisions. That being the case, there can be no possibility of inequality within such oneness. Indeed, Jesus identifies God as "equal." This suggests that God is equality itself, just as He might be considered love itself. And because this God, this Equality, created man in His own image, man must be wholly equal himself and not in any way special. By saying that he was given some of the things of his Father's, Jesus is making the point that he has been blessed by his Father, but so have others been blessed. This is not a claim of superiority by Jesus but a statement that says that no one created by God, by Equality itself, can be unequal. Jesus is saying to Salome that she is mistaken to think that he is better, more special, or closer to God than she is. The truth is that both she and he were created as one, and no power on earth can make it otherwise. One is reminded of the line in Mark (10:9) and Matthew (19:6): "What God has joined together, let man not put asunder."

The next line might be called Salome's dramatic conversion: "I am your disciple." It does not belong here. The preceding line leads naturally and quite logically to the following line that begins: "Therefore, I say…" Salome's sudden assertion of devotion to Jesus abruptly breaks the flow of this discourse. I suspect that, here again, we have evidence of a scribe who was intent on protecting the stature or dignity of Jesus. Just as modern commentators have done, this scribe took Salome's initial question to be haughty and disrespectful. Having made that judgment, he could not leave her insolence hanging like a dark cloud over this saying. There was no such cloud, but believing that there was, he had to soften this impression and justify her reputation as a loyal disciple of Jesus. So he inserted "I am your disciple" into the saying, believing that this would correct any false misconceptions about Salome and her respect for Jesus.

In his book *The Gospel of Thomas, Original Text with Commentary*, Uwe-Karsten Plisch comments on a keyword in 61c. It is the Coptic word for "destroyed" in the sentence, "Therefore I say, if one is destroyed, he will be filled with light." In the context of the saying, the word "destroyed" is not quite right. An ancient scribe, says Plisch, "mistook the last letter (of the Coptic word for 'to be alike') and thus wrote the meaningless 'destroyed.'"[1] The word for "to be alike" may also be translated as "to be equal." So here again, the idea of equality appears in this saying. The line in question, then, should read, "Therefore I say, if one comes to be equal, he will be filled with light." The connotation of that line is that if one sees himself as equal to all of God's children, he will not feel inferior. He will not artificially humble himself before others. He will accept others as being one with himself and everyone as being one with God. As a woman, this is particularly relevant for Salome, living as she is in a society largely ruled by men.

If, on the other hand, one is convinced that he or she is divided or separate (unequal), then that one will "be full of darkness." Until Jesus corrects her, Salome is in darkness. She does not understand his essential message that all of life is equal. Wholeness, being complete, admits no trace of separation or division between man and man or man and God. The mind that embraces this understanding, therefore, will be filled with the light of truth and love.

---

1 Uwe-Karsten Plisch, *The Gospel of Thomas, Original Text with Commentary* (Stuttgart: Deutsche Bibelgesellschaft, 2008), 151.

Saying 62

> **(62a) Jesus said, "It is to those who are worthy of (who seek) my mysteries that I tell my mysteries.**
> **(62b) Do not let your left (hand) know what your right (hand) is doing."**

Once again, instead of one saying here, we have two unrelated sayings. With the absence of an introductory "Jesus said" at the beginning of 62b, translators have assumed that the two sayings belong together. This missing intro to 62b, however, was more likely an omission by an ancient copyist. The two sayings have, in fact, quite distinct meanings, and in this commentary I will treat them separately.

The word "mysteries" does not refer to the Greco-Roman mystery religions of the first through third centuries CE, commonly known as the *mysteries*. There is no evidence of such a connection. Rather, it appears that the word "mysteries" is used here to refer to the Kingdom of the Father. In saying 5, that which is hidden, the Kingdom, is said to be "in front of your face," yet generally the seeker at first does not see it. The truth is that in the awareness of the Kingdom, man is one with his Father and one with all of creation. Once this is realized, the seeker is "astonished" (2). It is the most substantial discovery anyone could make, yet it is hidden from the awareness of most minds. It is a mystery, not because God wishes it to be mysterious but because man, lost in his identification with his ego, is afraid of it. The ego is fearful of its own dissolution, and would, in fact, cease to exist if the truth of man's oneness with God was fully acknowledged.

A tear in the papyrus has obscured a word in the first line usually translated as "worthy." That word choice, however, is a matter of conjecture. In his book *Unlocking the Secrets of the Gospel of Thomas*, Charles W. Hedrick proposes that a better choice than "those worthy" would be "those who seek," as in "I tell my mysteries to those who (seek my) mysteries." This is preferable, Hedrick argues, since the "primary strategy" of Thomas in saying 1 is "to encourage the experience of immortality by finding the interpretation of Jesus' words."[1] I agree that "seek my mysteries" works better in the context of this saying.

Jesus shares his mysteries only with those who prepare their minds to receive them. It is the responsibility of the seeker to free his mind of all the distractions and obstacles to the awareness of what Jesus calls in this gospel, the "Kingdom." That is the task of the seeker. No one can do this for him. He must seek this realization and work to make it manifest.

Next, we have 62b: "Do not let your left (hand) know what your right (hand) is doing." Although the word "hand" does not appear in the Coptic text, most scholars believe that the original saying would most likely have included it. This memorable aphorism has become so familiar that even those who know nothing of its source recognize it as a common idiom. It makes its single New Testament appearance in Matthew (6:1-4). There, its application is strictly external. The disciples are cautioned not to "practice their acts of righteousness before men" but to give to the needy without show. It is essentially a lesson on giving freely without pretense. Jesus tells his disciples that if they avoid such hypocrisy, they will find their reward in heaven.

In Thomas, the saying stands alone without embellishment. A general rule may be stated that, in these sayings, whenever a dichotomy is presented, an internal relationship is disguised as an external situation. In this case, the left hand is a metaphor for the ego-self, the part of the mind that accepts the ego's belief in separation. Conversely, the right hand is a metaphor for the true-Self, the part of the mind that accepts its true identity. So here again, we have the familiar duo of the lion and the man from saying 7 represented by different metaphors. Both sets of metaphors stand for the two identities that vie for supremacy within the mind. One is the true-Self, while the other is the ego-self. They are mutually incompatible and, in fact, a merging of the two is impossible; any attempt to do so will compromise the integrity of the true Self and strengthen the hold of the ego.

Jesus says, "Do not let your left (hand) know what your right (hand) is doing." The ego would not be the ego unless it sought to dominate the whole mind completely. What Jesus is saying here is this: do not let that happen. Have nothing to do with the ego. Starve it and isolate it by withdrawing all attention from it. Let it wither and die from inattention. Focus instead on the true-Self, represented here by the right hand. The true-Self is quiet and naturally loving. It is both serene and joyful. It is worthy of man's attention. The point Jesus is making is that man must live from that center of tranquility. Trust it. This is where the Kingdom is found. The alert reader will recognize the similarity of this message to the essential message of saying 57, the parable of the wheat and the weeds.

Additionally, this saying suggests that the left hand, representing the ego-self, wants to know what the right hand, representing the true-Self, is doing. It further suggests that it wants to know this in order to appropriate and misrepresent its wisdom. The ego must dominate all aspects of the mind's thinking to survive. While it cannot understand the true-Self, it will skillfully attempt to explain it away by reducing it to concepts and intellectual jargon. In this saying, Jesus warns the reader not to let that happen lest the ego devitalize the ineffable grandeur of the Kingdom to a conceptual dead end.

It is interesting to note that in ancient Rome, the right hand, *manus dextra*, was used to feed oneself while the left hand, *manus sinistra*, was used to clean oneself after defecation. Perhaps for that reason, the left hand was considered unclean and sometimes called the *manus diaboli*, the devil's hand.

---

1 Charles W. Hedrick, *Unlocking the Secrets of the Gospel According to Thomas* (Eugene, OR: Cascade Books, 2010), 118.

Saying 63

> **(63) Jesus said, "There was a rich man who had much money. He said, 'I will make use of my money so that I may sow, reap, plant, and fill my storehouses with produce, so in that way, I will lack nothing.' Those were his thoughts, but that same night he died. Let him who has ears hear."**

This rich man is a farmer. Farming is the source of his wealth. His financial security is additionally underscored by the use of the phrase "had much money." Yet, in spite of this, he fears poverty and worries about his future. The point is emphasized, however, that he is financially secure, which suggests that the chances of him falling on hard times are quite remote.

By the standards of the physical world, his plans are prudent, even admirable. He will not sit on his wealth but put it to work. He will sink it back into his business. He will sow, reap, plant, and fill his storehouses with the fruits of his labor. He tells himself that this action will secure his future. By doing this, he will lack for nothing. And then what happens? In a stunning turn of events, that same night, he drops dead. "Let him who has ears hear."

What readers sometimes miss when they encounter this parable is that, by the standards of the world, this man is wise. He responds to his fears in a seemingly reasonable and measured way. The saying accentuates this normalcy by running through the practical steps he plans to take. He will sow and reap, plant and fill his storehouses. He will invest in the future, which, by his standards, is a wise and shrewd thing to do.

How different is the same man in Luke's version of this story (Luke 12:16-19). In that version, the rich man is a fool. He overproduces without having a barn large enough to hold his harvest. He then decides to tear down his old barns and build larger ones. This time-consuming project, in the short run, is pointless. Finally, he thinks to himself, "You have plenty of good things laid up for many years. Take life easy; eat, drink and be merry." Here in Luke, the temptation is strong to dismiss such a man as a fool. But in doing so, we conveniently exclude ourselves from the possibility that we could ever do the same. In our condemnation of this man, we see him as an anomaly, someone so different from ourselves that, in comparison, we could never be so foolish.

In Thomas, however, the rich man cannot be so easily dismissed. He is not an obvious fool but a careful and intelligent farmer. It is not his lack of intelligence that is the problem; it is the seemingly wise but foolish belief system to which he has entrusted his life. It is a belief system based on fear. It is what colors and defines the world in which he lives. By a process of projection, the farmer sets up his world in a way that confirms his expectations. He fears loss, and true to his expectations, he suffers loss—not by losing his money but by losing his life. This is the way the mind works. Whatever is accepted as true becomes a platform for a self-fulfilling prophecy. The farmer cloaked himself in an airtight set of worldly defenses that was built on the assumption that the world is worth defending, and that if he defended it sufficiently, he would be safe. He was mistaken. In saying 56, Jesus states unequivocally that the world is a "corpse." This is the crucial point. The truth about this man is that the world he trusts and values is dead; it is a corpse. It is a projection of his fearful mind, and all of his worldly wisdom, all of his careful planning, counts for nothing. He lives in fear, and he dies in fear.

In Thomas, the real storehouse is always the Kingdom of the Father. It is the realm of oneness in which man enjoys a peace that is beyond understanding (17). It is a citadel of safety in which loss is impossible (32). It is where the projection of fearful thoughts is replaced by the extension of love and gratitude. In the Greek version of saying 36, man is "far better than the lilies which neither card nor spin." This suggests that when a man finds this treasure of the Kingdom, he needs nothing else. Consequently, there is no need to worry about the future. This is the teaching of Jesus in this gospel. Had the rich man known this, he would have sought his treasure and security from within and invested his labors in that quest.

When Jesus adds, "Let him who has ears hear," he is urging the reader to look beneath the surface of this parable, to see the man, not as an eccentric fool but as anyone who values the world more than he does the Kingdom of the Father. In this gospel, the Kingdom is not a heavenly realm of the future but a present reality (3a). It is found not in the rubble of pointless struggles but in the silent awareness that man, within himself, already has everything he could possibly want.

Saying 64

(64) Jesus said, "A man was having some guests. And when he had prepared the dinner, he sent his servant to invite the guests.
He went to the first one and said to him, 'My master invites you.' He said, 'I have some business with merchants. They are coming to me this evening. I must go and place an order with them. I ask to be excused from the dinner.'
He went to another and said to him, 'My master has invited you.' He said to him, 'I have just bought a house and have been called away for the day. I will be very busy.'
He went to another and said to him, 'My master invites you.' He said to him, 'My friend is getting married, and I am to prepare the dinner. I will not be able to come. I ask to be excused from the dinner.'
He went to another and said to him, 'My master invites you.' He said to him, 'I have bought a farm, and I am going to collect the rent. I will not be able to come. I ask to be excused.'
The servant returned and said to his master, 'Those whom you invited to the dinner have asked to be excused.' The master said to his servant, 'Go outside to the streets and bring back those whom you find, so that they may dine. The buyers and the sellers will not enter the places of my father.'"

Rarely is it noticed how strangely this parable begins. The master of the house "was having some guests." They had been received. There is no mention of how they came to be there but simply that these people were present. At this point, the story turns bizarre. After the host has prepared their meal, instead of serving it to his guests, he sends his servant out to invite these same people to the dinner. There is no mention of them having left, but apparently they are no longer in the house. One explanation sometimes offered for this curious detail is a Near Eastern custom of first inviting guests on principle and then sending for them later when the meal is ready. However, the guests in this parable are not initially invited on principle but are present from the beginning. They are there, and then suddenly they are not. Something is plainly going on here, but before

I propose that meaning, let me continue to examine this parable.

All four guests decline the invitation. The first man has a meeting with merchants with whom he has business. He must place an order with them. The second has just bought a house, and his attention is required for the day. The next man is preparing a banquet for a friend's wedding. Lastly, the fourth man has just bought a farm and is leaving to collect the rent.

In the Luke version of this parable (14:16-24), the guests' excuses seem comparatively feeble. For example, a man has just purchased a field. He desires to simply go and see it. In the Matthew version (22:1-14), the host is a king, and the guests are inexplicably hostile. Some of them seize his servants and kill them. Afterward, the king sends his army to kill these guests and burn their city.

In Thomas, the guests are not hostile and ask politely to be released. Moreover—and this is significant—in Thomas the guests all have legitimate excuses. Their explanations are reasonable, neither feeble nor hostile but ordinary. When the servant reports this back to his master, he is instructed to go out on the street and "bring back" whomever he finds. The servant does not invite these people; he simply brings them into the master's house.

What does all this mean? It is, of course, an allegory. The master, servant, guests, and people on the streets are all metaphors. From the perspective of non-dualism, its meaning can be understood as the failure of most people to recognize their opportunity to feast at God's table. The host is a metaphor for God. The guests are God's children (3b) who are lost in the world. They are never truly separate from Him, although they believe they are. In fact, they have always been at home in their Father's house. In Thomas, this theme of oneness with God is fundamental. So when the parable opens, the guests, who represent God's children (humanity), are present. There is no mention of how long they have been there, but the point is made that they are not elsewhere.

This is a thinly veiled story of man's relationship with God. The guests are present in the master's domain. There is no mention of them coming or going. They are there, although they appear to be out in the world, conducting business and taking their phantom lives seriously. The master sends to them a servant, a metaphor perhaps for the Holy Spirit. His true function is to remind them that their separation from God is not real and that they still are guests in their master's house, which is the Kingdom. The feast of God's love is waiting for their return, but it is not a return in space and time but a return in awareness to their present state of reality. (See my commentary on the Holy Spirit, saying 44.) They believe that they are separate and involved in the world, but in fact, they have never left their host's domain.

At this point, Jesus introduces a significant twist in the story. One would expect the guests to turn down the invitation based on their fondness for the pleasures of the world. But this is not the case. For Jesus, pleasure is apparently not man's primary attachment to the world. Rather, it is his devotion to what seems reasonable, responsible, and even admirable. The four excuses all fall into this category. The ego-mind is clever. Its alternative to the feast of God's love is to be right, proper, and firmly anchored within the dream of the world. Its loyalty is to the dream, not to the truth. It is precisely the same values that the rich farmer in the previous parable (63) entrusted his life to, only to die and gain nothing. The truth remains that the guests, though seeming to be awake, are asleep in their world of separation. Only when they awaken will they realize that, in reality, they have never left their master's home and that God's magnificent banquet is always theirs to enjoy.

After the four guests decline to attend the feast, the master tells his servant to go out into the streets and bring back those he happens to find. Notice he does not instruct his servant to *invite* these people; they need no invitation. They represent those who live simple lives. They are like the poor in saying 54—they will nothing, know nothing and have nothing. That is to say, they are content with their oneness with God. Their minds are open and spare. More than do the guests, they know where they belong and quickly join their host.

The concluding statement about buyers and sellers is generally considered by scholars to be a secondary interpretation, amended to this parable by a later scribe. Such interpretations are uncharacteristic of this gospel. Clearly, the author of this parable would not have weakened its message by narrowing its focus to only buyers and sellers. The intended target is everyone who is lost in his or her dream of the world.

Saying 65

> **(65) He said, "There was a good man who owned a vineyard. He leased it to tenants so that they might work it and he might collect the fruit from them. He sent his servant so that the tenants might give him the fruit of the vineyard. They seized his servant, beat him, and almost killed him. The servant went back and told his master. The master said, 'Perhaps <they> did not recognize <him>.' He sent another servant. The tenants beat this one also. Then the owner sent his son and said, 'Perhaps they will show respect for my son.' (But) those tenants, because they knew he was the heir to the vineyard, seized him and killed him. Let him who has ears hear."**

Some commentators have advanced the idea that the previous two parables (63 and 64) share a common theme with this one, which is that all three are critical of wealth. While it is true that each parable presents individuals with considerable wealth, and each parable indeed devalues this wealth to some extent, this is not the principal theme they have in common.

To identify that common theme, let us briefly review the previous two parables. In saying 63, what is striking about the rich man is that, by the standards of the world, he is a reasonable and prudent investor. He is the ideal businessman. Such a man would be esteemed in any society that values the world and accepts its values. Jesus does not condemn him. However, by investing in the world, he has invested in what is intrinsically temporary and limited. It never occurs to him to invest his life in what is limitless and eternal. In the words of saying 76, he fails to "seek after His unfailing and enduring treasure where no moth approaches to devour and no worm destroys."

In 64, the guests decline an invitation to feast with the master, a metaphor for God. Again, what is striking about these guests is that their excuses are perfectly reasonable. By the standards of the world, they do the right thing. They take care of business and attend to their friends. From their perspectives, these are responsible choices and wise investments of their time. However, with their eyes fixed firmly on what is shallow and transient, they pass up the opportunity to feast with the master. Thus, in this allegory of man's relationship with God, they choose the world and decline God's "enduring treasure."

In this parable (65), there is a lacuna or tear in the text that allows the vineyard owner to be identified as either a "good man" or as a "usurer." The missing letters can be restored either way. Most translators have settled on "good man," as there is no mention of moneylending anywhere in this parable. Moreover, just as the rich man of 63 and the guests of 64 were not condemned by Jesus, so too is this man not condemned. As a vineyard owner in first-century Palestine, he is a man entirely convinced of the rightness of his position. Yet, the question remains: Why is this man called a "good man?"

In the conflict between the owner and his tenants, the rightness or wrongness of either side is not the issue. Although it is hinted that the owner has not been fair to his tenants, this point is not developed. The owner of the vineyard is called a "good man" for the rhetorical purpose of urging the reader to see the story from his point of view. But the focus of Jesus is a not on what is just or unjust but on the extreme reaction the owner displays in response to the savagery of his tenants. Thus, the morality question should be dismissed from consideration.

Likewise, we should dismiss the idea that the owner metaphorically represents God and that his son represents Jesus. Clearly, we can see how tempting this interpretation would have been to orthodox members of the early Jesus movement. However, it is most unlikely that the author of this parable would have portrayed God as a fool and the death of Jesus as a senseless sacrifice. Rather, the parable focuses on a characteristic of the owner that was highlighted in the previous two parables. As the rich man does in 63 and as the guests do in 64, this man embraces the primacy of the world without hesitation. Unless this is seen, the allegorical meaning of this parable will not be understood.

Jesus says that the man is a "good man," but he is also extraordinarily foolish and naïve. Again we have a man whose attention is focused solely on his worldly investment. This is his pivotal mistake. This investment so consumes him that he is willing to chance the safety of his servants and his son for the fruit he claims to own. His gamble results in tragedy. Not only does he lose his investment but his servants are beaten, and his son is murdered. He fails to understand that he has placed all his trust in the world, a realm which is hopelessly undependable. He blindly and desperately tries to fix something for which there is no fix. His only sane recourse, at this point, is to stop his relentless slide into disaster, to open his eyes, and consider whether or not his allegiance to the world has been worth the losses he has suffered.

In Thomas, all choices consistently come down to a commitment to either wholeness and spiritual freedom or separation and spiritual poverty. A truly wise man will invest his life in the first and withdraw his investment from the second. In this parable, the vineyard owner's faith in the rightness of his position is so strong that he fails to notice that he is acting insanely. Thus, the point is made that choosing to identify with the world is fundamentally insane. The world is not man's home. It is a dream of separation from which one needs to awaken. Once again, the final line, "Let him who has ears hear," cautions the reader not to read this parable superficially. It is not a tale about a man who becomes a victim of the world. He is responsible for his own choices. This man is really anyone who passes up the chance to live from the abundance of spirit rather than from the emptiness of the world.

Saying 66

> **(66) Jesus said, "Show me the stone that the builders have rejected. That one is the cornerstone."**

This saying is based on Psalms (118:22):

> "The stone which the builders rejected has become the cornerstone."

A version of this saying from Psalms also appears in Matthew (21:42), Mark (12:10), and Luke (20:17), where the suggestion is made that the cornerstone represents Jesus. The words and phrasing are the same in all four biblical sources. In Psalms, the cornerstone is thought by most scholars to be an allusion to David, who, before becoming king, is rejected by Saul, his jealous predecessor. However, with the help of Jehovah, he overcomes his enemies and succeeds to the throne. Consequently, in the same way that a cornerstone unites the walls of a house and supports its structure, David becomes the cornerstone of the kingdom of Israel.

In Thomas, the phrasing is slightly different. Jesus says, "Show me the stone," as if the stone is not present or palpable, but something hidden or cast away. If the stone in Thomas represents Jesus, one would not expect him to be hidden. In fact, it is Jesus who does the asking, and he would hardly request to see himself. Rather, it is more likely that the cornerstone represents the truth. It is the truth that is "hidden" in sayings 5, 6, and 109, and it is the hidden truth that is identified throughout Thomas as the focus of his interest. By adapting this quote from Psalms, Jesus suggests that truth is greater than the prominence of any individual. Moreover, replacing David with the truth in this saying is consistent with the image we have of Jesus the iconoclast.

If we accept that the "cornerstone" is a metaphor for truth and that the "builders" reject this truth in the construction of their house or building, then it follows that their house is built on lies or illusion. Their preferred cornerstone represents the opposite of truth. In fact, what we have here are two houses—one that Jesus wishes to build on the cornerstone of truth and the other, built by the "builders," on the cornerstone of lies. Allowing for this interpretation of saying 66 then, we begin to understand its relationship to 71:

> Jesus said, "I will destroy this house, and no one will be able to build it [up again]."

The implication here is that the house in saying 71, which Jesus wants to destroy, is the same house built on lies in 66, which the "builders" have constructed. That leaves two questions to be answered: What do the two houses represent, and who are the "builders?"

Although the word "house" is not mentioned in this saying (66), a large house or building is implied. In my commentaries on 48 and 71, I point out that in Thomas, the word has several connotations. In one saying (64), the "house" is simply a physical structure that a man has purchased. It may have no more significance than that. However, in the above-quoted saying (71), the word has a negative connotation and apparently refers to something that is not physical. My position is that in seven out of the eight sayings where "house" appears (16, 21, 35, 48, 71, 97, and 98), its author employs it not as a physical house but as a metaphor. It represents a thought structure that either supports and gives shelter to the truth of the Kingdom or stands against it, giving shelter to fear and guilt. It represents two different thought systems, two modes of evaluating perception. In Thomas, the first house is built not of beliefs but of insight and direct experience. The second is built entirely from the belief that separation is real, and it is this second "house" that Jesus wants to destroy. It is this house that was constructed without a legitimate foundation. It is missing the cornerstone of truth, and without this cornerstone, the house cannot long stand. This is what Jesus teaches in this gospel.

Who are the "builders" of the second house? They are the collective egos of all the separate ones, working together to construct an edifice of beliefs based on fear and guilt. The sole function of the ego is to deny man's home in God. To this end, it will twist logic so profoundly that sanity and insanity appear almost indistinguishable. The builders of this world reject the cornerstone of truth, the truth that God and His creations are one and indivisible. However, when that cornerstone is found and secured in place, the structure built around it will stand tall and strong and be a refuge to all who seek its blessings of certainty and peace. The good news of this gospel is that this cornerstone has been found, and the structure built upon it has been, and always will be, open to all who wish to enter.

Saying 67

> **(67) Jesus said, "He who knows the all but lacks (awareness) of himself, lacks everything."**

> **(67)** ***Jesus said, "He who knows the all but lacks (awareness) of himself, lacks the place (the Kingdom), all of it." (My restored version, based partially on Thomas Paterson Brown's interlinear version)***

In my restored version of this saying, I have retained the literal translation of the final phrase. That phrase is, "lacks the place, all of it." In most translations, the Coptic word for "place" is considered idiomatic, so it does not appear in the final drafts. However, in other Thomas sayings, the word is a code word for the Kingdom; therefore, its appearance here should not be overlooked. In Jean Doresse's book, *The Secret Books of the Egyptian Gnostics*, he writes about the significance of this word in an earlier saying (24): "In Hebrew, God is often referred to by the paraphrase *Maqom*, which means 'the Place.'" Regarding this saying (67), he says, "Here again, and perhaps also in the following saying (68), the Place is a paraphrase for God, like the Hebrew Maqom." Indeed, in Thomas, "place" nearly always refers to a worthy state or junction in which man and God are experienced as one. In saying 24, the disciples say to Jesus, "Show us the *place* where you are." Likewise in 76, the followers are urged in the literal translation to "seek after...the *place* where no moth approaches to devour and no worm destroys." The Coptic phrase for "bridal chamber" in 104 is literally translated as "the *place* of marriage," suggesting a place of ultimate union. In these and other sayings, the word "place" appears to refer to the Kingdom, the realm in this gospel in which man and God are experienced as one.

In Thomas, the world is a "corpse," and the only thing worth knowing about this corpse is that it is dead. To "know the all" is not to know this dead world and all of its details but to know the light that is not of this world. To "know the all" in Thomas is to be enlightened. It is not to know the height of every mountain or the number of fish in the sea, but it *is* to know what is real in the light of truth. (See my commentary on 77.) In saying 61, to be "filled with light" is to be enlightened. Yet paradoxically, this saying (67) states that even he who knows everything, if he lacks awareness of himself, he lacks everything. This paradox challenges the reader to look beyond enlightenment as the final achievement of Jesus's teachings and stresses the immense importance of Self-awareness.

The key phrase in this saying is, "lacks (awareness) of himself." Jesus says that if one lacks this awareness of himself, he lacks the "place" or the Kingdom entirely. This is not about the need to understand intellectual concepts. What this saying is suggesting is that the seeker must not only know the "all," but he must also know that he *is* the all. There is truly nothing that exists outside of his Self. He is spirit, and all that is spirit is one with him. The entirety of the spirit realm is his identity as a child of God (3b). Any follower of Jesus must own that identity, claim that identity, and experience the indescribable bliss that this awareness reveals to him. If he does not know this Self, he will lack the Kingdom, "all of it."

There are parallels between this saying and two others:

> (77a) Jesus said, "I am the light that shines on everything. I am everything. From me did everything come forth, and unto me did everything extend."

> (82) Jesus said, "He who is near me is near the fire, and he who is far from me is far from the Kingdom."

In 77a, Jesus describes his identity as he experiences it. To him, he is "the light that shines on everything." He *is* "everything," by which he means he is everything that is real. He is both that which acts and that which is acted upon, both subject and object in the world-releasing realm of non-duality. Yet, this inconceivably sublime encounter with truth was not unique to Jesus. Mystics throughout history have reported similar experiences of alignment with the all. Moreover, there is no evidence in Thomas that Jesus considers his identity as the Son of God solely his own. The central theme of his teaching is the understanding that man—any man or woman—is one with his creator. Saying 82 essentially asserts that as long as anyone lacks this same identity, he is far from the Kingdom. It is not a matter of merely listening to the words of Jesus and intellectually agreeing with him. Awareness of the Kingdom is a consequence of joining with his identity in all its fullness.

Saying 68

> **(68) Jesus said, "Blessed are you when they should hate and persecute you. They will find no place where you have been persecuted."**

> **(68)** *Jesus says, "Blessed are you when you are hated and persecuted (diwke); but they will not find a position in that place to which they shall pursue (diwke) you!" (Jean Doresse translation)*

(68) ***Jesus said, "Blessed are you when they should hate and persecute you. (For) they will not find the place (Kingdom) where they would pursue you." (My restored version)***

Translators of this saying have found its language obscure and possibly corrupt. As a consequence, interpretations of its meaning are many. A careful study of its design, however, reveals hidden clues. Jean Doresse, in *The Sacred Books of the Egyptian Gnostics*, made the observation that the "place...is no doubt the same place as mentioned in the preceding paragraph (saying 67), that is to say, the Kingdom..." As we have seen in previous sayings, Jesus uses "place" as a code word for the Kingdom. Here again in this saying, the word points to a realm of being that is totally unlike the realm of the world.

Doresse also translated the Greek loanword *diwke* as both "persecuted" and "pursue." Its primary meaning is "pursue," but also "persecute" by implication. Therefore, it appears to have been used here as a play on words, suggesting that the hatred and desire to "persecute" was thwarted by the inability to "pursue" the persecuted individual to within (the Kingdom). The persecuted one is blessed, because he has found a "place" of refuge within himself, where nothing can touch him, nor can anyone or anything "pursue" him there. That same "place" is mentioned in saying 60 in a similar context: "You too, look for a place for yourselves within rest, lest you become a corpse and be eaten." This "place" or Kingdom is a refuge, not in some future time but in the present, where harm, hatred, and persecution cannot follow.

According to this gospel, man's natural state is safety, and nothing can change that. (See my commentaries on 36 and 37.) However, one can believe that he is unsafe and suffer from that illusion. In rest, man abandons his ego and surrenders completely to God. In rest, he experiences his spirit-Self which is pure consciousness. He thus becomes aware that he is not his body and that this "corpse" of a world is not his home. In this awareness, illusions have no power to pursue or bring pain to this sacred "place."

As mentioned before, however, all threats in Thomas are internal threats generated by the ego. In saying 22, the Kingdom cannot be entered until one makes the "inside like the outside and the outside like the inside." In other words, one cannot see the truth until he understands that such dualities are meaningless. What is experienced as outside is merely the projection of what is inside. Persecution by outside forces is only possible, then, when one believes in separation. When a man abandons that belief, he realizes that he is not a victim of the world. When he lets go of that belief, he enters into the awareness of the Kingdom, where the manifestations of such beliefs cannot "pursue" or follow him.

In both Matthew (5:11-12) and Luke (6:22-23), a similar saying is represented as a beatitude in which persecution is an external phenomenon. For his loyalty to God, he who is persecuted for his beliefs is rewarded in heaven. In Thomas, this is not the case. Blessings are never deferred, but always present for those who are willing to look past nonexistent limitations and fully embrace the present moment.

Saying 69

> **(69a) Jesus said, "Blessed are they who have been persecuted (pursued) within. It is they who have come to know the Father in truth.**
> **(69b) Blessed are the hungry, for the belly of him who desires will be filled."**

Here we have two beatitudes linked together in one saying. It is quite possible that the two were always linked, as each supports the other around a common theme. Specifically, both refer to an inner hunger or need to go within to satisfy that hunger. As in the previous saying (68), the Greek loanword translated here as "persecuted" has as its primary meaning "pursued," and only by implication does it mean "persecuted." In other words, it is a play on words, something that occurs quite often in Thomas. However, unlike the previous saying, this is not a presumed pursuit from without but a clear pursuit from within. Something within is causing the mind discomfort. This is the discomfort of spiritual hunger. This suggestion not only explains the first beatitude found here but defines the kind of "hunger" alluded to in the second beatitude.

It is spiritual hunger that is causing the mind to feel discomfort. If an individual seeks to escape from this hunger by filling his mind with worldly distractions, he will experience it as a kind of "persecution," a nagging unsettledness that persists and incessantly pleads for attention. As long as this restless emptiness continues, the seeker will feel under attack from an uncooperative world, each distraction failing to gratify the hunger. However, the play on words of persecute/pursue suggests another possibility.

The seeker can experience this continual failure to find satisfaction as an unavoidable feature of a hostile world, or he can feel "pursued" by the very thing he needs the most, union with the Father. Using the generic term *Son* to include both male and female, it is the Father who pursues His Son. This is the prime hunger—the Father for his Son and the Son for his Father. Until this core hunger is satisfied, nothing will change. And each time the seeker chooses to look for fulfillment where there is none, a faint voice, like an ancient memory, will whisper in his inner ear, "Go within, my Son, go within." By going within, the Prodigal Son comes home, and what seems like a curse is revealed as a blessing. The insatiable hunger for completion propels the seeker to find satisfaction, not in the world but in the quiet center of his being.

In 69b, spiritual hunger, if fully acknowledged, leads inexorably to spiritual fulfillment. Unlike physical hunger, spiritual hunger can be ignored for long periods of time, denied entirely, or called something else. It can be called restlessness and be appeased by anything that will turn the mind's attention to something else. Yet, that will work only in the short term. The pain of separation, which is what spiritual hunger is, cannot be ignored forever. So the first step in healing the pain of this hunger is to acknowledge it, to accept that something is missing beyond the physical needs of the body. Such an acknowledgment, of course, can be difficult for anyone who identifies with the body. It will seem to him that by merely accepting this premise of spiritual hunger, he will place in jeopardy all the pleasures and satisfactions his body brings to him daily. He might also fear that, by this admission, he will compromise his ability to make changes to his environment and attend to the physical security of himself and others.

It is, of course, the ego that fears the spiritual. It sees the spiritual Kingdom of the Father as a threat to its existence, and so it is. If spiritual hunger were to be seen for what it is, the ego would instantly come under scrutiny. An honest appraisal of the ego would then reveal that its promises are hollow and undependable. As the clarity and peace of the Kingdom begin to dawn on the mind, the desire to return to this spiritual realm becomes overwhelming. However, to finally "know the Father," one must clearly know that he is God's one Son, along with all of God's creation. He must know this despite the fact that such oneness is completely beyond all intellectual (egoic) understanding. He must find this true Self beneath the illusion of his little-self, which is separate, incomplete, and hungry.

One's empty "belly" will not remain empty when all thoughts of separation and exile are laid aside. To an open and forgiving mind, nothing can stop the flow of God's love from satisfying this craving. When the false self of the ego is unmasked, the true-Self is revealed. This is how the Son and the Father find each other.

Saying 70

> **(70) Jesus said, "If you bring forth what is within yourselves, what you have will save you. If you do not have that within yourselves, what you do not have within you will kill you."**

> **(70) *Jesus said, "If you share what you have in you, what you have in you will save you. If you do not share what you have in you, what you do not have in you will kill you." (My restored version)***

This is a difficult saying, made more difficult by the presence of textual corruption in the first clause of the second sentence. In my restored version, I have rendered this line as, "If you do not share what you have in you…" This was suggested by a translation advocated by Elaine Pagels in her book *The Gnostic Gospels*. The Pagels version is not strictly supported by the Coptic text, but it does present a logical response to what otherwise appears to make little sense. Here is the Pagels version:

> Jesus said, "If you bring forth what is within you, what you bring forth will save you. If you do not bring forth what is within you, what you do not bring forth will destroy you."

As Pagels recognizes, a prominent theme of this saying is the importance of bringing forth what is found within. The literal translation of the Coptic word *jpe* is "beget" or "bring forth." Jean Doresse translated this as "share" in the sense of bringing forth to share. From that understanding, we can proceed to examine how this concept relates to "having" and "not having." There are two ideas here that are presented. The first is that man has within him something that is essential to his existence. The line that asserts this is: "What you have will save you." In other words, there is something independent of external circumstances that assures man's safety. The second idea is that this something must be shared to be operative; it cannot be stagnant. It must be given forward to secure the safety of the giver.

This something must be love, since love is the only thing that increases when shared. When given away, it blesses both the one who gives and the one who receives. In fact, love must be shared to remain love. It saves because it reminds the individual that he is not abandoned but joined with all of life. If love is not shared, this refusal to share is experienced as a denial of love itself and, therefore, a denial of man's connection with life. The inevitable result is fear. In this saying, this refusal to share love is said to kill, because it denies that which is an essential component of life.

Although Pagels recognizes that the phrase "bring forth" is an essential element of this saying, her rendition overstates its function. The word *jpe* appears only once, in the first line. Her version gives the impression that it appears four times. While it is true that its appearance in the second line was likely omitted by an ancient scribe, overemphasizing its role obscures the subtle meaning of the words for "have" and "do not have."

The problem with the standard or most common translation is that it presents a contradiction. The first sentence states that the saving quality (love) is "within yourselves," while the second sentence says that it is possible for you to "not have *that* within yourselves." The word "that," of course, refers back to "what is within." Thus, it asserts that one can have something and not have it at the same time. Pagels corrects this contradiction by replacing "If you do not have that within yourselves" with "If you do not bring forth what is within you." This restores logic to the saying, but by ignoring the "have" and "do not have" statements, a pattern is obscured and the saying's meaning is oversimplified. This may be visualized as an ABC/abc pattern, which demonstrates how it works:

A. "If you share what you have in you, (if you share love)
B. what you have in you (love)
C. will save you.
a. If you do not share what you have in you, (if you do not share love)
b. what you do not have in you (fear)
c. will kill you."

As shown, lines A/a are about sharing or not sharing, lines B/b about having or not having, and lines C/c about the consequences of sharing or not sharing. There is a symmetry and poetry about this saying that is only hinted at in the standard translation. Indeed, such fondness for symmetry can be seen throughout both Thomas and the New Testament gospels. One example is saying 83, a saying that also suffers from textual corruption. But beneath its obscure references, the same ABC/abc pattern can be observed.

The standard translation gives the impression that "what you have in yourselves" in the first sentence is the same quality that "you do not have in yourselves" in the second sentence. As mentioned before, that would constitute a contradiction. Therefore, "what you do not have" must refer to a different quality. If love is the quality referred to in the first sentence, then the absence of love (fear) would seem to be the quality referred to in the second sentence (what you do not have). This absence of love from the mind does not necessarily result in hate, but it always results in fear. Hate may arise from fear, but fear always comes first. As mentioned before, fear is the natural consequence of the mind's refusal to share love. Additionally, when love is denied to any part of the Kingdom, it is denied to the whole of it. Consequently, by refusing to share love with even one individual, the ultimate love between he who refuses and his Source is denied and fear is the result.

By implication, "what you do not have in you" is fear. That prompts the question: Why does it say this, that fear is something that you do not have in you? The non-dualistic answer is that, regardless of what the ego maintains, there is no separation between man and God. Therefore, fear is impossible, being an effect without a cause. Since God cannot be fearful, being love itself, anyone in union with God cannot be fearful either. Only in his dream of separation does man experience fear. It is an illusion, just as the world is an illusion. In this saying, fear is "what you do not have in you." Yet, while you remain asleep to the truth, you nevertheless feel its pain and suffer its consequences.

In this saying, sharing love strengthens the conviction that love is all there is. Man is love, just as God is love. It is not something separate from their common natures. This is what man must understand to wake up. If he does not share love with others who he mistakenly thinks are separate from himself, his entrenchment in the dream becomes deeper. His sense of abandonment becomes more acute, resulting in fear. But while he sleeps, this experience remains only in his dream world. The truth is that there is no fear in him. He remains as God created him, and God did not create a fearful creation. When Jesus further says, "what you do not have (fear) within you will kill you," he means that in man's dream of separation, his preoccupation with fear will appear to kill him. A nonexistent quality (fear) is experienced within a nonexistent world (the dream), resulting in a nonexistent state (death). In truth, man is at home in God, and his separation from Him never occurred. When he wakes up to this realization by going within and sharing his love, he will know true safety.

Saying 71

> **(71) Jesus said, "I will destroy this house, and no one will be able to build it [up again]."**

Many commentators have written that it is almost impossible to discern what this saying means. On its surface, it appears to be about the destruction of a house that, for some reason, can never be rebuilt. Why would Jesus destroy a house? Perhaps this is a reference to the Temple in Jerusalem? Did Jesus want to destroy the Temple, a structure sometimes referred to as the "house of God?" There is no evidence of that in Thomas or in the Bible. Furthermore, a temple can be rebuilt.

Is this "house" his body? That would seem more likely. In Matthew (26:61) and Mark (14:58), witnesses testify to hearing Jesus say that the Temple would be destroyed and rebuilt in three days. In John (2:19-21), it is explained that Jesus indeed said this, but that he was speaking not of the

Temple but of his body. However, in Thomas, a house is never compared to either a temple or a body. It could refer to the idea of a body as a representation of separation. But why would Jesus limit his destruction to only one manifestation of separation? The real question is this: Is it not more likely that the "house" that Jesus wants to destroy represents the structure and the sum total of everything to which he is opposed? This, I think, is what we should be looking for. What was Jesus opposed to?

From what we have seen so far, Jesus seems to have opposed, not physical structures, but a structure of beliefs, a "house" of beliefs. In particular, it was those beliefs that maintain that man is a limited being, endlessly fragmented and existing in a world that is separate from God and the wholeness of creation. We further have seen that, in this gospel, Jesus teaches that what is separate from God is like a "grapevine planted outside the Father (40). It is like a corpse (56) or world without life. And so, if God did not create this corpse, this grapevine, this world, what is it? Since it was not created by God but fashioned in the mind of man, it must be an illusion. What Jesus is opposed to in this saying is the promulgation of illusions.

A house is a structure. It is constructed as a shelter, but in ancient times, more than today, it had a defensive function. It was the final refuge from one's enemies. Notice how well this metaphor of "house" serves to represent a thought structure, made to shelter and protect either the belief in separation or the awareness of wholeness.

In Thomas, the word "house," appears in eight sayings (16, 21, 35, 48, 64, 71, 97, and 98). In seven of these sayings, 64 being the possible exception, the metaphor serves to offer refuge and safety to whichever thought system is examined. In 48, the "house" is that of oneness, which is the Kingdom or domain of the Father. In this saying (71), the house is one that Jesus wants to destroy, so that no one may build it up again. It stands for the structure of the ego, constructed from the bricks and mortar of guilt and fear. It is defended by a host of defense mechanisms including projection, denial, and identification with the body. However, the house of oneness is a place of true refuge, safety, and power. The contrast between these two thought structures is found throughout this gospel in a variety of expressions. Saying 10 states essentially the same thing as this saying but without the use of this "house" metaphor:

> Jesus said, "I have cast fire upon the world, and behold, I am guarding it until it blazes."

In 108, Jesus urges his followers to "drink from his mouth." It is an invitation to immerse themselves in his words of wisdom. It is also an appeal to share his safety in the refuge of the Kingdom. When they seek refuge in the ego's belief structure, they, in essence, drink from the ego's mouth. They buy into its lies. So, it is the ego's house that Jesus wants to destroy. It is this belief structure he wants to dismember, brick by brick and beam by beam, until the light of truth can easily penetrate its dark defenses.

Saying 72

> **(72) [A man said] to him, "Tell my brothers to divide the possessions of my father with me."**
> **He said to him, "O man, who has made me a divider?"**
> **He turned to his disciples. He said to them, "I am not a divider, am I?"**

This is a story about a man who asks Jesus to talk to his brothers. It is also a story with wider implications. First, let us think about that desperate man. His father has died, leaving three or more sons. No arrangements were made for the disposition of his property. As a result, one son feels he has been denied the proper share of his father's estate. He asks Jesus to intercede on his behalf. He says, "Tell my brothers to divide the possessions of my father with me." It is really more a demand than a request. He is convinced that he is a victim of other men's greed. In his state of anger and righteous indignation, he insists that Jesus intervene and come between him and his brothers.

In response, Jesus says to him, "O man, who has made me a divider?" It is a rhetorical question since anyone familiar with his philosophy would know that he stands not for division but for wholeness. It is the central tenet of all that he teaches. For this reason, it is a perfect opening for Jesus to reaffirm this fundamental idea.

To further press home the point, Jesus asks his disciples, "I am not a divider, am I?" The literal translation of this is, "Truly, do I exist as a divider?"

The Coptic word for "exist" can be found in four other sayings. It generally means to exist in or dwell in, as the light exists or dwells within a man of light (24). In another saying (61), there is the statement, "I am he who exists from He who is equal." In both 61 and in this saying (72), Jesus refers to his essential nature. He is someone who exists not in division as a divider but in union with the divine. He is one with God and also one with everything that exists. In other words, division is the very antithesis of who he is and what he stands for.

Saying 73

> **(73) Jesus said, "The harvest is plentiful, but the laborers are few. Beseech the Lord, therefore, to send forth laborers to the harvest."**

The first line of this saying speaks of a plentiful but unspecified "harvest." In nearly identical versions in Matthew (9:37-38) and Luke (10:2), it is strongly suggested that this "harvest" is the bounty of evangelism. In both gospels, the disciples are subsequently chosen, and instructions are given for the success of their mission. They are told to heal the sick, perform miracles, and preach the message that "the Kingdom of heaven (or God) is near." In Thomas, however, the closest reference to anything like evangelism comes in saying 14, when Jesus tells his disciples:

> "When you go into any land and walk about in the districts, if they receive you, eat what they set before you, and heal the sick among them."

This passage comes at the end of a saying in which Jesus urges his disciples to reject pious practices such as fasting, praying, almsgiving, and the dietary laws. The focus is not on evangelizing but on those practices that Jesus considers excessive or potentially perilous. Additionally, to merely "walk about in the districts" is not the same as evangelizing." Neither is "healing" necessarily linked to spreading the gospel. Evangelizing involves speaking, and it is precisely this that Jesus cautions against in the last line of 14. He says, "For what goes into your mouth will not defile you, but that which comes out of your mouth—it is that which will defile you."

This saying (73) is not about evangelizing but about seeking fulfillment for oneself. Fulfillment is the "harvest" of this saying. It is the goal of this gospel and the heart of its teaching. It is the wealth one gains from knowing one's true identity (3b). The message here is that this "harvest" can now be gathered, but there are few who labor to claim it for themselves.

This is the first of three sayings (73, 74, and 75) that compares the "many" or "plentiful" to something less, or in the case of 75, something seemingly less but actually more. Unlike 73, the other two sayings make their point and end on that note. This saying has an additional statement attached to it. That additional comment appears foreign to Thomas and more reminiscent of the culture that produced the New Testament. That line is: "Beseech the Lord, therefore, to send forth laborers to the harvest." It is not original to this saying, and indeed, the first sentence would be stronger without it.

The New Testament version of this saying is nearly identical to this Thomas version. It is found both in Matthew (9:37-38) and Luke (10:2):

> "The harvest is plentiful, but the workers are few. Therefore ask the Lord of the harvest to send out workers into his harvest field."

Scholars disagree about when Thomas was written. Many claim that it is a secondary work, based loosely on the New Testament gospels. If that were true, it would explain why this saying (73) in Thomas is so similar to the Matthew and Luke versions. While I disagree with this general assessment of the dependence of Thomas on the synoptic gospels, I nevertheless believe that someone in antiquity appropriated the second sentence of these New Testament versions to explain the first sentence and original saying here in Thomas. For this scribe, the emphasis in Thomas on personal fulfillment was not sufficient enough to ignore this additional comment on evangelizing that he found in Matthew and Luke.

This borrowed sentence has additional problems. In the New Testament, the word "Lord" appears over 400 times. It is used primarily as an honorific, a word or title expressing respect for God or Jesus. Here in this saying, the term is used specifically as an honorific for God. Elsewhere in Thomas, the word is found in 64 and 65, but in neither saying is it used directly to honor

God or Jesus. It also appears in the next saying (74), where it seems to have no other function than to refer to its use in this saying (73). Consequently, the word as an honorific is not characteristic of Thomas; therefore, it must be considered suspect.

A more significant problem with this second sentence is that it advocates a prayer of supplication. This form of prayer is forcefully denounced in saying 14: "If you pray, you will be condemned." Whether for more laborers or for a better world, such prayer pleads that an external problem be fixed externally on the level of the world. In Thomas, however, there are no external problems. All problems arise from one cause, the failure of man to realize his oneness with God and God's creation. In saying 3, ignoring this connection results in poverty. The idea that God would "send forth" laborers for whatever purpose is inconsistent with a major theme in Thomas. The problem is not out there; it is always within. That is the focus of this gospel. It is not concerned with evangelizing in any form.

The phrase "The harvest is plentiful" may be compared to this line in saying 113: "The Kingdom of the Father is spread out upon the earth, and men do not see it." The harvest is everywhere. It cannot be limited to space and time. It is always ripe and ready to be picked. Yet, the laborers are few. Thus, Jesus identifies the problem this way: God's love is free, and its blessings are everywhere. But man is fearful of that love. What more evidence could there be, as Jesus says in saying 28, that man is "blind in his heart?"

Saying 74

> **(74) He said, "O Lord, there are many around the drinking trough, yet there is nothing in the cistern."**

The image that comes to mind here is of people assembled around a drinking trough like a herd of thirsty animals. They wait for water, stubbornly believing that it will come. Meanwhile, the cistern, the reservoir for the water, is empty. This is a stunning image and a powerful metaphor for misplaced trust. Consider this similar passage from Jeremiah (2:13):

"My people have committed two sins:
they have forsaken me,
the spring of living water,
and have dug their own cisterns,
broken cisterns that cannot hold water."

In the Thomas saying, the many who gather around the drinking trough have, in a sense, dug their own cistern. In forsaking their Source, they have made a world of separation and idols. It is a broken and empty world. There is nothing in this cistern of a world that truly satisfies. As long as they depend on its empty promises, they seek in vain for what is real and alive. When they awaken to the truth, they will then know that the world of the ego can never quench their thirst. They will know that within their minds, there is a spring of living water, which, when discovered, will end their waiting forever.[1]

Some commentators maintain that the words "O Lord" imply that the speaker is a disciple addressing Jesus. If that is the case, the sayings 73, 74, and 75 might be considered a dialogue between Jesus and one of his followers. However, there are several problems with that reasoning. First, this saying (74) begins, as some other sayings in Thomas do, with the words, "He said." Where this happens, this always refers to Jesus. Moreover, referring to a disciple as "he," without identifying that disciple, is implausible. In Thomas, "disciples" ask questions and make comments, but single, anonymous disciples do not. And since no disciple is named, we cannot assume that this is a dialogue.

Second, the expression "O Lord" has no apparent function in this saying. It adds nothing to its meaning. As an exclamation, it is quite uncharacteristic of Thomas. It seems more than coincidental that the word "Lord" turns up here immediately following its use in 73. In that saying, the word appears as part of a highly suspect sentence in which the "Lord" is beseeched to send out laborers to the harvest. My suspicion is that a later copyist, perhaps one who harbored an orthodox understanding of Jesus, sought to identify him with this "Lord," in the sense of elevating Jesus to the status of God, as the second person of the Trinity. So, rather awkwardly, he added "Lord" to the beginning of this saying. Without a "Jesus said," in this introductory phrase, the scribe may have felt justified in identifying the speaker as the "Lord" of the previous saying.

The Coptic word for "nothing" may also be translated as "no one." Some commentators prefer the second half of this saying to read: "but there is no one in the cistern (or well)." The meaning of the saying then becomes: Many are content to drink from the trough, but the true seeker completely immerses himself in the living water of the cistern. While this is possible, the theme of misplaced trust, which is common to both this saying and the Jeremiah quote, is ignored. In this scenario, spiritual freedom is a matter of degree; more of it is better than less. That is never the position of this gospel. In Thomas, spirituality is an all-or-nothing proposition. The "many" have no access to the living water precisely because they see themselves as "many." The living water of God's love is only accessible to those who see themselves as one with Him. Moreover, as a metaphor, throwing oneself into either a cistern or a well is problematic, as it suggests the possibility of drowning. So at best, it is a mixed metaphor, not about drinking or consuming truth but possibly about drowning in it.

The empty cistern metaphor works well to affirm the futility of seeking the Kingdom where it is not, a prominent theme in Thomas. The "many" look for salvation in the things of this world. But this cistern/world is broken, and, as Jeremiah (2:13) states, a broken cistern cannot hold (living) water, a metaphor for the loving grace of God.

---

1 On a deeper level, there seems to be the possibility of a hidden message here based on the literal meaning of the Coptic words for "drinking trough" and "cistern." These given translations fit the context but ignore the literal translations which are respectively revealed as "separation" and "sickness." Therefore, a better understanding of this saying might be conveyed as: "Oh Lord, there are many around the drinking trough of separation, yet there is nothing in the cistern of sickness." The "sickness" is the illness of the mind referred to in this book as the ego. Since the ego is simply a complex of false beliefs fueled by the mind, it is "nothing." In the realm of the world, however, there are "many" who look to the principal manifestation of the ego, the belief in "separation," as real and desirable. In truth, it is neither. The ego's promises are empty. Consequently, the "many" wait in vain to quench their thirst. The living water of oneness, the awareness of this loving grace of God, is their only hope for fulfillment, not "separation."

Saying 75

(75) Jesus said, "Many are standing at the door, but it is the solitary ones who will enter the bridal chamber."

The way this saying is usually interpreted is this: Many seek the blessings of spiritual life, but only those who isolate themselves will eventually succeed. Success depends on withdrawing from society and taking the single path of isolation and self-denial. This indeed is the route that many take to achieve their goal of spiritual freedom. However, there is another way this saying may be interpreted.

The key word is *monachos*, a Greek loanword that means the "single ones" or "solitaries." From this, the English word *monasticism* was later derived. This, of course, suggests that the "single ones" are those who take up the austere lives of monks or anchorites. While there is nothing here which conclusively rules out that meaning, it runs counter to the general philosophy of this gospel. In fact, there is no idea more fundamental to Thomas than the idea that man finds his identity not in separation but in wholeness. Yet, this saying seems to say the opposite, that those who seek isolation will enter the bridal chamber.

However, *monachos* has also been translated as the "whole ones." We have seen its use before in 16 and 49, where this translation is crucial to the understanding of those sayings. Such "whole ones" do not find meaning in isolation but always in relationship, in completion but never in separation. Whole ones are whole precisely because they see their faces in the faces of others, their destinies in the destinies of others. They find themselves in others, not in spite of them and certainly not in isolation from them but because they *are* them. They find themselves in oneness with others.

The "many," on the other hand, are fragmented. They are many within and without—within because each of them has separate interests, separate worries, and separate goals; without because everything they experience of space and time is separate and in constant flux. Consequently, their minds are filled with a multitude of conflicts and problems. In contrast, the "whole ones" recognize that man has but one problem, the problem of separation, and one solution, the abandonment of ego identification. They are whole because they have released everyone and everything from judgment and have chosen love and forgiveness over fear and hate. In this way, they have learned that wholeness is their natural state.

Wholeness cannot be understood by the intellect. Intellectually, it can only be hinted at by establishing what it is not. It has nothing to do with the joining of bodies. Bodies are forms, and true union is only possible on the level of spirit-mind. It has nothing to do with forms of any kind. It is the union of spirit with spirit. What then is spirit? Spirit is what never dies. It is changeless and eternal. It is man's true identity. In uniting with spirit, man looks beyond the world, beyond all illusions, and in that silence, he remembers who he is.

The literal translation of the Coptic term for "bridal chamber" is "place of marriage." As I have mentioned before, the word "place" in Thomas is a code word for the Kingdom. Therefore, the "bridal chamber" is the place where man joins with God in a kind of spiritual consummation. It is not a specific place but a spiritual realm, not above or below but wherever man lays aside his separate identity and embraces his oneness with everything. It is not in isolation but in joining that man realizes his true identity in oneness. It does not ultimately matter whether he surrounds himself physically with others or whether he seeks the silence of a cave. All that is required is that he free his mind of all thoughts and concepts that divide what God created as one. In that state of emptiness, beyond judgment, the fullness and rapture of the Kingdom is experienced.

Saying 76

> **(76) Jesus said, "The Kingdom of the Father is like a merchant who had a consignment of merchandise in which he found a pearl. That merchant was shrewd. He returned the consignment and bought the pearl alone for himself. You too, seek after His unfailing and enduring treasure where no moth approaches to devour and no worm destroys."**

The merchant or consignee is an agent for someone else. This is a crucial point. The merchandise is not his own. His business is to sell it for a commission or a fee. He receives a consignment, and among its contents he finds a pearl. At this point, most translators have the merchant sell the merchandise and buy the pearl for himself. However, the words in question may also be translated as "he gave the consignment back." That is to say, he gives the consignment back to the owner, minus the pearl. The pearl he buys for himself. See how closely this translation conforms to the wording in saying 8:

> And he said, "The man is like a wise fisherman who cast his net into the sea and drew it up from the sea full of small fish. Among them, the wise fisherman found a fine large fish. He threw all the small fish back into the sea and chose the large fish without difficulty. Whoever has ears to hear, let him hear."

In both sayings, the protagonist returns the product of his livelihood without attempting to profit from its sale. There is no valid reason why the fisherman could not keep the many small fish and the one large fish as well. Nor is there any reason why the merchant could not sell his consignment for profit and also purchase the pearl. In both cases, these men relinquish their customary professional practices. In truth, they appear to relinquish even their rational minds, while keeping for themselves what the world would consider a poor choice.

It is important to understand how radically unconventional these transactions are. Both men choose an option that has nothing to do with worldly profit and what no sane merchant or fisherman would ever do. Likewise in 107, the shepherd abandons his ninety-nine sheep to look for the one sheep. In a sense, these men abandon their professions to possess a singular, life-changing treasure. Indeed, in this saying, Jesus tells us that the merchant is "shrewd." The hidden message in all of these parables is that the choice of spirit over the world is always the shrewd choice, regardless of how it appears to the egoic mind.

From the viewpoint of the ego, the way of the spirit is insane. The ego values the things of this world and treasures particularly those feelings and perceptions that enhance or give pleasure to the body. From its perspective, it is incomprehensible how anyone could deny this solid and unassailable realm. The fully realized Self, on the other hand, is free. Where the ego sees problems, the Self sees wholeness. It is fully awake, and what previously was an impossible dream of pointless struggle and exile is now forgotten. The true insanity is over, and what remains is an order of bliss and peace to which nothing in the world can compare (17). All of this is possible for the one who is willing to question everything this world teaches and accept nothing that is unworthy of his divine nature. This is the path metaphorically chosen by the merchant, the shepherd, and the fisherman in these parables.

This saying then addresses the listener: "You too, seek after His unfailing and enduring treasure where no moth approaches to devour and no worm destroys." In a magnificently poetic way, the pearl is identified as a metaphor for eternal fulfillment. In effect, Jesus is telling his audience to seek the Kingdom of the Father and not waste their time with that which dies and is consumed by the world. The pearl is not a mere bauble; it represents the end of all seeking. When found, nothing more is needed; nothing more has any value. We are told in the literal translation to "seek…the *place* where no moth approaches." The "treasure" is equated with a place. As in previous sayings, the Coptic word for "place" is a code word for the Kingdom. Only in the realm of the Kingdom, not in the realm of the ego/world, can true value and genuine freedom be found.

Saying 77

> **(77) Jesus said, "I am the light which is above them all. I am the all. From me did the all come forth, and unto me did the all extend. Split a piece of wood, and I am there. Lift up the stone, and there you will find me."**
>
> **(77) *Jesus said, "I am the light that shines on everything. I am everything. From me did everything come forth, and unto me did everything extend. Split a piece of wood, and I am there. Lift up a stone, and there you will find me." (My restored version)***

The word "light" appears in seven sayings. It obviously has significant meaning for the Jesus of this gospel. In saying 24, there is a light within a "man of light." There is no reason to believe that this refers only to Jesus. It appears to pertain to anyone who "shines" with the inner light of truth and love. The universality of light is a concept expressed throughout Thomas. One dwells in the light in 11. It is shared in 33. The disciples come from the light in 50. One is full of light in 61, and in 83, the light exists in both man and God. In none of these sayings, except in this one (77), is the light mentioned specifically in connection with Jesus. Only here is Jesus identified as a man of light. He says of himself, "I am the light." But actually, this is no more true for him than it is for the "man of light" in 24. Therefore, Jesus should not be seen as special in this regard. He is not claiming to be special. He is the light—he is everything—but in the fullness of the Kingdom, so is every man and woman created in God's image.

There is a problem in the first sentence. It is usually translated as "I am the light which is above them all." This appears to imply that Jesus sees himself as superior and thus separate from creation. This rendering makes the saying internally inconsistent, with Jesus being both one with everything and above everything. It is also inconsistent with the gospel as a whole. In saying 22, making the "above like the below" is essential for entering the Kingdom. In other words, within the Kingdom there is no above or below because within that realm, these dichotomies are meaningless. Furthermore, saying 108 suggests that he who understands what Jesus understands will be like him, neither inferior nor superior. To make sense of this sentence, I have opted for a translation suggested by Wim van den Dungen: "I am the light that falls on all." By implication, the shining of the light, not the superiority or elevation of the light, is what appears to be the intended meaning here. My version of this is, "I am the light that shines on everything." Jesus is both the light and everything on which the light shines. By extension, he is both love and the object of love. Again this is not unique to Jesus. In the awareness of non-duality, it is true of everyone.

What is "the all?" What is everything? I prefer the word "everything" here for two reasons. First, it is the literal meaning of the Coptic word. Secondly, it avoids the temptation to understand this concept in terms of Gnostic cosmology. The word "everything" has no ancient echoes or specific implications as "the all" does. "Everything" is simply all that truly exists. In this saying, Jesus asserts that he is everything. This cannot mean that he equates himself with the world, since in saying 56 he calls the world a "corpse," and in 10 he casts fire on the very idea of a physical world. Rather, this is an acknowledgment that he is one with the spiritual Kingdom of the Father, which in Thomas is everything. Outside of this realm, nothing exists.

When Jesus says that he is everything, he is affirming the truth as he sees it. There is nothing more to it than that. It is not the ravings of a hyperactive ego but a confirmation of his enormous faith and trust in God. In truth, it takes humility, not arrogance, to claim oneness with all that is. By embracing the Kingdom's reality of total oneness with God, man surrenders his separate will for the will he shares with God. He abandons the lie of his separate, egoic identity for the truth of his real identity in the limitless realm of spirit.

Jesus says that from him "everything came forth," and unto him did "everything extend." This is true for everyone who shares God's mind. In saying 50, the "sign of the Father" is a "movement with rest." Receiving and extending love is the "movement" part of that equation. Whether called love or light, it is what man is and what he extends. Outside of this love, nothing exists.

My third question is answered in the final lines of this saying. What does "everything" include? It includes all of life. Even the tiny creature that hides beneath the "rock" is everything. So too is the worm within the "wood." This is not to say that bodies or physical manifestations are real, but life is real in whatever manifestation it might be seen with the body's eyes. Those little specks of life are each the whole of life, each seemingly lost and yet found in the vision of Jesus. This saying is about the supremacy of wholeness. For that reason, it perfectly expresses the non-dualism that lies at the core of this gospel. (See also the use of the rock/wood expression in the Greek version of saying 30.)

Saying 78

> **(78) Jesus said, "Why did you come out into the field? To see a reed shaken by the wind? And to see a man clothed in soft garments [like your] kings and your great men? Upon them are soft garments, and they are unable to know the truth."**

Thomas is a highly metaphorical gospel. In this saying, metaphors are used quite artfully. We have Jesus confronting listeners who have come out into a field apparently to hear him speak. He asks rhetorical questions of them, odd questions about a "reed" and a "man clothed in soft garments." The man is not identified. Because of his soft clothes, he is compared to "kings" and "great men" who, despite their wealth and power, are "unable to discern the truth." The saying gains momentum when we realize that this man dressed in soft garments is not a real man. He is the Jesus of their expectations. He is the great teacher about whom everyone has heard so much. Such a man should wear fine garments, not the rough and threadbare clothes in which they find Jesus. They expect their speaker to be well-dressed, but instead they encounter him in the clothes of a poor man. This appears to be the surface meaning of this saying. However, as nearly always in Thomas, there are hidden depths of meaning to be found just below the surface.

Commentators have admitted that without a narrative to give this saying context, there seems to be little that can be said about it. A context is provided in Matthew (11:7-9) and in Luke (7:24-26), where a version of this saying is used to introduce John the Baptist. However, there is no evidence in this saying that it has anything to do with John.

A possible clue is found in the Coptic word for "field." This is sometimes translated as "desert" or "countryside." However, the word is translated as "field" in two other sayings, 21a and 109. In 21a, a "field" is clearly used as a metaphor for the world. In 109, it is just as clearly used as a metaphor for the mind. However, in this saying (78), the "field" is a metaphor for the world. Consider what happens when "world" is substituted for "field" in the first sentence: "Why have you come out into the (world)?" Perhaps a better way of stating this question is, "Why have you left your home in spirit and come out into the world of separation?" Jesus then asks the follow-up question: Is it "to see a reed shaken by the wind?" He seems to be saying that when one abandons the inner world for the outer, this is what you will find, "a reed shaken by the wind," a metaphor for that which is frail and subject to the vagaries of an unpredictable world. The reed is exposed to, and at the mercy of, the world. So it would seem that Jesus is asking essentially this question: Why would you wish to leave the security and peace of the Kingdom to experience the insecurity and instability of the world of separation?

We are also presented with an image of a man dressed in soft clothes, an image solely in the minds of those expecting Jesus to be so adorned. This man of their imagination is dressed like "your kings and great men." But we are told that these men are unable to discern the truth. Though richly attired, they are ignorant of what really matters. Fine, soft clothes mean nothing, and in a sense, they protect the wearers from the harsh extremes of the world no better than the "reed" is protected from the wind. Both the soft clothing and the reed represent the flimsiness and unreliability of the things of this world. Why would anyone leave the safety and certainty of the spiritual realm for the danger and meaninglessness of such a world? That seems to be the underlying question of this saying.

In Thomas, the world is not an evil realm. As Jesus insists in saying 56, it is a corpse, a place devoid of life and meaning. In this saying, it is represented by the bleak and barren image of a single reed shaken by the wind. Likewise, wealth and worldly power mean nothing here, having nothing to do with truth. The truth lies elsewhere, in another realm altogether, in what Jesus calls the Kingdom. This is a place discovered not by coming "out" but by going within.

Saying 79

> **(79) A woman from the crowd said to him, "Blessed is the womb that bore you and the breasts that nourished you."**
> **He said to her, "Blessed are those who have heard the word (logos) of the Father and have truly guarded it. For there will be days when you will say, 'Blessed is the womb that has not conceived and the breasts that have not given milk.'"**

> **(79)** ***A woman from the crowd said to him, "Blessed is the womb that bore you and the breasts that nourished you."***
> ***He said to her, "Blessed are those who have heard the rational principle (logos) of the Father and have truly guarded it. For there will be days when you will say, 'Blessed is the womb that has not conceived and the breasts that have not given milk.'" (My restored version)***

A woman from the crowd, impressed by Jesus, honors him by bestowing blessings on his mother. She says, "Blessed is the womb that bore you and the breasts that nourished you." In response, Jesus seizes on the opportunity to shift the focus from bodies to spirit and to raise the question again of man's true identity. The question is: Are we our bodies? The general assumption is that we are. Is this true? And if we are not bodies, are we *in* bodies? Non-duality maintains that neither proposition is true. We are not bodies, nor are we *in* bodies. A better way of understanding this is that we are spirit experiencing ourselves as bodies. We are spirit, but in a sense we have fallen asleep, and in sleep we have dreamed a dream in which separation is possible. Then, what are bodies? They are illusions; they are not real, but to the ego-mind, bodies are seen as proof that separation is real.

Jesus turns aside the well-meaning comment of the woman by saying that blessings should go instead to those who have "heard the word of the Father and have truly guarded it." A more accurate translation of this would be, "Blessed are those who have heard the *logos* of the Father and have truly guarded (or watched over) it."

Although the Coptic word for "word" is found elsewhere in Thomas, only here in this saying is the Greek loanword *logos* used, indicating a specific meaning other than "word." Classical philosophers preferred to define *logos* as the rational principle that governs the universe. The idea of a "rational principle" of the Father seems to fit better in the context of this saying where a principle is being explained, not a passage from scripture. The word "kept," as found in some translations as referring to the "word," is not quite right either. The literal meaning of the Coptic word *arex* is "guarded" or "watched over." In saying 10, it is generally translated as "guard."

In the prologue to the Gospel of John, the logos is identified as the person of Jesus. Here in saying 79, that claim is not made. Jesus merely states that those who have heard the divine, rational principle of the Father and have truly guarded it are blessed. Before one can understand the point of this saying, which is that man's true "womb" or Source is God and not the womb of his human mother, one must hold fast to the divine principle (logos) of oneness. Man is one with his Source, and anything that appears to contradict this principle is false.

Next, Jesus says, "For there will be days when you will say, 'Blessed is the womb that has not conceived and the breasts that have not given milk.'" The truth is that God, who neither creates bodies nor gives milk, is man's Source.

Spirit is created by spirit from the spiritual womb of God and sustained or nursed by that same spirit. This is who man is. This is his reality. This is the reality that Jesus fully realized. So when the woman praises his earthly mother, he gently corrects her. His mother is not his Source or his womb; God is. Man is spirit like his Father.

Separation is not God's will; therefore, it does not exist. All expressions of separation likewise do not exist. This includes the entire world of space and time. All such illusions are the product of the mind of man. He is wholly spirit but believes himself trapped in the fragile flesh of bodies.

This understanding of the primacy of spirit over flesh is supported by several sayings in Thomas. In 22a, those who enter the Kingdom are compared to infants being suckled. The implication is that those who enter the Kingdom do so by feeding directly from the spirit Father/Mother. In 29, the body is called "this poverty," the spirit called "this great wealth." In that saying, Jesus finds it amazing, incredulous really, that the spirit should find its home in the body. In 87, the soul, the spirit-Self, is wretched when it depends on the body. Perhaps the strongest evidence in support of this idea comes in 101, where Jesus says, "My mother [bore me], but my *true* [Mother] gave me life."

Saying 80

> **(80) Jesus said, "Whoever has known the world has found the body, but whoever has found the body, of him the world is not worthy."**

This saying and saying 56 are nearly identical. Here, the world is compared to the body; in the earlier saying, the world is compared to a corpse:

> (56) Jesus said, "Whoever has known the world has found a corpse, and whoever has found (this) corpse, of him the world is not worthy."

These two sayings work together to identify the characteristic that both the world and the body share in common. That characteristic is death. Both are essentially dead. If the world is a corpse, as claimed in saying 56, all aspects and features of the material world are also dead. Therefore, the body is dead. It is "found" or recognized when the world is "known" or recognized as a corpse.

Both sayings further state that for him who makes this discovery, "the world is not worthy." This appears to be more than just a casual expression of praise. What Jesus is saying here is that to recognize the body as something dead is to be independent and free of the world. Furthermore, to be free of both the world and the body is to recognize that man is spirit, existing neither as a body nor in a body. The world is not worthy of man because the world is a fantasy, not a reality. The world was never alive except in man's dream of separation. As long as he takes it seriously, as long as he acquiesces to its limitations and material idols, he will remain in darkness.

The Greek words used in these sayings are *ptoma* for "corpse" and *soma* for "body." It is conceivable that this saying's use of *soma* was a copyist's error, based on its similar spelling to *ptoma*. This might have led to the erroneous duplication of saying 56, based on the misidentification of *ptom*a for *soma*. However, it may equally be maintained that these similarly spelled words were chosen precisely to highlight the equivalence of the two proposals. In both sayings, to have true knowledge of the world is to recognize the corpse-like characteristic of the world in whole (56) or in part (80). It is an axiom of non-dualistic philosophy that everything in the world of phenomena, where perception is the sole means of discernment, is essentially illusory. Like the world, the body is fundamentally an effect of man's thoughts. Those thoughts are the cause of that which is perceived. What mystics have known, long before the time of Jesus, is the importance of controlling one's thoughts. Consistently loving thoughts help dissolve the blocks to the awareness of God's Kingdom. Fearful thoughts project a fearful world.

God did not create corpses, nor did He create death. To believe that He did is to believe that He created something in opposition to Himself. That makes no sense. It is to believe that in opposition to love, He created hate; in opposing life, he created death. Furthermore, a dominant theme of this gospel is that God is one with all of life and that dualisms of any kind are blocks to the awareness of the Kingdom (22). Therefore, if death were real, God would be a victim of His own creation. He would suffer just as man suffers. However, man made the body as he made the world, not as anything real, but as a part of his dream of separation. Jesus refers to the world as a corpse to point out that it is not alive. It was never created; therefore, it is not real.

As it does here, the body comes under scrutiny in several other Thomas sayings. In 29, the body is considered inferior to spirit and referred to as "this poverty." As we saw in 79, the body is not man's Source. Man was born of spirit and is nourished by spirit. When he awakens to this astonishing truth, he will cease to identify with his body and find complete freedom as a child of God in spirit.

Saying 81

> **(81) Jesus said, "Let him who has grown rich be king, and he who possesses power, let him deny it."**

It is typical of Jesus in these sayings to lead the listener/reader in one direction and then to suddenly yank him back in another. In this saying, he appears to urge his listeners to let a man who is rich in the worldly sense become king. Then he tells them to let him who has power—presumably the same man—deny that power. This makes no sense. It would seem that for a king to deny himself power, he would not wish to be a king in the first place. Again, we see an absurd situation, the same absurdity that we find in the parables of the fisherman (saying 8) and the shepherd (107). As in those parables, the answer to this conundrum is that in the Kingdom, what seems nonsensical is the truth. And the truth is that only spiritual power is real. Worldly power is an illusion.

In this saying, the man who "has grown rich" is not a man who functions in the external world. If he did, there would be no one powerful enough to let him "be king." Worldly kingdoms are not so easily established. Rather, he who "has grown rich" is the same inner man who "lets" himself seek for meaning in saying 2. In that saying, the seeker proceeds through the various stages of spiritual empowerment until he finds the truth, which then astonishes him. He "lets" himself do this. He allows himself this choice. And at the end of his search, he reigns, just as he does in this saying.

Here, this inner man has "grown rich," not in the things of this world but in the fullness of spirit. With such a treasure, what use does he have for the things of this world? What is there in the world that has any value compared to what he has now? In the words of saying 3, he has discovered who he is. He is a Son or child of the Living Father. Could there be any greater wealth than this?

This saying (81) has a twin which is nearly identical to it:

> (110) Jesus said, "Whoever has found the world and become rich, let him deny the world."

As we have previously seen, finding the world is the same as finding a corpse (56). He who makes this discovery—that the world is not his true home—also discovers that the world is not worthy of him. He is worthy of much more. The Kingdom of the Father is his home. Along with the Father, he reigns over all lesser things. In fact, whatever does not share this realm of the Father is not real. The "power" Jesus speaks of in this saying is worldly power. It is the power of illusion, and the pull of illusion is strong. However, to retain his sovereignty over illusion he must deny this false power completely.

In our present saying (81), as in 110, the primary translation of the Greek loanword *arna* is "deny." Most translators have opted for another possibility, which is "renounce." Indeed "renounce" works in this saying but only in a limited sense. The only way that spiritual wealth and real power can dawn on the mind is for the things of this world to be utterly denied. Worldly power is an illusion, and only the complete denial of that power can wipe the slate clean. It cannot be toyed with. It is either denied totally or truth, which knows no exceptions, will not be known. So, this saying may be restated in this way:

> Let him (the seeker within) who has grown spiritually rich be king (prevail over the limitations of the world), and he (also this inner seeker) who possesses the least bit of worldly power, let him deny it.

Saying 82

> **(82) Jesus said, "He who is near to me is near the fire. He who is far from me is far from the Kingdom."**

It would be wise to approach this saying with caution, as it presents Jesus in a way that can be understood both positively and negatively. In saying 10 and again in 16, Jesus casts fire upon the world. On the face of it, this fire appears destructive and fearsome. However, when we examined these sayings earlier, we learned that the target of Jesus's displeasure is not a physical place or even a condition but the idea of a separate world. It is this idea that he opposes. This is the target of his fire. However, here in this saying, fire is linked to something positive. He equates it with himself and with the Kingdom. This correlation of fire with the Kingdom is not explained, and only by looking at this gospel as a whole can we attempt to clarify the connection.

In Thomas, The Kingdom of the Father has no fearsome or negative connotations. In saying 20 it is compared to a mustard seed. In 22 it is compared to infants being suckled. In 76 it is a merchant who discovers a pearl, and in 107 it is a shepherd who finds a lost sheep. For there to be any consistency between this saying (82) and these others, the fire that is linked with the Kingdom must be a loving fire, a healing fire. It is perhaps what Pierre Teilhard de Chardin had in mind when he wrote these words:

> The day will come when, after harnessing the ether (space),
> the winds, the tides, gravitation, we shall harness for God
> the energies of love. And, on that day, for the second time in
> the history of the world, man will have discovered fire.[1]

The love Chardin is speaking of here is unconditional, a love that blesses everything and asks for nothing in return. The fire he speaks of is one that casts light and warmth on a world rich in material progress but poor in the awareness of the Kingdom.

A proverb by Aesop, written centuries before the time of Jesus, is this: "Whoever is near Zeus is near the thunderbolt." In Greek mythology, Zeus was a capricious god, and familiarity with him and with the other Greek gods and goddesses could be hazardous. This Thomas saying (82) was adapted from that proverb. But here, instead of a "thunderbolt," we have "fire." Instead of "Zeus," we have Jesus himself. Yet, despite these substitutions, this saying still conveys a powerful image. Jesus is presented as a daunting figure, the embodiment of fire. Of course, when we realize that his "fire" is a loving fire, we are not afraid. Unlike Zeus, Jesus is not capricious. His fire is not destructive, and how this fire is experienced depends on the observer's responsiveness to love.

For those who identify with their egos, love is a threat. Such a fire is what those who cling to their ego defenses fear more than anything else. To those tyrannized by their inner lion (7), love is fearful because, for them, it is the one thing that can utterly consume the ego. Again, the ego is their cherished identity. In their view, if the ego dies, so will they. But as we have said before, the true Self never dies. The ego is simply the false belief that man is separate from his creator and separate from all of life. When the ego is exposed to such love, it cannot maintain this belief in separation. The love that Jesus personifies overwhelms the objections of the ego, and, consequently, the lion of saying 7 is consumed by the true Self.

There is ample evidence in Thomas that Jesus believed himself to be one with God and all of life. In 61, he says, "I am he who exists from He who is equal." He is one who exists from equality itself. In 72, he asks the rhetorical question, "I am not a divider, am I?" In 13, he tells Thomas that he is not his master. He is not special. To be special is to be separate, and this idea of separation is what he opposes. The principal message of this gospel is the power of oneness. In 106, he says that "when you make the two one" you can metaphorically move mountains.

Everything in Thomas points to the conviction that man is not his body; like Jesus, he is spirit. This is the identity of the entire Sonship. The only difference is that Jesus knew he was spirit, and knowing this, he also knew that he shared God's divinity. So, when he asserts in this saying that "he who is near me is near the fire," he is saying that he who is undivided and knows that he is one with Jesus will also know that he is one with God. There is no separation. He who is far from Jesus—that is to say, distant in the awareness of this union—is, consequently, far from the awareness of God's Kingdom. This is not a statement of someone whose ego has portrayed him as a Zeus-like god but a statement of someone who has realized his oneness with God and seeks to share it with his fellow man. By doing this, he shares the awesome fire of God's love.

1 Pierre Teilhard de Chardin, *The Evolution of Chastity* (February 1934) as translated by Rene Hague in *Toward the Future* (New York: Harcourt Brace Jovanovich, 1975), 86.

Saying 83

> **(83) Jesus said, "The images are manifest to man, but the light in them is hidden in the image of the light of the Father. He will become manifest, but his image will remain concealed by his light."**

> **(83)** *Jesus says, "The images are visible to humanity, but the light within them is hidden in the image. {} The light of the Father will reveal itself, but his image is hidden by his light." (Patterson, Robinson, Berlin Working Group [BWG] translation)*

> **(83) *Jesus said, "Images are manifest to man, and the light within them is hidden in the (man's) image. The light of the Father will be manifested, and his (man's) image will be hidden by His (God's) light." (my restored version based on above BWG translation)***

This saying appears to be quite difficult—which it is, though not impossibly so. But before anything can be said about it, two problems need to be addressed. The first is determining where sentences begin and end. The second is deciding who is being referred to, whether man or God. Once these two uncertainties are resolved, this saying reveals a meaning that is not unlike the other Thomas sayings. Here again, the spirit prevails over the world. At first, the world's images seem solid and undeniable. They hide the "light." But when fully exposed to the light, which is the Father's light, the light of truth prevails.

There is a problem with the standard translation. The first sentence,

"The images are manifest to man, but the light in them is hidden in the image of the light of the Father," makes no sense. No matter how it is parsed, it is hopelessly convoluted and obscure. The BWG translation solves this problem, at least partially, by moving the end of the sentence back six words to follow the word "image." It then omits the following "of," presumably a scribal error, and begins the next sentence with "The light of the Father." In Coptic, as in Greek, there are no periods or full stops. The end of a sentence is determined by its context. So, moving the end of the sentence in this way is quite justified. By doing this, what is manifested by man—namely, the images—is addressed in one sentence, while what will be manifested by God—the light—is addressed in the other. In addition, I have rendered the final "his image" in my restored version to refer to man's illusory image, not to the Father's. The Father is pure spirit; He has no "image" and He knows it. There is no evidence in this gospel of God having a body or material "image."

In my restored version, I have arranged the lines to emphasize the ABC/abc pattern. The A/a lines both contain the word "manifest," as the C/c lines both have "hidden." The B/b lines contrast "light" with "image." A similar ABC/abc pattern can be found in saying 70. Here is my version, based on the BWG translation:

A. Jesus said, "Images are manifest to man,
B. and the light within them
C. is hidden in the (man's) image.
a. The light of the Father will be manifested,
b. and his (man's) image will be
c. hidden by His (God's) light."

We need to be careful about how we define the words "images" and "light." In this saying, images are representations of the things of this world in form. Consistent with the non-dual nature of this gospel, they are unreal, being projections of the mind and nothing more. Also being unreal, they are neither good nor bad. They are nevertheless experienced as real. The world is the total experience of its perceived images.

In Thomas, the Greek loanword for "image" is *eikwn*. It appears in three other sayings (22, 50, and 84). In all three of these other sayings, however, the word takes on a slightly different meaning than it does here in 83. It is often translated as "likeness." A likeness is a resemblance to something material, but it could also resemble something spiritual. For example, when we say that someone is godlike, we are comparing that person to a spiritual being. Here in this saying, an image is not a representation of something spiritual. That is clear from the way "images" are contrasted with spiritual "light." One may even substitute the word "materiality" for "image." The sense is the same. The images here are strictly physical representations of a physical world.

The light mentioned here is, of course, spiritual light. In saying 24, light exists within a man of light. In 61, when one experiences himself as equal to all of life, "he will be filled with light." Light is equated with God himself in 50. So, light is the very essence of God and the key to man's happiness. But man's egoic defenses must be abandoned before he can experience God's presence as light.

The world of images or form is manifest to man because that is what he chooses to see. It is an illusion, but that is precisely what a man, overwhelmed by guilt and fear, chooses to experience. He is in darkness, and nothing outside of that darkness makes any sense to him. The darkness seems to protect him from what he does not understand. He does not see the light, although it is all around him. It is hidden or shielded by the very images he so values. "The light in them is hidden in the image." The light is everywhere (113), though it is hidden, not by God, but by man's refusal to look beyond the darkness.

When man decides to wake up to his true identity, "the light of the Father will be manifested." It was always present, but his choice to awaken will make it manifest or palpable to the mind. He will then experience the glory of the Kingdom because he will have abandoned his old ego defenses and welcomed the truth. Where before, he only saw images of separation, now, he will see only wholeness and light. This extraordinary phenomenon is represented in the final line:

> "The light of the Father will be manifested, and his (man's) image will be hidden by His (God's) light."

Where before, the images hid the light from his awareness, now, the light will hide the images. As light operates by shining, there is a suggestion here that the darkness of man's world will be shined away by God's light.

The light of God is antithetical to the images of man. Something seemingly as ethereal as spiritual light has the power to hide or completely shine away precisely what seems most solid to man, the world of form. This saying demonstrates once again the utterly insubstantial nature of the world when understood from the viewpoint of this gospel.

Saying 84

> **(84) Jesus says: "When you see your likeness, you rejoice. But when you see your likenesses that came into existence before you, which neither die nor become manifest, how much will you bear?"**

> **(84)** ***Jesus said, "When you look upon your likenesses, you rejoice. But when you should look upon your (true) likenesses, which came into being before you, which neither die nor do they manifest, how much (more joy) will you bear!" (My restored version)***

Two identities or likenesses are compared with each other in this saying. The self that man believes himself to be, the physical self or body, is compared to the Self that comes into being before the body or ego does. It says that this earlier likeness will never die, nor will it manifest. To never manifest means that it will never express itself in physical form. This is the spiritual-Self.

There are two problems here. The first is the use of the word "likeness" in two languages. The first "likeness" is represented by the Coptic word *eine*. I take its meaning to be synonymous with the idea of identity. When "you look upon your likeness (or resemblance)" you see your body as in a mirror. That is your presumed identity. If you can look without judgment, you may be pleased with what you see and experience joy. The saying continues: "But when you see your likenesses that came into existence before you…" Here the Greek loanword *eikwn* is used, which can mean "likenesses" but also "images." Some translators prefer the word "images" here, although "likenesses" appears to fit the context better. This second, but earlier, likeness or identity "does not die." It is spiritual, and therefore it cannot be a physical object. In the previous saying (83), the word *eikwn* is used to describe physical objects. That is not the case here. Indeed, in the two other sayings in which this word appears (22 and 50), the contexts favor "likeness." So, only in 83 does the word *eikwn* mean "images" and not spiritual likenesses or identities as it does here.

The second problem is a minor one but something that might confuse the reader. The first "likeness" mentioned is written in the singular form even though the speaker is addressing more than one person. The three appearances of the word "you" are all written in the plural form. I take this to be either a scribal error or a reference to each person in the group, focusing on each individual's common experience. For the sake of clarity, I have opted for the plural form of "likeness" in my restored version.

In this saying, the spiritual-Self, with which the physical-self is compared, precedes the body and will never die. It says, "They neither die nor become manifest." The Self is immortal and shares this likeness or identity with God. Because it is spiritual, it is beyond space and time. It is not restricted to the limitations of the world. What follows is particularly important in understanding the theology of this gospel: it does not "manifest" as a body, and therefore, it is spiritual, fixed and unchanging. If this is the case, then the body must be an illusion. What cannot "manifest" cannot manifest as a body or be trapped in a body. It cannot be what it is not. Such an impossible manifestation can only be a feature of man's dream of separation. The body, therefore, is a false self, a likeness only in man's mind.

The "joy" the body experiences cannot be compared to the immense joy experienced when the spirit-Self realizes its freedom. Of the spirit-Self, it says, "How much will you bear!" The question then is, how much of *what* will you bear? The only experience mentioned in this saying is that of "joy." This concluding statement, then, seems to be that when you look upon or experience this unlimited, all-encompassing Self, how much more joy will you bear or experience! The use of the word "bear" suggests an experience of splendor that is overwhelming.

This idea of a spiritual reality buried or hidden from consciousness but longing to be liberated is found throughout this gospel but particularly in sayings 18 and 19. In 18, the "beginning" and "end" are in one "place," that place being the Kingdom. In other words, in the Kingdom there is no time, nor are the beginning and the end separate states. In the non-duality of this gospel, such dichotomies as "beginning" and "end" are meaningless. In the words of 18, if a man takes his place in the beginning (realizing his spiritual reality), he will "know the end (which is also the beginning) and will not experience death." In 19, Jesus says, "Blessed is he who came to be before he came to be." Again, coming into being means to realize one's true Self, a self that existed before man dreamed of his second coming in a separate body in a separate world. Dreams, however, are not real, and man will someday wake up to his true identity in God and the knowledge that nothing real has ever separated the Son from the Father.

Saying 85

> **(85) Jesus said, "Adam came into being out of a great power and a great wealth, but he did not become worthy of you. For had he been worthy, [he would] not [have tasted] death."**

Adam came into being as a man in an epic story. He was the representation of the first man. But also in that story, Adam became the symbol of man's separation from God. This is a saying about both Adam, the man of that story, and Adam, the symbol for man's seeming separation from his creator.

Before man (as Adam) chose separation, metaphorically represented by the eating of the apple, he had no conception of sin or shame. He only knew, much as a baby knows, the warmth of his father/mother's womb (Eden). Then, he fell asleep (Genesis 2:21) and, stretching the metaphor in Genesis a bit, dreamed a dream in which the concept of limitation played a central part. From that dream, he never woke up, even to this day. Adam represents here not only himself but all of mankind. And like Adam, man still sleeps and dreams his dream that he is separate from his Father and all that exists.

There is a tear at the bottom of the codex page on which this saying is written. Here, scholars are fairly confident in restoring the final words, "he would not have tasted death." The phrase "taste death" appears in three other sayings (1, 18, and 19). In saying 111, the word "see" replaces "taste." It says, "The one who lives from the Living One will not see death." In all five of these sayings, there is the suggestion that if a man achieves a certain level of understanding, death will not be "seen" or "tasted." It does not say that he will hold on to his body forever. It merely suggests that he will not "taste" or experience death as an experience of loss. Like the world, the body is a "corpse" (56 and 80), so the experience of letting the body go should not be one of loss but of gain. However, to experience this gain, one must be awake and not fear the loss of anything.

When Jesus says that Adam is not "worthy of you," he is additionally saying that the body is not worthy of man. Adam represents a spirit who came into being from a "great wealth," but believing himself to be a body, he lost sight of that wealth and his own spirit nature. As one who chose form over substance, the body over spirit, he became unworthy as a role model for those who chose to wake up to their true spirit nature, as he did not. In this saying, Jesus confirms that those unnamed disciples, whom he addresses here, are awake to this spirit nature in which death, as an experience of loss, is meaningless. They are free of all beliefs in limitation; therefore, Adam, as a symbol of the body's limitations, is not worthy of their reverence.

Saying 86

> **(86) Jesus said, "[The foxes have their dens] and the birds have their nests, but the son of man has no place to lay his head and rest."**

In responding to this saying, I see an opportunity here to tie together some related themes in Thomas that, when thoroughly explored, should enhance our understanding of this gospel. Hence, I will spend a little more time on this brief saying than might otherwise seem necessary.

The phrase "son of man" appears over a hundred times in the Old Testament, especially in the Book of Ezekiel. In what is also called the Hebrew Bible, it refers simply to human beings, both ordinary and special. It may be translated "son of Adam." It is not a title for anyone. Only in Daniel (7:13) does it refer to a future, unnamed, messianic figure seen by Daniel in a vision. He describes this person as "like a son of man." He says of him that he saw him "coming with the clouds of heaven" and that "nations and men of every language worshiped him." In the New Testament, Jesus refers to himself repeatedly as "the son of man" in such a way that, within the first few centuries after his death, this became a messianic title for him. To what extent this term was truly self-referential or placed in his mouth by the evangelists to affirm Daniel's prophecy is not clear. In any case, the Church eventually proclaimed that Jesus was the messiah whom Daniel had prophesied. So in addition to being referred to as the "Son of God" in the early church—a title which suggests a messianic mission—he was also called "the son of man," also a messianic title, apparently referring to the prophecy in Daniel.

The word "messiah," of course, does not appear in Thomas. Jesus is not described here as someone who will judge the "living and the dead," as he is in Acts (10:42). In Thomas, he does not perform miracles or rise from the dead. The phrase "son of man" appears only once, here in saying 86. The plural expression of this appears in 28 as "sons of men." The term "sons of man" in 106 appears to be either a scribal error or a deliberate revision. I explain this in my commentary on that saying, where I argue that the original phrase was likely "Sons of God," but later changed to "sons of man." My theory is that a later scribe could not accept that ordinary mortals should be described as divine in the way that Jesus apparently was in the New Testament. Nevertheless, in Thomas, the two phrases—son of man and Son of God— are not equivalent, as they seem to be in the Christological sense in the New Testament. The following list shows where these references can be found.

son of man:

"sons of men" (28)
"son of man" (86)

Son of God:

"Sons of the Living Father" (3)
"Son of the Living One" (37)
"Father...Son and...Holy Spirit" (44)
"sons of man" (106) This was likely a scribal revision, the original phrase being "Sons of God." (See my commentary on this saying.)

The phrase "Son of God" frequently appears as a reference to Jesus in the New Testament. In that source, it was spoken of Jesus by others, by Jesus about himself, and twice by a voice speaking from heaven. It specifically alludes to Jesus as the Messiah and, in part at least, to his birth by the Virgin Mary. In Thomas, the nearly identical phrase "Son of the Living One" does not allude to Jesus alone (37), nor to his status as a messiah. Nor does it have anything to do with anyone's physical birth. This "Son" in Thomas refers to God's one creation, His beloved one, who exists beyond space and time and in oneness with his Father. He is the one Self and the true identity of every living creature. He is neither male nor female, young nor old. He is beyond all dualities of every kind (22). He is one with all of life and with God. To the ego-mind, he is incomprehensible. The ego-mind can only understand this as a concept, but never the reality behind the concept.

Throughout Thomas, Jesus compares, by way of metaphor and allegory, the experience of the "son of man," who lives in ignorance of his divine Self, with that of the "Son of the living One." Likewise, there is an implied reference in Thomas to a *kingdom of man* that Jesus contrasts with the "Kingdom of the Father." Though never explicitly stated, the opposite realm of the Kingdom of the Father must be the kingdom of man. This is the realm of separation and isolation in which man believes he inhabits. But in truth, he does not exist in this realm; it is illusory. There can be no opposite of what is all-encompassing, and the purpose of this gospel is to remind him of that.

An essential theme in Thomas is that man experiences within himself two selves. One is real; the other is not. The real Self is the one Jesus calls the "Son of the Living One," (37) a synonymic term for the Son of God. As we saw in 84, man's true likeness, this immortal Self, is wholly complete. He does not die or manifest as a body. He, therefore, has nothing to do with the world of form. He can dream he is a "son of man," however, and propelled by fear and guilt, take this dream very seriously. This is the means by which he experiences form and separation. In this saying (86), Jesus calls the subject of this dream "the son of man" to distinguish him from the "Son of God." Although they are the same man, one identity sees himself as alone and separate; the other knows with certainty that he is safe and loved by his creator. Thus, the true Self of every man or woman is the "Son of God;" the false-self or illusory-self is called in this saying, "the son of man."

In saying 3b, it states: "When you come to know yourselves, then you will become known, and you will realize that it is you who are the Sons of the Living Father. But if you will not know yourselves, you dwell in poverty, and it is you who are that poverty." To realize one's true identity is to know that one is a Son of God. This is who man is. If he thinks that he is not this, he is mistaken, and the consequence of this ignorance is spiritual poverty and misery.

Why then does man experience himself as a limited thing within a body? Coming from such wealth, why does he now sleep in ignorance of this wealth? The Gospel of Thomas does not answer this question directly. If the world is a dream, it would seem that the answer could never be found within the dream but only in a mind that is fully awake. So perhaps, for now, this must remain a mystery. Nevertheless, what is not a mystery is the pain and exhaustion that man experiences while still entangled in this dream of loss and exile. It is this exhaustion to which this saying (86) alludes.

Some commentators maintain that this "son of man" is Jesus. Even more believe that this refers to those followers of Jesus who, by their loyalty to their master, experience much hardship and exhaustion. I propose a third alternative. Man experiences two selves. Either he is awake, and he knows himself to be a Son of God, or he sleeps (102) and believes himself to be a son of man. As a son of man, he appears wedded to the earth. He further appears to be a creature born of dust. He is convinced that fate has made him a victim of a world from which death is the final release. He lives a roller-coaster existence in which God, if acknowledged at all, is understood as some distant and uncaring, absentee administrator. While convinced of this identity, he cannot possibly find rest. Like the Prodigal Son, he roams the world in a futile attempt to find satisfaction. The foxes have their dens, and the birds have their nests, but the man who cuts himself off from his Source has no home and no rest. Only when he remembers who he really is will he return to his true home, a *place* from which he never left except in his dream. Once again, we encounter here the word "place," which in Thomas is often used as a code word for the Kingdom. So, it is the Kingdom to which this "son of man" needs to return.

Echoes of this son of God/man dichotomy can be found throughout Thomas. The lion and man confrontation in saying 7, although employing different metaphors, dramatizes the struggle between two diametrically opposed identities. There is no middle course; one identity must consume the other to be wholly itself. One must die for the other to live. Saying 42 restates the same theme: "Come into being as you pass away." It is an internal action, entirely within the mind of man, but allegorized in Thomas in parables and aphorisms. Even the phrase that has puzzled readers for centuries, "Do not let your left hand know what your right hand is doing (62)," sets the false identity, represented by the left hand, against the true identity of the right hand. There cannot, in fact, be any true cooperation between these two identities, as one is the denial of the other. The inevitable triumph of the Son of God over his shadow self is perhaps most succinctly stated in 61a:

> Jesus said, "Two will rest on a bed: the one will die, and the other will live."

In that saying, life arises not on a battlefield but on the bed of peace. But as long as man refuses to wake up from the meaningless battlefield of his dream world, as in this saying (86), he will have no place to lay his head and rest.

Saying 87

> **(87) Jesus said, "Wretched is the body that depends on a body, and wretched is the soul that is dependent on these two."**

There are many ways in which a body can depend on a body. All of them spring from a single thought: I am separate. Without this thought, there is no need for dependency, since what is whole needs nothing outside of itself. Into this dream we call the "world," children appear to be born who naturally need their mothers. Lovers cling to each other, feeling incomplete in themselves; and, at the end of "life," the infirm need help from their family or their government. So, in this dream of separation, dependency seems essential, yet it is not love in the ultimate sense. Yes, love is there in all of these occasions of tenderness and caring. It is genuine love and not to be devalued, but pure love is of a different order.

In my commentary on saying 22, I wrote of the reciprocal love of mother and child as being the ideal metaphor for the mutual love of man and God. This is true, although it is still just a metaphor and not equal to the love that is not of this world. Such love only gives and asks for nothing in return. It recognizes everything and everyone as perfect and worthy without exception. It is unconditional and freely accessible in any and all circumstances. Any judgment that such perfection is too good to be true, that it cannot exist, rests solely on the belief in lack. And while lack can be imagined, it was not created by God. Therefore, by the logic of this non-dualistic gospel, lack is not real, and ultimately, physical dependency is, at best, redundant.

The Kingdom is a realm in which God's love flows freely to his creation. Nothing can stop it, but its presence can be denied. In this earthly realm, born of denial, man sees himself as weak and undeniably dependent—not on God but on the physical world. In fact, the illusion of the physical world was made precisely to replace God and banish Him to a far-off heaven. In this astonishingly insane situation, man cannot help but suffer. He has cut himself off from his Source and suffers the consequences. As long as he identifies with his body, it will be the focus of his pain. The source of this pain, however, is not the body; it is man's choice to see himself as separate from God's love. When at last he acknowledges God as his true Source of strength and not the world, he will then know his wholeness, and this wholeness will fully support and embrace him.

In this saying, a body that is dependent on a body is wretched because, in this limited relationship of body to body, oneness is dismissed and misery is unavoidable. When the world of duality is taken seriously, unhappiness is the result. Jesus goes on to say that it is not just the body that will be afflicted by man's belief in duality but the soul as well. In the context of Thomas, the soul/mind is not external to the body but beyond the body, as truth is beyond illusion. It is not the brain, yet it manifests as the brain in man's dream of limitation and separation.

The mind/soul has within it the knowledge of its wholeness, although this is suppressed by the powerful belief system we call the ego. Within the soul is the constant struggle we see in saying 7 of man and lion, of truth and illusion. As long as this struggle continues, it will continue to bear witness to the two bodies of this saying and take the belief in dualism seriously.

It will, in fact, depend on this dualistic view of reality to confirm its belief in separation.

As long as the soul takes "these two" bodies (duality) seriously, it will thirst for completion and hunger for love. This is why the "soul that is dependent on these two" will be "wretched." The world of duality is like a drinking trough that has gone dry (74). There is nothing there to nourish the soul. Only spirit can do that. To find relief, the soul must focus on spirit and nothing else. Only from that quiet cistern of living water will its thirst be quenched.

Saying 88

> **(88) Jesus said, "The angels and the prophets will come to you, and they will give to you those things that you (already) have. And you also, give them what is in your hands, and say to yourselves, 'When will they come and take what is theirs?'"**

The following quote regarding this saying is taken from the book *The Five Gospels* by Robert W. Funk, Roy W. Hoover, and the Jesus Seminar:

> The meaning of this saying is simply unknown. Fellows attributed its character to the general tendency in Thomas to indulge in obfuscation and esotericism—to make assertions that are mystifying, secretive, dark, impenetrable.[1]

Such skepticism about Thomas is undoubtedly shared, not only by the fellows of the Jesus Seminar but among many others as well. To be fair, the Jesus Seminar has supported the study of this gospel as no other scholarly group has. It must be kept in mind, however, that most people are unfamiliar with the philosophy and practice of non-dualism. Consequently, they will almost unavoidably interpret these sayings in the context of their own worldview. Yet, in the light of non-dualism, patterns can be seen in Thomas that are unmistakably suggestive of a consistent message. Indeed, out of its darkness and obscurity, light and clarity can still be salvaged, meaning can be found, and a new appreciation of this gospel can be discovered.

It seems quite likely that both confusion and skepticism about Thomas were present from the beginning of its existence. It was written not to be easily consumed and digested but to challenge the reader/listener to question his most basic assumptions. It should not be surprising, then, that scribes working on this gospel fifty, one hundred, or perhaps two hundred years after its creation, would further obscure its message in a misguided attempt to soften its radical stances or harmonize its language with orthodox ideas.

The ultimate source of love is God, but without the help of those who have actualized their oneness with God, His love can seem quite distant. Those conveyors of love who have realized this oneness are the "angels" and "prophets" of this saying. They represent the full range of help, from tender care to spiritual guidance. The Greek loanword *aggelos* means "messenger" as well as "angel." In the context of this saying, anyone offering love and guidance may be considered an angel or a prophet. It would be a mistake, I think, to understand these terms too narrowly.

When love is extended unconditionally to another, it finds itself. It acknowledges and confirms what is already there. Two minds join as one, and in that joining, love is experienced as a celebration of wholeness. Each mind is already whole, but love awakens the awareness of that wholeness. In the acceptance of love, love is returned. The experience of sharing love in this way increases its impact on both the giver and the receiver.

The concluding question—"When will they come and take what is theirs?"—is a clever way of saying that giving freely of love always adds and never subtracts. Giving is receiving. The "angels" and the "prophets" already have "what is theirs." In freely giving love, they have lost nothing. Nothing is ever lost in the transfer of love. This is the opposite of what the ego teaches, that giving is a sacrifice. To the ego, for someone to gain, someone else must lose. However, with this exchange of love nothing is sacrificed. For a brief moment, the artificial barriers of the ego break down, leaving only the experience of utter fullness and completion for both the givers and the receivers. Inspired by the loving gifts of the "angels" and the "prophets," those identified as "you" in this saying respond in kind. The question they then ask themselves is essentially this: Having given what we have, why do we feel so full and complete, as if we had not given at all? Their minds, unaccustomed to the exchange of such generosity of spirit, are staggered by what they feel, and nothing in their experience of limitation and separation can account for it. The message of this saying is that true giving is always a gift to oneself.

1 Robert W. Funk, Roy W. Hoover, and the Jesus Seminar, *The Search for the Authentic Words of Jesus* (New York: Macmillan, 1993), 519-520.

Saying 89

> **(89) Jesus said, "Why do you wash the outside of the cup? Do you not comprehend that he who made the inside is the same one who made the outside?"**

"Why do you wash the outside of the cup?" The question presumes that Jesus has no issues with washing the inside of the cup. But it is the washing of the *outside* that he questions. In this highly metaphorical gospel, the "outside of the cup" can be seen as a metaphor for the world. This appears to be a reasonable proposal. To say that Jesus is referring to the outside of the body trivializes his message by implying that he is opposed to body hygiene. However, what is less clear is the identity of the "he" who made the "outside" and the "inside." Most people would say that God made the world. But nowhere in this gospel does Jesus say this or even imply this. To him, the world is a "corpse" (56). Would God have created a corpse? That would seem unlikely. The other option, the one that Thomas appears to support, is that man made the world as an illusion in a dreamlike state of emptiness, blindness, and intoxication (28). He then made this illusion his home.

In saying 22, Jesus tells his listeners that they will enter the Kingdom only when they "make the inside like the outside and the outside like the inside." The suggestion is that they were the ones who *made* this duality of "inside" and "outside," and, therefore, it is their responsibility to *unmake* it. In other words, it is their responsibility to wake up to the truth that all is one and that the concept of "inside" and "outside" is meaningless. Moreover, in this saying, the "he" who makes the "inside" and the "outside" appears not to be God but man. Nowhere else in Thomas, except here, is the Father identified merely as a "he" without elaboration. Jesus could have easily said that the Father made the inside of the cup and also the outside. But instead, he teases the listeners with the implied question: Who is this? The ambiguity of this "he" appears intentional to stimulate inquiry.

Returning to our first question, why would Jesus want only the inside of the cup washed? Presumably, the "inside" refers to man's mind, where thoughts and judgments are generated. For someone as concerned about interior states of mind as this Jesus apparently is, this would seem to be a reasonable place to wash. But why wash the inside exclusively? Either the outside (the world) does not matter to Jesus, or he believes that the outside images will conform automatically to the inside condition. From the evidence of this gospel, the outside does indeed matter to Jesus, but only as a place where man suffers exile and death. He calls the world a "corpse," and it is this empty realm that he compares negatively, elsewhere in Thomas, to the fullness of the "Kingdom." What matters more to Jesus is the inside. It is on the inside, on the level of the mind, where choices are made that will determine the condition of the outside world. In actuality, there is no outside. The outside is merely a screen on which the inside is projected.

The screen itself is a projection of the belief in separation. The outside will be experienced only as long as man values separation and believes in the reality of inside/outside. As saying 22 suggests, the Kingdom will be entered only when one sees all dualities as one without distinctions. In truth, there is only oneness, and that is why Jesus asks the question, "Why do you wash the outside of the cup?" For this Jesus, making changes to the world is not a sensible thing to do. On the other hand, making changes to the way one thinks about the world is entirely sensible.

The message of this saying is that by washing the inside of the cup (the contents of the mind), by cleansing it of its egoic beliefs, the outside of the cup (the world projected by that mind), will conform to the inside automatically, being inseparable from it. "He" (man) who made the inside (the contents of his mind) is also the "one" who made the outside (his mind's projections). Going back to the initial question, why then should one not wash the outside of the cup? One should not because one cannot; there is nothing there to wash. The illusion called the "outside" is merely a projection of an inner condition. As in a movie house, a film is viewed on a screen. What is seen on that screen seems real; it is not. The film may portray the end of civilization, but there is nothing anyone in the audience can do about it. Changing anything real by manipulating the projections on the screen is futile. That would be like washing the outside of the cup. In an unreal world, true change cannot take place. Real change and real healing can only happen within the mind. That is the fundamental assumption of non-dualism in a nutshell and, apparently, of this gospel as well.

Saying 90

> **(90) Jesus said, "Come unto me, for my yoke is easy and my lordship is mild, and you will find rest for yourselves."**

> **(90)** *Jesus said, "Come unto me, for my yoke is easy and my burden is mild, and you will find rest for yourselves." (This is based on John Dominic Crossan's version which in turn was based on a suggestion by Helmut Koester.)*

"Come unto me." What a stunning invitation! It is a call to leave one's fears and doubts behind and follow the legendary teacher and mystic, Jesus. But more than that, it is an open door, a summons to share the same consciousness as Jesus. That is what makes this saying so extraordinary. This is his "yoke"—one that is designed for two—which he is offering to share. It is not his yoke in the sense that he alone owns it. It is his because he shares the burden in tandem with another. He says, "Come unto me," not "Come unto my yoke." He invites the listener/reader to pull alongside him in the same yoke. By pulling together, Jesus and his coworker affirm their oneness with each other.

Such sharing entails the coming together of two wills to make one will. In saying 108, Jesus says, "He who will drink from my mouth will become like me. I myself shall become he, and the things that are hidden will be revealed to him." This is the way truth is revealed. From these sayings, it can be seen that freedom is not found in isolation but in joining, in making the "two one" in an affirmation of oneness.

This principle of one will is represented by the yoke, an implement for bringing together the equal efforts of two into a single force. It is, in fact, this equality of effort that makes the yoke effective. Here again, we have what is the principal theme of this gospel, that only in oneness—in one effort, in one goal, and in the awareness of one spirit—does man find his way home. Jesus offers his yoke to everyone, without distinctions of any kind. But before joining is attempted, anything that causes an imbalance between the two must be rejected. Pride would make cooperation impossible, particularly spiritual pride. In this effort of the two working as one, both must be humble and abandon all claims of specialness and divine approval.

Jesus also says that his yoke is easy. What makes it easy is precisely the abandonment of separate interests. There is no power in having separate interests, only in having a common goal. When that goal is the Kingdom, the immense power of God's grace is released and made accessible (106). Nothing can be denied to one who joins with his brother to find the Kingdom. By accepting the yoke of Jesus, all obstacles to the awareness of God's love will dissolve and melt away.

In his book *In Fragments, the Aphorisms of Jesus*, John Dominic Crossan casts doubt on the originality of the word "lordship" in the phrase "my lordship is mild." The Gospel of Matthew (11:28-30) has a version of this saying that represents the phrase as "my *burden* is mild." Crossan discounts the dependency of this saying on Matthew, as a whole, but argues for a suggestion by Helmut Koester that "burden" is more original to this saying than is "lordship." He maintains this for two reasons. First, the words "burden" and "rest," in connection with this saying, reappear in two later works, Pistis Sophia, 95, and Dialogue of the Savior, 141:3-6. Secondly, "the force of the aphorism seems intensified if there is some comparison made between heavy or difficult burdens (from elsewhere) and light or easy burdens (with Jesus)."[1] I would add that the word "lordship" appears incongruous in a saying that asks the listener/reader to join him as an equal in the use of the yoke. Moreover, in this gospel, Jesus does not present himself as a lord to be obeyed, not as a "master" (13) but as an example to be followed. I suspect that, here again, an ancient scribe has substituted the word "lordship" for "burden" to support or inflate the stature of Jesus. For these reasons, I have restored the more apt word, "burden," to this saying.

---

1 John Dominic Crossan, *In Fragments, The Aphorisms of Jesus* (Eugene, OR: Wipf & Stock, 2008), 257.

Saying 91

(91) They said to him, "Tell us who you are so that we may believe in you."
He said to them, "You examine the face of the sky and the earth, but you have not recognized the one who is before you, and you do not know how to read this moment."

(91) ***They said to him, "Tell us who you are so that we may believe in you."***
He said to them, "You examine the face of the sky and the earth, but you have not recognized what is right in front of you, and you do not know how to read this moment." (My restored version, based on a Stevan Davies translation)

Just as we do now, the people who engage with Jesus in this saying look to authority for validation about what they should believe: "Tell us who you are so that we may believe in you." Concealed within that plea is an assumption. His listeners assume that Jesus is someone special, someone unlike themselves. Perhaps he is the Messiah, a prophet, or maybe a man of great learning. In other words, he has qualities that they apparently lack. By being assured of his superiority, they can then trust his words to be true. This, they believe, is the way to acquire wisdom—find someone who has special credentials and accept what he or she says as true. Two thousand years later, we continue to do exactly this. We look for a teacher of high acclaim or a book in which to believe, and our spiritual odyssey stops right there. Here, Jesus teaches quite a different strategy for accessing wisdom.

In this saying, Jesus teaches that each individual is responsible for his own seeking and finding. He states in saying 5, "Recognize what is in front of your face and that which is hidden from you will become plain to you. For there is nothing hidden which will not become manifest." One has to follow his own spiritual path and not simply believe what others see or believe. In these two sayings (5 and 91), the truth is "in front of your face" or "right in front of you." That means that the truth, though hidden behind a screen of false beliefs, is always present and available. Here, Jesus addresses the inclination to look beyond one's own experience and blindly follow the lead of others. In a similar saying (24), his disciples ask him to "show us the place where you are." He answers them by saying, "There is a light within a man of light, and he lights up the whole world. If he does not shine, he is darkness." The light is the source of everything that is true. It is this eternal light of truth in everyone to which Jesus points. This is where he is, in that place of light.

In this saying (91), Jesus tells them, "You examine the face of the sky and the earth." In Matthew (16:1-3) and Luke (12:54-56), this assertion is taken literally. In those versions of this saying, the sky and clouds are read for signs of good or bad weather. It is more likely, however, that this line was intended as a metaphor. To "examine or read the face" means to understand the surface of things, the appearance of things. A superficial understanding of the sky and earth will not take the seekers of wisdom very far. But the truth is so much closer. It is right in front of them. Likewise, they are unable to "read this moment." Their minds are focused on the past and future. But truth is not found in either the past or the future. It is found only in the present moment. (See my commentary on 59.) So not only do they not know *where* to look for truth, they do not know *when* to look for it.

My adaptation of the Stevan Davies translation (above) demonstrates how this saying might be alternately worded. He has replaced the standard phrase, "the one who is before you," with "what is right in front of you." The difference between these two versions is that the first refers to a person (presumably Jesus), the second to a thing (presumably the truth). This contrast stems from the word in Coptic that may be translated as either "the one" (he) or "what" (it), depending on the context. Either translation is acceptable. In his book *The Gospel of Thomas, Annotated & Explained*, Davies writes that this saying (using his own translation) rejects the principle, found in the Gospel of John, that Jesus himself was the primary route to salvation. He says of the Gospel of Thomas, "When Jesus is asked about himself, he answers in terms of the whole world, deflecting attention from himself to the condition of reality."[1] This deflection works for this saying in the Davies translation but fails in the way it is rendered by most translators. That version has Jesus referring to himself as "the one" who should be "recognized." It contradicts an essential idea in this gospel that

Jesus is not the sole route to wisdom but the one who points to or "measures out" the truth (13). He invites the seeker to share his "yoke" in saying 90. He points to the truth, but that which he points to and speaks of must be approached and embraced by the seeker himself. No matter how liberated and profoundly wise this master may be, it is not enough to depend alone on the authority of Jesus.

1 Stevan Davies, *The Gospel of Thomas, Annotated & Explained* (Woodstock, VT: Skylight Paths, 2003), 112.

Saying 92

> **(92) Jesus said, "Seek and you will find. But the things you asked me about in past days and what I did not tell you then, now I do desire to tell them, but you do not seek after them."**

Marcel Proust wrote: "We do not receive wisdom, we must discover it for ourselves, after a journey through a wilderness which no one else can make for us, which no one can spare us, for our wisdom is the point of view from which we come at last to regard the world."[1]

A wise man who has found the truth for himself can point in the direction from which he came, but he cannot take anyone there. That journey must be made by the seeker himself. Jesus says, "Seek and you will find." To seek is to go on a journey. A spiritual journey is one which has as its goal the awareness of God's love and freedom from the world's limitations. Jesus makes the promise that by seeking for it, it will be found. He makes the same promise in sayings 2 and 94. He knows about this because he has found this awareness and freedom for himself. In this saying (92), he again encourages others to make this journey for themselves.

The remainder of the saying seems bizarre and confusing. After assuring his disciples that true seeking is always successful, he seems disappointed in them. When they previously asked him about matters important to them, he declined to answer. Now that he is willing to answer, they no longer seem interested. He reproaches them for this. He appears to scold them for their inconsistency. But is this the correct interpretation of this saying, or is there something else going on here? I suspect that this is a shell game—not a shell game intended to deceive but one that challenges the listener to pay attention.

The key to this enigmatic saying lies in the initial statement, "Seek and you will find." This is the shell in which the pea is placed. The truth never leaves this shell. It is the principal message of this saying. When the disciples asked questions of Jesus in the past, he refused to answer. In effect, he was saying to them: I can point to the truth, but you must seek it for yourselves. The obstacles you have placed in front of the truth are yours to remove. I removed my own internal blocks to this awareness, and that has opened my eyes. Now, you must do the same. In refusing to spoon-feed his disciples, his response to their questions was not indifference but kindness. The mark of a good teacher is his ability to point his students in the right direction but then step back and allow them to find the truth for themselves.

Later, Jesus tells them that he is willing to answer their questions. Now, however, they no longer inquire. We are led to believe that they are indifferent, that they have given up. But this is an empty shell. It is not what is going on here. The truth is that his disciples did indeed seek the truth within themselves, and they found it, just as Jesus said they would. By refusing to help them at that crucial juncture, they were free to do the work for themselves. Now, when he offers to answer their questions, they already know the answers. They have found the truth for themselves, which is the only way it can be found.

The faith that Jesus had in his disciples was not misplaced; neither was his promise empty, that by seeking they would find. They did seek, and they found the truth. They are now silent. They no longer need to inquire further; in their silence, nothing can be added. So here in 92, instead of a disappointed teacher, we find a teacher who is entirely successful. He has achieved the highest goal for any teacher, to teach so well that he is no longer needed.

---

1 Marcel Proust, *Within a Budding Grove, Seascape, With Frieze of Girls* (London: Chatto & Windus, 1924).

Saying 93

> **(93) <Jesus said,> "Do not give what is holy to dogs, lest they throw them on the dung-heap. Do not throw pearls to swine, lest they turn <them> into [mud]."**

> ***(93) <Jesus said,> "Do not give what is holy to dogs. Do not throw pearls to swine, lest they turn <them> into [dung]." (My restored version)***

As shown in the above standard translation, this saying has several curious features. Compare it to the parallel saying in Matthew (7:6):

> "Do not give what is holy to dogs; do not throw your pearls to pigs. If you do, they may trample them under their feet, and turn and tear you to pieces."

Missing from this Matthew version, but present in Thomas, is the phrase, "lest they (the dogs) throw them (what is holy) on the dung heap." Even for this gospel, this is a very odd expression. Dogs, of course, do not "throw." Nor do they have any obvious connection with dung heaps. Who "throws" in this saying (93), and in the Matthew version as well, are identified in the second sentence as his listeners who are cautioned not to "throw pearls to swine." Moreover, what is thrown, referred obscurely as "them," apparently alludes to the pearls, which are not mentioned in this first sentence but only in the second. The problem is that no one talks this way. It puts the cart before the horse, or more precisely, the "them" before the "pearls." A Thomas scribe apparently thought that the idea of giving what is holy to dogs needed additional emphasis, so he added this "lest they throw them on the dung-heap" extension to match the "lest they turn them into mud/dung" extension in the following sentence. By doing this, he created an absurdly awkward and nonsensical phrase. It is uncharacteristically vague and discordant, which makes it unlikely that it was a part of the original saying. Matthew's simple, but direct, statement, "Do not give what is holy to dogs," was likely the correct wording here.

Did Jesus truly see some individuals as dogs or swine? This is an important question. The "dogs" and "swine" of this saying appear to refer to certain undesirable people who are unworthy of what is holy. At that time, calling a person a "dog" or a "swine" was a gross insult. It was the same as saying that one was unclean or debased. Matthew's version goes even further. In his gospel, the dogs threaten to "tear you to pieces," a metaphorical reference to hostile individuals, not to actual dogs. Yet, is such a blanket condemnation of human beings consistent with Thomas? Can anyone believe that the Jesus of *this* gospel could call anyone a dog or a pig? Could the author of "Love your brother like your soul, guard him like the pupil of your eye" (saying 25) actually support this view of debased human beings?

Surely the answer is no. These "dogs" and "swine" are not metaphors for people but metaphors for manifestations of the ego. The ego dominates that part of man's mind that clings to illusions. It is itself an illusion, yet as long as it is fed by fear and guilt, it will seem very real. The free mind cannot oppose the ego directly because to do so is to accept its reality. One overcomes the ego by aligning oneself with what is true or holy. By doing this, the ego is denied nourishment, and its hold on the mind is loosened. In this saying (93), when Jesus speaks of giving "what is holy to dogs," he is urging his listeners not to align their holy minds with the world of separation, the world of the ego. That world is false, and being false, it is not holy. When he says, "Do not throw pearls to swine, lest they turn them into mud," he means that a man should not deny his true identity as a child of God. To do so is to align with the ego and give it the power to turn this sacred identity into something base and unworthy. Man's innate holiness must be protected and not tossed away. In truth, it cannot be lost, but the one who identifies with the world will believe the ego's lies. It will tell him that he is merely a thing of this world, a victim of forces beyond his control. But God's children cannot be debased; they can only think they are debased. What remains forever safe in the mind of man is the treasure of his union with God. This can be ignored or thrown away but never lost.

It should be emphasized that in this view, the world is neither good nor bad. It is merely an outer embodiment of an inner condition. In themselves, dogs and swine are innocent animals. But as metaphors, they represent the things of this world that are manifestations of a troubled mind. Whenever man forgets his identity as God's Son, even for the briefest of moments, he looks to what is unholy and unworthy. He looks to what is illusory. In his confusion, he invests his sacred life, represented by the pearls, in the emptiness of the world, rather than in the wholeness of the Kingdom. Regardless of what he experiences, however, he is safe. His foray into madness is but a dream from which he will awaken when he is ready.

There is a lacuna or gap at the end of this saying that obscures the final words. Several restorations have been suggested. Turning pearls into "mud" makes no sense. Swine wallow in mud, but, strictly speaking, they cannot produce mud from pearls. However, they can produce "dung" from whatever they consume. This appears to be the more appropriate word and the word I use in my restored version. It is conceivable, as well, that the scribe who attached the phrase "lest they throw them on the dung-heap," referring to the dogs, got his "dung" idea from this concluding word.

Saying 94

> **(94) Jesus said, "He who seeks will find, and [he who knocks] inward will be let in."**

This saying is such a familiar one to most people that on the surface of the mind it barely causes a ripple. What is lost is nearly always found. Doors open to those who persist in knocking. We take these things for granted. The question then is why is this saying included in this collection? Why are these words even worthy of attention? The question is answered when the reader discovers what Jesus means by "find" and what he means by being "let in."

What is found in this gospel is a truth so life-changing and profound that on confronting it, the seeker is utterly astonished (2). It is like the treasure found in a field (109), or like the sheep for which the shepherd abandons his entire flock (107). It is promised in 17: "I will give you what no eye has seen, what no ear has heard, what no hand has touched, and what has never occurred to the human mind." It is so far beyond human comprehension that it resembles nothing the mind has ever experienced. This is how the treasure is presented in this gospel. It cannot be described, but only hinted at. In Thomas, the seeker is guided to abandon every other activity, every other goal, and seek only the oneness of the Kingdom.

Outside of this, nothing has any meaning.

Where is this truth found? The correct reading of the second half of this saying answers that question: "He who knocks will be let in." It is found within. The one who seeks within is the one who finds. In his book *In Fragments*, John Dominic Crossan carefully analyzes this line which, due to a tear in the papyrus, is partially missing. He accepts the phrase "he who knocks," which is widely acknowledged by scholars, but adds to this the word "inward," based on the partially obscured word that follows.[1] "He who knocks inward" is one who ignores the chatter of the surface mind and, instead, seeks meaning from within. Within is the only place where truth can be found. Trying to find it in the things of this world is like chasing one's tail—an imaginary tail at that. The world is merely a representation of one's thoughts. In the world, one goes round and round, seeking for something that is not there.

To knock at the inner door is to abandon all futile efforts to find meaning in the world. It is to surrender completely and say with conviction, "I know nothing, Father. Show me what I need to know." By doing this, the mind becomes quiet, and in this stillness, the truth of man's relationship with Him is known. It has so long been forgotten, but now it is remembered. In his consummate wholeness, man is God's Son. The Prodigal Son has come home. A door is opened within the mind, and the Son is invited in.

---

1 John Dominic Crossan, *In Fragments, The Aphorisms of Jesus* (Eugene, OR: Wipf & Stock, 2008), 100.

Saying 95

> **(95) Jesus said, "If you have money, do not lend it at interest. Rather, give it to one from whom you will not get it back."**

Reading the first line, "If you have money, do not lend it at interest," one would expect the follow-up line to read, "but lend it *without* interest." Instead, the saying urges the listener to give the money to someone who will not give it back. In effect, it says, do not lend either at interest or without interest. Do not lend at all, but *give.*

In ancient Israel, imposing interest was forbidden by Mosaic Law. At that time, Israel was not a commercial society, so lending had the primary function of aiding the poor. In first-century Palestine, however, business was very much a part of everyday life. Lending at a reasonable rate of interest—to non-Jews, in particular—was necessary for the effective functioning of trade. Therefore, it was permitted at this level. Nevertheless, among the religiously observant, the issue remained controversial. There were many Jews who would not sanction this disregard of the ancient law and were quite vocal about it. Then, into this discussion steps Jesus to say that the issue is irrelevant. What is his idea? Do not lend at all; instead, give freely.

How should such a radical idea be understood? It is important to recognize that what Jesus teaches in this regard is consistent also with what non-dualism maintains. With non-dualism, there is no "other." There is no separate giver and no separate receiver. There is no separation between the two. In the world, giving to get is the norm. When a person gives, the expectation is that he will be repaid in some way, if only in gratitude or the esteem of the community. But in Jesus's vision, giving is receiving. He means this quite literally. First of all, for him, nothing in the world has any value (56). The world is something dead and meaningless; therefore, everything within it is also dead and meaningless. The world offers nothing worth keeping. Consequently, nothing is lost by giving it away. What is gained by giving, however, is the joy of extending love to another. In that extension, oneness is experienced—if only for a brief moment. Both the giver and the receiver gain in this exchange. Neither loses. (See my commentary on saying 88.)

Ultimately, only love can be fully given and fully received; every other transaction is ego-driven and, therefore, shallow and tentative. As an extension of God, who is love itself, man is also love itself. By sharing love, he becomes increasingly aware of who he is. He thus becomes aware of his oneness with the Source of love. So when someone freely gives money away, it is a gift of love, not because money in itself has value, but because the thought behind the gift comes from love. In this transaction, both parties gain. The recipient gains by being the receiver of love. The giver gains because by giving love, his identity in love is confirmed and enhanced.

In this saying, Jesus urges his followers to give money to one who will not give it back. This is unconditional giving and unconditional loving. It expects nothing in return. The very act of giving is the gift itself.

Saying 96

> **(96) Jesus said, "The Kingdom of the Father is like a woman. She took a little leaven, hid it in some dough, and made large loaves of it. Let him who has ears hear."**

Commentators have pointed out that in this parable, the Kingdom is not compared to the "leaven," as it is in Matthew (13:33) and Luke (13:20-22), but to the "woman." In his book *The Gospel of Thomas, Annotated & Explained*, Stevan Davies proposed another option. He said, "The Kingdom is not like a thing but like a person in action; the Kingdom is what someone does." This is closer to the truth, but this too, I think, is not quite right. Rather, I see this and other Thomas parables as comparing the Kingdom to a *situation*, one that is often unusual or even bizarre. Into this situation are cast actors that play out their metaphorical parts. In this way, the unique characteristics of the Kingdom of the Father are illustrated. For example, in the realm of the Kingdom, a large fish (8) and a treasured sheep (107) are presented in contrast to many small fish and ninety-nine sheep. The hidden message is that in the Kingdom, the one spiritual treasure is preferred to the multitude of worldly substitutes. By means of this vehicle, an entirely different way of looking at life is presented, one that overturns the conventional rules and expectations of the world. It is not just what someone does; it is a situation that dramatizes how man's most fundamental assumptions may be challenged.

Quite often in the parables of Thomas, we find an element that is unexpected or even peculiar. That unexpected element in this parable is the phrase "she hid it in some dough." The word "hid" or "concealed" is the acknowledged translation, although the presumed Coptic word in question is obscured by a tear in the papyrus. However, "hid" is also the preferred translation in the Matthew and Luke versions. In spite of this, some New Testament translators insist that the intended word must have been "mixed". One mixes yeast into dough; one does not hide it there. As we shall see, however, "hid" was specifically chosen to convey a meaning essential to the overall message of this parable. The Coptic word for "hid" also appears in saying 39, and in no way is the idea of "mixed" suggested in that instance.

In that parable, the Pharisees and scribes "hide" the keys of knowledge. Likewise, in this parable, the woman hides the yeast. If the two parables are compared, the suggestion is that what is hidden acts as a kind of key to something. In effect, this key opens the dough to the possibility of becoming bread. Both the key and the yeast have the same function within their respective parables—to unlock the potential for something quite extraordinary.

This parable is often compared to another one, that of the mustard seed:

> (20) The disciples said to Jesus, "Tell us what the kingdom of heaven is like." He replied to them, "It is like a mustard seed. It is the smallest of all seeds. But when it falls on tilled soil, it produces a great plant and becomes a shelter for birds of the sky."

In both sayings, something minute helps produce that which is comparatively great. In both sayings, the medium or soil of this transformation is cultivated. In this saying (96), the "dough" is prepared to receive the "leaven." The analogy is that into a mind that has been prepared to receive it, a spiritual truth is introduced. It is both small and seemingly inert, yet it goes to work gradually to change a life, and the result is astonishing. The leaven (96) and the mustard seed (20) represent only a hint of God's love and presence, a faint light, a dim memory of grandeur with extraordinary potential.

Returning to the conspicuous choice of the word "hid," a woman hides leaven in the dough. Metaphorically, she might represent wisdom or perhaps the Holy Spirit. However, she cannot be either since in Thomas that which is free of fear does not "hide." Only man hides. In 39, the Pharisees, being human, hide the keys of knowledge, denying its bounty not only from themselves but from everyone else. Here in 96, Jesus combines the idea of the "hidden" with the idea of the small, but generative, leaven. If the "woman," a metaphor for humankind, were already aware of her divine identity as a child of God, she would have no need to hide anything. However, her mind is split between that which is governed by her ego and that which seeks the truth (7). Like the Pharisees, the woman hides the generative factor, but unlike them, she hides it where it is most needed. Metaphorically speaking, her ego is wary of the leaven's power, just as man is wary of God's love. She is cautious, so she "hides" it within, not completely aware of its potential. This is how most people come to the awareness of the Kingdom. Their contribution to the process is quite limited. All that is needed is a little willingness to prepare the ground or dough of the mind to receive the seed or leaven of God's light. Then, once accepted into the mind, God does the rest. A miracle occurs—one that the ego-mind could never have imagined.

Saying 97

> **(97) Jesus said, "The Kingdom of the [Father] is like a woman who was carrying a jar full of meal. While she was walking some distance (from home), the handle of the jar broke and the meal emptied out behind her onto the road. She was unaware; she had not noticed a problem. When she reached her house, she set the jar down and found it empty."**

> **(97) *Jesus said, "The kingdom of [man] is like a woman who was carrying a jar full of meal. While she was walking some distance (from home), the handle (ear) of the jar broke and the meal emptied out behind her onto the road. She was unaware; she had not noticed a problem. When she reached her house, she set the jar down and found it empty." (My restored version)***

Suppose for a moment we consider the possibility that the initial phrase of this parable, as originally composed, read, "The kingdom of man" rather than "The Kingdom of the Father." I believe that restoring the words "kingdom of man" here is justified and reveals the real intention of the author. The problem is that the parable, as presented, is internally inconsistent and makes no sense. The "Kingdom" here is uncharacteristically associated with loss and failure, not with gain. The "meal" that the woman carries is seen as having value, but it is lost despite all her efforts to bring it home. This is not the Kingdom of the Father as described in the Gospel of Thomas. In this gospel, the author's intent was clearly to portray the Kingdom as one of treasure found, not of treasure lost. Here, it is compared to failure—not failure redeemed but utter failure. I propose that scribal error was the cause of this substitution, and that by restoring "the kingdom of man" for "the Kingdom of the Father," the parable not only makes sense, it does so quite forcefully.

In support of this restoration, consider these points. It appears quite likely that if Jesus had a name for the realm of truth, called in this gospel the "Kingdom of the Father" and sometimes the "Kingdom of Heaven," he also would have had a name for its counterpart, the "kingdom of man," or as it might be called today, the "kingdom of the ego." If Jesus had devoted his life to describing what it means to embrace the Kingdom of the Father, he also surely would have occasionally described what it means to embrace its opposite. In saying 63, he describes this opposite, although he does not name it. This is the parable of the rich man. No one would assume that what happens to this man represents the Kingdom of the Father. The story instead represents the dynamics of the Kingdom's opposite, the devastating forces of the ego. The rich man's ego, with which he identifies, values the world and the things of this world. It is in this world that he foolishly places his trust. That story illustrates the consequence of making the *kingdom of man* one's home.

Likewise, just as we have this contrast in Thomas between the realm of the Father and the realm of man (63), so too do we have a contrast between the "Son of the Living One" in saying 37 and the "son of man" in 86. In my commentary on saying 86, I argue that the phrase "son of man" makes far more sense in describing one who identifies with the world than it does in describing Jesus. It should be expected, in fact, that this gospel would examine both "kingdoms" for their value and fitness to be the home of God's creation. Having a free will, man has the choice of seeking security in God's realm, the realm of oneness and peace, or looking to the things of this world for security. If he chooses God's realm or Kingdom, he will discover that he is a Son of the "Living Father" (3b). If he chooses man's realm of separation and death, he will instead see himself as a body and, therefore, a son of man. Thus, in Thomas, there are two, seemingly, antithetical realms of existence. There is the realm or Kingdom of the Father versus the kingdom of man. Likewise, there are two antithetical identities, the Son of God versus the son of man. The teaching of this gospel points in one direction: one realm is the true home of God's Son, and the other is not. One identity is true and characterized by spiritual wealth; while the other is illusory and characterized by spiritual poverty (3b).

Returning to this saying (97), whereas the Gospel of Thomas describes the Kingdom of the Father as one of completion and union with the divine, the situation in which this woman finds herself is one of disintegration and loss. She metaphorically carries the weight of the world on her shoulders. The contents of her jar represent the sum of all her hopes and dreams. She is invested in values which she believes will reward her, not in the present but at the end of her journey. She is a metaphor for every man and woman who ever walked this bitter world from birth to death. Not long after she starts her trek, the handle of the jar breaks and the treasured contents begin to leak out. She notices nothing wrong, being certain that the world will not fail her. She stubbornly staggers on, almost in a trance, unaware of what is happening. Ultimately, her trust in the world leads her to a kind of death. Her treasure is lost; her jar is empty. Yet, that is the journey on which all people travel who trust in the world and not in their Source.

This is an allegory, of course, and it is futile to seek meaning in the shape and position of the jar. However, one detail appears significant. The leak occurs at the point at which the handle is attached to the jar. The literal meaning of the Coptic word for "handle" is "ear." In both Biblical Greek and Aramaic, there are similar linguistic links between the words for "handle" and for "ear." Such handles look like ears, and this resemblance probably explains why in all three languages the word for "ear" is also a word for "handle." In this parable, the handle may be metaphorically seen to be broken when the woman's inner ear ceases to listen. Her inner ear, which is her connection with Spirit, is broken. In essence, her connection with God is severed, and so she struggles on, oblivious of her true treasure, which is the Kingdom she has buried within her mind. However, *God* does not abandon the woman. By stubbornly clinging to what she thinks is her treasure, *she* abandons God. She is not a hapless victim of the world or of God. She has made a choice, as did the rich man in 63, to place her trust in the world. However, the world is not worthy of trust, so the consequences of her choice are predictable. She has made her home in the kingdom of man, not in the Kingdom of the Father, and this is the fundamental tragedy of her story.

Saying 98

> **(98) Jesus said, "The kingdom of the father is like a man who wanted to kill a powerful man. In his own house, he drew his sword and thrust it into the wall in order to find out if his hand had the strength (to do this). Then he slew the powerful man."**

On the face of it, this parable makes little or no sense. Why would Jesus speak about an assassin plotting to kill a "powerful man?" As with many other sayings in Thomas, if you try to understand it literally, you will miss its deeper meaning and also its value.

Everything that happens in this parable happens within the mind, and all the elements of this story are metaphors. The "powerful man" is a metaphor for the ego, and the "house" is a code word that we have seen before. In this story, it represents the structure of the ego's belief system. For a problem to be corrected, it must be corrected on the level on which it was made. In Thomas, all fundamental problems exist on the level of the mind. Therefore, it is only there that meaningful change can take place. This is a theme that can be found throughout these sayings. It is the ego which is always the underlying problem in any situation.

Let me restate what the ego is, as understood from the perspective of non-dualism. Primarily, it is the belief in separation. It is a complex of ideas centered around the belief that man has a separate mind, which is apart from other minds. Additionally, this separate mind is wholly contained within a separate body, which is apart from other bodies, and these bodies inhabit a world in which everything, including space and time, manifests in separation. Like a "house," the ego is a structure, a structure of beliefs, in which a man chooses to live and make his home. It lacks the cornerstone of truth (66); yet, to a mind obsessed with fear and guilt, it appears to offer shelter. There is nothing new about the ego. As a recognized phenomenon, it can be traced back more than 2,500 years to India where it is described in the Upanishads. It was called *ahamkara*. How Jesus came to understand this concept is unknown. However, there is no reason to believe that he could not have discovered its basic principles on his own. It is not that complicated. Every mystic who seeks to realize his oneness with the divine must eventually recognize the ego's function. It is what impedes his efforts. It is the mechanism within his mind that he must learn to quiet and ultimately silence.

The dedicated seeker eventually arrives at an understanding about his ego. He realizes that a major impediment to his spiritual fulfillment is his belief that he is small, helpless, and a victim of the world. However, the truth is that he is not small and helpless, and the world of separation is not real. He further recognizes that these beliefs arise in the part of his mind called the ego-mind, and that this part can behave quite despotically in defense of its beliefs.

In this saying, the "powerful man" is the ego. The seeker or true "man" is the uncertain and cautious assassin. His "sword" is the sword of inquiry. This man is roughly equivalent to the "man" in saying 7, just as the "powerful man" here is equivalent to that saying's "lion." Both the "powerful man" and the "lion" represent the tyrannical force, the ego, which seeks to retain its power over the whole mind. The man in this saying, however, is uncertain. He thinks of his enemy as someone existing outside of his "house." Furthermore, he wonders if he is strong enough to carry through his intention to slay this powerful man. So, as an experiment, he thrusts his sword of inquiry into what appears to be the solid stone wall of his "house." Notice how absurd this scene appears, reminding the reader of the seemingly absurd nature of the Kingdom.

Here is where the saying pivots. Here is where the genius of its author shows itself. The final line says this: "Then he slew the powerful man." The implication seems to be that having successfully tested his strength in piercing the wall of his house, he *then* goes out and kills the powerful man. This is the literal meaning of that sentence, but is there not a hidden meaning here that cuts though the absurdity of that scene? The key Greek loanword in this final line is *tote*. It means "then" or "subsequently," but it can also mean, as in English, "at that moment." We are led to believe that the man practices slaying the strong man in the house and "then" goes out and does the deed. However, the other option is that when the sword of inquiry pierces the structure of the "house," which is the structure of the ego, *at that moment* the "powerful man," the ego, is slain. For the slayer, the powerful man is not someone or something outside of himself; it is the very "house" in which he lives. It is the structure of beliefs in which he lives and calls his home. When he challenges the seemingly impenetrable tyranny of this ego/house and resolutely pierces its structure, *at that moment* it yields its false beliefs and releases its hold on the mind. The problem is resolved at its source, on the level on which it was made. There is no need to go anywhere or do anything more than this.

As we have seen before, a single word in a saying can be a vital clue in its interpretation. In this case, it is the word *tote*, which has a double meaning. When such a clue is found, it has a powerful and transformative effect on the direction and meaning of the saying. We have seen how the word "hid" had this same effect in saying 96. With this clue, here in 98, the parable ceases to be impenetrable. Its wall of obscurity is breached, and its powerful and liberating message is revealed. In any moment of the day, it is possible to break through the structure of beliefs that bind us to this seeming fortress of a world. We need wait no longer. Our adversary stands before us and within us. Our "hand" is strong, and our "sword" of inquiry is sharp. But more importantly, the "powerful man" is vulnerable and, having no cornerstone of truth, his defenses are weak.

Saying 99

> **(99) The disciples said to him, "Your brothers and your mother are standing outside."**
> **He replied to them, "Those here who do the will of my Father are my brothers and my mother. It is they who will enter the Kingdom of my Father."**

The disciples tell Jesus that his brothers and his mother are standing outside. In contrast to the biblical versions of this saying (Matthew 12:46-50; Mark 3:31-35; Luke 8:19-21), his family does not ask for admittance. It might be assumed that they are asking for admittance, but it is not stated. No one is actually turned away. No one is rejected, since no one is yet asking for admittance. Contrary to how it appears, this dialogue is not about rejection. It is about the primacy of oneness in contrast to the conditional quality of earthbound loyalties.

We know from studying his other sayings that the Jesus of this gospel was a master of the metaphor. Thus, what appears to be a straightforward story is often more than that, an invitation to make sense of a strange relationship or absurd situation. In this saying, the relationship of Jesus to his family is curious. We know from saying 25 that he advocates the love of "brothers." He says that you should love your brother like "your soul." By "brother," he apparently includes all men and women in the generic sense, related by kinship or not. Additionally, we know from saying 71 that he is not a "divider." He teaches inclusion. He professes that oneness is the reality of God's children. Therefore, it appears likely that he is using his family here in 99 as a metaphor for family ties and, by extension, for any claim of loyalty outside the realm of the Kingdom.

We have here an inside and an outside. The inner/outer dichotomy seen in this dialogue is also explored in saying 40. There, the grapevine is "planted outside of the Father, but being unsupported, it will be pulled up by its roots and destroyed." The point of that saying (40) is that, in truth, there is nothing outside the Father. There is only illusion there, and what is illusory is unstable and cannot last. In the present saying, the concept of conditional love in familial relationships is the unsound grapevine. The family of Jesus is used as a metaphor for that concept. As an idea, it is "outside," while the idea of the unconditional love of Jesus and his disciples is inside. And like the grapevine, conditional love will be destroyed, not by violence or external forces but from the mere fact that it is not anchored in the reality of the Kingdom's inclusiveness and wholeness. Thus, being insubstantial, it will fade naturally from the mind.

Although it is not stated, Jesus and his disciples reside in a *house*. Here again is that familiar code word, a metaphor for either a structure made of the Father's love and light or one of empty beliefs. In this case, it stands for the correct perspective required to enter the Kingdom. It is where duality is understood to be a dream, and non-duality the proper home of God's children. Indeed, outside of this house, there is only illusion. There is actually no inside or outside (22). Outside is where the brothers of Jesus and his mother believe themselves to be. Yet, they are mistaken.

So when Jesus says that "those here who do the will of my Father are my brothers and mother," it is another way of saying that his loyalty is always to the truth and to unconditional love. Outside of the inclusive love of all of God's children, family loyalty means nothing. His family is the entirety of the Kingdom. It is the whole of creation, not just a part of it. Although appearing to exclude his family, he does not because, outside the Kingdom, there is nothing. Outside of truth, there is only illusion. For this reason, all of God's children are wholly equal and worthy of love.

When man accepts God's will, he will see that the happiness of his brother, defined as every man and woman, is essential to his own happiness. He will guard him like the pupil of his eye (25). This is what "do the will of my father" means. It means to accept this wholeness. It is not exclusive love that Jesus is promoting but inclusive love. When man accepts God's will, he will then enter the Kingdom and know with certainty that he is one with all of creation.

Saying 100

> **(100) They showed Jesus a gold coin and said to him, "Caesar's men demand taxes from us."**
> **He said to them, "Give to Caesar the things that are Caesar's, give to God the things that are God's, and give to me that which is mine."**

Consider the elements of this story. There are important differences between this Thomas version and the versions in Matthew (22:15-22), Mark (12:13-17), and Luke (20:22-26). In this Thomas rendition, the coin is a "gold coin," an *aureus*, and it is shown to Jesus by unnamed individuals. In the synoptic gospels, the coin is a silver *denarius* with a value of one twenty-fifth that of the aureus. In the synoptic versions, Jesus asks the men to hand him a coin in order to show them that the image on its face is that of Caesar. In Thomas, no such request is made. In the synoptic gospels, his visitors are comprised of Pharisees and Herodians intent on trapping Jesus into making statements that implicate him in some offense. In Thomas, there is no hint of this.

To understand this saying, it must be read as it is and not be confused with its synoptic variants. Those stories have Jesus outwitting his hostile opponents who are intent on arresting him for making reckless comments. In this story, his visitors are waving a gold coin in front of his face. They appear upset. Jesus does not ask for the coin to make a point; it is those who have the coin who make the point. The point is that they are losing a lot of money every year to Rome. The high value of the coin represents their high tax burden, their resentment of Roman oppression, and, perhaps more significantly, the value they place on the material world. Consequently, this confrontational act appears to challenge Jesus on the issue of what has value and what does not, or in the context of his sayings, what is real and what is not. It is as if they were saying, "Look, this is real. This is not an illusion. If we do not pay this amount in taxes, we will be in very real trouble."

The answer Jesus gives these men does not directly challenge their erroneous thinking. They are too fearful for that. They would probably not accept the truth. The truth as Jesus understands it, as reflected in his sayings, is that no one owns anything that is separate from God. That is because nothing exists outside of God's Kingdom (sayings 40 and 56). Nothing, in fact, belongs to Caesar that is separate from God. So when Jesus says, "Give to Caesar the things that are Caesar's, give to God the things that are God's," what he is actually urging these men to do is to give nothing to nothing and all to all. This does not mean that they should not pay their taxes. It means that, in the larger view of life, it does not matter. Paying taxes is a part of living in the world. On the level of the world, it is necessary. It buys time while the real work of finding true freedom goes on. It is judicious temporarily but nothing more. The truth remains that attention paid to the world is attention paid to a dream. It is nothing. The primary focus should rest on the Kingdom.

Despite the circumstances, the truth must always be honored and kept in mind. In this saying, Jesus refuses to compromise the truth. It is wisely cloaked, however, in a clever phrase that appears to argue for compromise. The men with the coin would probably not understand the subtlety of his answer, but on reflection they might later. His closest disciples likely would, knowing the way he thinks.

In truth, the core of his teaching is always on the level of awareness, not behavior. In a sense, what the men do is irrelevant. What is important is the understanding that, essentially, man has only one problem—the problem of separation—and one solution, which is the abandonment of all beliefs that support that concept. In general, all of his sayings address this problem and promote this answer. All difficulties that man encounters arise because of this one unanswered problem of separation. Everything belongs to God, and since man is not separate from God, everything belongs to him as well. It is the Kingdom of the Father that all life shares, and beyond this one central fact, nothing else matters.

Many scholars maintain that the final phrase, "and give to me that which is mine," is a later accretion to the original saying. It seems to unnecessarily muddle a tight and crisp comparison of what belongs to God and what belongs to the world. But also, it has Jesus insisting that something belongs to him alone, something that belongs to neither Caesar nor to God. This admission that he is separate from God as well as from the world is, of course, inconsistent with the other sayings of this gospel. Again, I suspect that this additional phrase was fabricated by a scribe who sought to elevate the status of Jesus while woefully misunderstanding his essential message.

Saying 101

> **(101) <Jesus said,> "Whoever does not hate his father and his mother in my way cannot become a disciple to me. And whoever does [not] love his [Father] and his Mother in my way cannot become a disciple to me. For my mother [bore me], but [my] true [Mother] gave me life."**

The first line of this saying is nearly identical to the first line of saying 55 but with the additional phrase, "in my way." In my commentary on that earlier saying, I made the point that this declaration of hatred should not be understood as a rejection of certain individuals, whether parents or siblings, but rather as the complete rejection of the *concept* of conditional love. It is this concept that should be renounced, not the people themselves. Unconditional love presupposes that all people, without exception, are worthy of love. Love is the pull of oneness, and oneness, as implied in this gospel, is God's creation; separation is not. That premise requires that there be no separate selves. For this reason, any inclination to see anyone as less than worthy of God's complete and unqualified love is not only an attack on that one, it is an attack on all. That is why the Jesus of Thomas would not advocate hating anyone. He would certainly not deny the mutual love between parent and child and wish to isolate one from the other. Having said this, the question remains, why does Jesus appear to support the concept of family loyalty (conditional love) in the second sentence of this saying while disapproving of it in the first?

He does not. The paradox between these two statements is striking, yet, the confusion is resolved in the follow-up explanation. That explanation distinguishes between one's biological mother and one's "true" Mother or spiritual Mother. Part of this final line, referring to one's biological mother, is missing due to a lacuna in the text. Consequently, the identification of these missing words has been debated by translators for years. Thomas Paterson Brown proposed perhaps the most credible solution. Based on the available letter space in this gap and the final two extant letters, Brown suggested that the best literal reconstruction should be "my mother for did she [bear my body forth]," the missing words being "bear my body forth."[1] So in plain English, the final line would read: "For my mother *bore me*, but my true Mother gave me life."

The mother who "bore" Jesus would, of course, be his biological mother, while his "true" Mother, who gave him life, would be his Father/Mother God, his creator and Source. The reference to God as a feminine figure should not be a problem. One must remember that in saying 22, a condition of the Kingdom is the rejection of such dichotomies as male and female. The author of these sayings would, therefore, have no hesitation in referring to God as his Mother if it serves the rhetorical function of the saying.

Here in 101, Jesus does not condemn parents. Nor does he teach hatred for mothers who bear their children in innocence and love. He condemns no one but promotes the love of the Father/Mother creator over the exclusive and conditional love of human parents. In saying 15, he explains how all of God's children can be loved unconditionally—that is, by acknowledging their divinity as God's children. In that saying, Jesus offers this remedy:

> "When you see one who was not born of woman, prostrate yourselves on your faces and worship him. That one is your Father."

The truth is that none of God's children are "born of woman." Only within the dream of separation do they seem to be. God's creation is forever one in wholeness with its creator. In this sense, no one is special; no one is loved above anyone else. When Jesus withholds his approval of worldly ties and loyalties, it is only because such ties deny the unconditional oneness of God and all that extends from God. God made man as an extension of Himself. Man's true Self is he who was not "born of woman" but of God. If an individual continues to sleep and dream of separation, he will not know this Father/Mother who gave him life. His understanding of love will be as something that is entirely temporary and conditional. Moreover, he will not understand anything that Jesus says in his public ministry and, for this reason and this reason only, he cannot be "his disciple."

---

1 Thomas Peterson Brown, *Hypertext interlinear of the Gospel according to Thomas*, http://freelyreceive.net/metalogos/files/th_interlin/th101.html.

Saying 102

> **(102) Jesus said, "Woe to the Pharisees, for they are like a dog sleeping in a manger of oxen, for he neither eats nor does he let the oxen eat."**

An ancient Greek fable, attributed to Aesop, reads:

> A dog lay in a manger, and by his growling and snapping, he prevented the oxen from eating the hay which had been placed there for them. "What a selfish dog!" said one of them to his companions; "he cannot eat the hay himself, and yet he refuses to allow those to eat who can."

There are several existing versions of this fable. But what mainly distinguishes them from this Thomas saying is that, in them, the dog is awake. He growls and snaps, whereas in Thomas he sleeps. In Aesop's fable, he is a selfish dog; he is hostile to the oxen and prevents them from eating. In Thomas, his mere sleeping presence is enough to keep the oxen from eating. Therefore, since Jesus compares the sleeping dog to the Pharisees, it is they who metaphorically sleep in this parable. It is the Pharisees whose sleeping, in the practice of their faith, prevents others from consuming or experiencing spiritual nourishment.

In saying 39, the Pharisees and scribes hide the "keys of knowledge." Not only do they not enter the realm of knowledge themselves, but by hiding the keys they prevent others from entering as well. In effect, the same is said of the Pharisees in this saying. The keys of knowledge are like the oxen's fodder or hay. Though not explicitly mentioned, this fodder is a metaphor for spiritual nourishment. The "dog," of course, cannot eat hay, suggesting perhaps that the Pharisees prefer their own refined form of spiritual nourishment. Nevertheless, while in sleep they cannot partake of this either. As for the "oxen," they represent people who presumably are served or protected by the Pharisees. Yet they are so intimidated by these spiritual masters that they, likewise, cannot partake of spiritual nourishment and, consequently, go without.

The word "woe" appears in only one other Thomas saying, 112, where Jesus says, "Woe to the flesh that clings to the soul; woe to the soul that clings to the flesh." In a similar saying, 87, the Greek loanword for "wretched" is used in a related context: "Wretched is the body that depends on a body, and wretched is the soul that is dependent on these two." The implication is that the word "woe" in Thomas suggests a meaning more like "wretched" than "damned." The Pharisees are wretched because, like the dog, they are unaware of the spiritual wealth that remains unconsumed as they sleep. They are doubly wretched because, as they prevent others from partaking of this wealth, they deny themselves the joy of sharing it. Yet, they are not to be damned; they are simply asleep and, therefore, they need only to awaken.

In the New Testament, Jesus condemns the Pharisees in decidedly violent language. In this saying, they are not villainous. They are metaphors for those who sleep, lost in the dream of duality. Moreover, it is only what they represent that he opposes. The Pharisaic way is one of strict laws and precepts in which salvation is promised for good behavior. In other words, salvation is deferred, and between promise and reward comes meticulous sacrifice. His teaching, on the other hand, is that salvation is freely attainable, waiting only for man to fully awaken to it. In this saying, it is metaphorically called "fodder." But call it fodder, grace, or vision; it is man's bread, his connection with God's bounty. Once he becomes aware of this spiritual sustenance, he keeps it, not by saving it for himself but by sharing it with his fellow creatures. In this way, everyone joins in the feast, and the wholeness of creation is celebrated together.

Saying 103

> **(103) Jesus said, "Blessed is the man who knows where (from what district or part) the plunderers are coming, that he may rise and muster his domain (Kingdom) and gird up his loins before they come in."**

This saying has much in common with saying 21b. In that saying, the "thief" is coming with the intention of carrying away goods, just as the "plunderers" in this saying threaten to do the same. In both sayings, preparations are made to deal with the threat. In both, the "owner" or "man" is admonished to "gird his loins." Literally, this means to lift the tunic and tuck it into a belt or girdle below the waist. In other words, it is a preparation for confrontation. In both sayings, something is threatened, whether the "house of his domain" in 21b or the "domain" itself, as here. In the former, the field of action is smaller, a house in which the owner "begins his vigil." Here, the scene expands to that of a "domain" in which the man's forces are mustered.

There is a double meaning to consider in this parable. The Coptic word that is generally translated here as "domain," is the same word translated as "Kingdom" elsewhere in Thomas. Keeping in mind how fundamental the word "Kingdom" is in the overall teachings of Jesus, we can hardly ignore its presence in this saying. Therefore, it is reasonable to assume that, metaphorically, the one who is threatened in this saying is the man who defends the Kingdom of the Father.

Likewise, the phrase that is literally translated as "in which part" is more often rendered as "where." This "where" is not an unreasonable choice, but it overlooks the double meaning of the word for "part." The Greek loanword for "part" may also be translated as "district." A superficial reading of this saying would logically have the plunderers come from a neighboring district. However, when "part" is considered, the same sentence can be understood as an attack by the plunderers who serve what is partial or limited against the man who serves what is whole, which is the Kingdom. Thus, Jesus employs this play on words to suggest a deeper meaning for what might otherwise appear mundane.

In Thomas, of course, the Kingdom of the Father is not a worldly domain. It is a spiritual domain in which man has his being. Within this Kingdom, there is only wholeness; there is no "part" of anything. This is the realm to which the man in this parable is loyal. Therefore, this seeming story of an external event is really an allegory of an internal event that pits the forces of the ego against the man who defends the Kingdom. Once again, the story takes place entirely within the mind.

The forces of the ego are referred to as "plunderers." These may be understood as fear and guilt, the principal weapons the ego uses to block the awareness of God's love. The ego is not a thing or a being; it is a structure of beliefs that support the false idea of separation. A part of man's mind has accepted these beliefs as true, and it is this part that is called the ego-mind. Without the support and power of the ego-mind, the ego structure of beliefs would collapse. But until that happens, the mind of man is split between two thought structures or identities. One is the part of the mind that takes separation seriously; the other is the seeker and defender of the truth. He is represented as the "man" in this saying, as well as in saying 7, and the "owner" in 21b. Both sides in this split of identities draw their power from the mind. If the whole mind decided to identify completely with the Kingdom, the ego would be drained of all power and cease to exist.

In Thomas, all threats are internal threats, generated internally. From the non-dualistic point of view, the ego is always the only threat that man faces. All else, all seemingly external threats, are projections of a fearful mind and thus illusory. Even the ego is illusory, as it was not created by God but fashioned by man as an impediment to God's love. In this saying, the man is blessed because he is vigilant and aware of the danger posed by his internal plunderers. He also knows where—in what part of his mind—these egoic thoughts will enter his consciousness. He "rises," which suggests that he awakens as if from sleep, and musters his domain or Kingdom. In other words, he awakens to the awareness that his real strength comes from God, and it is this power with which he arms himself. He girds his loins with this power, and stands with truth against illusion. His weapons, however, are not the weapons of war but of peace. It is the confluence of truth, peace, and love that undermines the ego and demonstrates its emptiness and absurdity.

Saying 104

> **(104) They said to [Jesus], "Come let us pray today, and fast." Jesus said, "What is the sin that I have committed, or in what way have I been won over? But when the bridegroom leaves the bridal chamber, then let them (him) fast and pray."**

Unnamed companions ask Jesus to join them in prayer and fasting. We know from saying 14 that he sees no value in either practice, at least in the narrow sense of supplication and sacrifice. Accordingly, he asks, "What is the sin that I have committed?" His question implies that he sees himself as wholly innocent, and that an innocent man has no need to pray or fast. Indeed, it may be said that from the viewpoint of non-duality, God created man as an extension of Himself, and like Himself, he is wholly innocent and incapable of committing sin. It follows then, that man does not need God's forgiveness any more than God needs man's forgiveness. Sin is a meaningful concept only for those who believe that man is separate from God and deserving of His wrath. Neither proposition is supported by the Jesus of this gospel. Thus, Jesus has no need for exercises in supplication or sacrifice to restore his pristine relationship with God. That relationship is fixed forever in innocence and love.

Jesus then asks, "In what way have I been won over?" I employ here the phrase "won over," instead of the more common translations of being "overcome" or "defeated." In the context of this saying, it is his core teachings and convictions that are being challenged. In what way, he asks, has his core teaching changed or been won over? In effect, he is saying that his companions must not know him very well if they would suggest he join them in the pointless exercise of atoning for sin.

In the next line, Jesus illustrates metaphorically why prayer and fasting are unnecessary. The "bridal chamber" is a metaphor for the Kingdom. It represents a kind of consummation of wills where man unites in love with his Source. This is not a special or restricted place; it is found wherever man is willing, if only for a moment, to abandon his worldly idols and limitations and experience the union of man with God. When any of God's children are ready to forgive themselves for their imaginary "sin" of separation from His love, then they will rest in the discovery that God is joined with them and always has been. If, however, they should insist that prayer and fasting are requirements for the forgiveness of sin, then in that conviction, God's Kingdom becomes an impossible dream. In truth, the Kingdom is man's home, a home he never left. He can ask for guidance to realize it, but in fact, he already has it and is it. To enter the bridal chamber of the Kingdom is to realize one's natural state.

The final line uses the word "them" to inexplicably refer to unnamed others who will "fast and pray." I take this to be a scribal error, or possibly an attempt to make Jesus the sole "bridegroom," elevating him above all others. However, the sense of this sentence is more evident when "them" is replaced by "him." The bridegroom is then correctly understood as anyone who is free to claim the bridal chamber as his rightful home or, conversely, anyone so foolish as to leave it and engage in practices that deny his Father's love.

The "bridegroom" is not Jesus in isolation. The bridegroom is anyone, including Jesus, who is willing to abandon what has no value in exchange for everything. The saying states, "But when the bridegroom leaves the bridal chamber, then let (him) fast and pray." Why would anyone want to abandon what is everything to pray and fast for nothing? Indeed, he would not, and that is the point. For Jesus, this would be unthinkable. If someone else wants to do the unthinkable, he says, then let him "fast and pray."

Saying 105

> **(105) Jesus said, "He who knows (not) the Father and the Mother will be called the son of a harlot."**

The subject of family arises frequently in Thomas. The relationship of man to God is likened to that of a son to his father. In this capacity, the word "Father" appears in 20 sayings. Saying 101 reads, "my mother bore me, but my true Mother gave me life." Whether the divine is called a Father or a Mother, it is clear that Jesus teaches in this gospel that man's ultimate loyalty belongs to the divine parent, not to the human parent. The divine procreator is the "true" procreator, the real Source of life. The divine parent resides in the realm of God's Kingdom, while the body and, by implication, the relationship of bodies to other bodies, lies within the realm of the ego's kingdom, the illusory world.

The phrase "knows the Father and the Mother" is found nowhere else in this gospel. In 69, "know the Father" clearly refers to God, whereas only here in 105 do we find "know the Mother" or even "the Mother." It appears clear that this phrase must be referring to the Father/Mother God as mentioned in 101, rather than to human parents. Why Father/Mother? In the context of this saying, a non-dualistic equivalent to earthly parents was needed. It expresses the idea that God is neither male nor female, having no separation within His being, but encompassing all expressions of love.

Also in this gospel, the word "know," when followed immediately by the object of knowing, always suggests a profound revelation that leads to something good or worthwhile. For example, such rewards are experienced in not tasting death in saying 18, in being blessed in 69, and in being superior to the world in 56 and 80. The problem with this saying, as it is presented here, is that knowing the divine Father/Mother results not in something positive but in something negative. Here, the one who "knows" will be called the "son of a harlot." This does not fit the pattern found elsewhere in Thomas, therefore, an explanation is required.

Various theories have been advanced. The most common one is that "son of a harlot" refers to the illegitimacy of Jesus himself. The third-century theologian Origen reported on a tradition that Jesus was the illegitimate child of Mary and a Roman soldier named Panthera.[1] However, as tempting as it is to read into this saying an allusion to the man himself, there is no compelling reason to do so. It appears more likely that the phrase "son of a harlot" was not meant as a reference to him but used metaphorically in a gospel that is conspicuously metaphorical.

In their book *The Fifth Gospel*, Stephen J. Patterson and James M. Robinson suggest another possibility. In a footnote on this saying, they say, "As the text has been transmitted, an original negation may have been left out, so that we can understand the text as follows: "Whoever will not know father and mother…”[2] If we accept this possibility, a negative cause results in a negative effect. One who does not know the Father/Mother God will be called the “son of a harlot,” a metaphor for illegitimacy. One who does not know his true Source will, as a result, experience feelings of abandonment and illegitimacy. God will not reject this one; it is this one who will reject God.

In the first century, babies of prostitutes (harlots) were often killed at birth and their bodies callously discarded. In fact, throughout the Roman world, infanticide was not an uncommon solution for the problem of unwanted babies. This saying (105) compares the fate of those unfortunate children to the fate of one who rejects his divine Source. The one who knows his true Father/Mother knows the fullness of life in the Kingdom. He who does not know this fullness, who looks to the world for completion, will inevitably suffer the consequences. Though completely innocent, like a newborn baby, he will nevertheless experience spiritual illegitimacy.

---

1 Origen, “Contra Celsum,” *New Advent*, Book I, Chapter 32, http://www.newadvent.org/fathers/0416.htm.

2 Stephen J. Patterson and James M. Robinson, *The Fifth Gospel, The Gospel of Thomas Comes of Age* (Harrisburg, PA: Trinity Press, 1998), 30.

Saying 106

> **(106) Jesus said, “When you make the two one, you will become sons of man, and when you say to the mountain, ‘Move away,’ it will move away.”**
>
> **(106) *Jesus said, “When you make the two one, you will become Sons of God, and when you say to the mountain, ‘Move away,’ it will move away.” (My restored version)***

The theme of oneness runs throughout this gospel in various expressions, including this one of making “the two one.” If we look back to saying 22b, the same phrase can be found there but explained by several examples. Among them is this passage:

> "And when you make the male and the female one and the same, so that the male not be male nor the female female..."

Commentators have called this the integration of opposites and, to define it more precisely, have used such words as "merging," "subsuming," and "reconciliation." However, I contend that none of these words go far enough to convey the idea here. If we take another example mentioned in saying 22, the inside/outside dichotomy, and extend it in the same way that the male/female illustration was extended, we have:

> "And when you make the inside like the outside and the outside like the inside, (so that the inside not be inside nor the outside outside)..."

There is no credible reason to assume here that what is true for one dichotomy should not be true for all of them. If we apply this same extension to all the other examples mentioned in 22, we can observe that this oneness is not integration. It is not the merging of one thing with another so that elements of each can be found in the other. It is the utter abandonment of duality itself. To "make" this happen is to see beyond the limits of duality with the mind's eye to the oneness of the Kingdom. It is to appreciate the simple and beautiful wholeness of everything by acknowledging the meaninglessness of a dualistic world. In the words of saying 18, it is to "take (one's) place in the beginning" before an entirely different view of reality was conceived. In this view, polarities and differences of all sorts were conjured up in the mind to support its belief in separation. The world, in fact, was made this way, not as an actuality but in a dream, as an enormously complex set of images, all projected onto the screen of consciousness. In short, what we call the world was not created in any true sense but "made" or fabricated in the mind. Yet, what can be made in this way can be unmade, not by destruction but by waking up to the truth that the images on the screen are not real.

In this saying, we have the same idea of the "two" restored to "one." Only now, as a result of discovering that oneness, man discovers its power. In 22, Jesus says that by making the two one, man can enter the Kingdom. By entering the Kingdom of the Father, one realizes that all of creation is spirit and that outside of this spiritual realm there is nothing (40). From the tiniest particle to the largest celestial event, there is nothing that separates man from his creator. There is only the illusion of space, time, and, of course, mountains, the "mountain" being a metaphor for any limit that delays man's coming home to oneness. Moving such a mountain would be a miracle, but the real miracle is man's awakening to what is real. It is this that will demonstrate to him that he is the true Self, the Son of God.

I have restored the phrase "Sons of God" to this saying to take the place of "sons of man." I do this for several reasons. First, the designation of "sons of man" in this saying makes no sense. Literally, it means "sons of Adam," and in the Old Testament it refers merely to human beings. In the New Testament, Jesus appears to support his identity as the Messiah when he accepts this label for himself. The question is, however, did Jesus really see himself this way, or did the evangelists place this phrase in his mouth to connect him with the prophecy in Daniel (7:13-14)? That prophecy refers to a future leader as "one like a son of man." (See my commentary on saying 86 for a more thorough explanation of this connection.) In this saying (106), however, we have no evidence that by merely being a human being, even an exalted human being—a messiah—can someone move mountains. Some commentators have suggested that becoming a "son of man" implies that such a person becomes more *truly human*. However, not only does this identification appear inadequate to move mountains, whether metaphorical or not, it conflicts with the use of the phrase in 86, where the "son of man has no place to lay his head and rest."

Here in 106, an ancient scribe might well have considered "Sons of God" to be an unacceptable description of ordinary mortals. Such a lofty identification of anyone, other than Jesus, would have likely seemed not only mistaken but scandalous. So, he changed the phrase to "sons of man." By doing so, however, he made an extraordinary claim for one who simply realizes his humanity.

It appears unlikely that Jesus ever referred to himself as the "son of man" in the messianic sense. The Jesus of this gospel does not do so. He defines that phrase quite differently. In 86, the "son of man" is not a specific man but any man who chooses to identify with his body. He is any man who sees himself as a limited individual, a son of Adam. Consequently, he finds no rest in this identity. However, there is another option. In sayings 2 and 3b, the one who seeks makes the astonishing discovery of his identity as a child of God. In those two sayings he finds "rest" as he could never do as a "son of man." As a "son of man" he denies his connection with the Father, which may be compared to self-imposed exile. And while the "foxes" and "birds" of 86 have their places of rest, he has none. In saying 3b, this choice to identify with the body results in spiritual poverty. On the other hand, if such a man chooses to identify with his true spiritual nature, as a child of the living Father, the result is spiritual wealth.

In this gospel, "son of the living one" (37), a synonym for Son of God, is not a special title but an assertion that follows from the conviction that man is not many but one. He is the one I have called in this book the "true Self." He is God's one creation, and that oneness not only includes all of life but God Himself. Creation does not have a beginning or an end. Strictly speaking, creation is extension, so that in the triumph of love, nothing is separate. There is no place where God ends and man begins. Man is the Son of God, but in the spiritual sense. In this non-dualistic gospel, man is the extension of perfection. He is not in any sense the son of man. He is not a mere body made from other bodies. He is free of all limitations, and the Kingdom is his home. Outside of this divine realm, he is merely a dream figure submerged in his own dream.

Saying 107

> **(107) Jesus said, "The kingdom is like a shepherd who had a hundred sheep. One of them, the largest (greatest) went astray. He left the ninety-nine sheep and sought after the one until he found it. After he had toiled, he said to the sheep, 'I love (want) you more than the ninety-nine.'"**

The similar, though not identical, versions of this story in Matthew (18:12-14) and Luke (15:4-7), have been firmly anchored in the Christian psyche for centuries. In the Luke version, the lost sheep is compared to a sinner who repents of his sins. The shepherd tells his friends later that "likewise, there will be more joy in heaven over one sinner who repents than over ninety-nine righteous persons who do not need to repent." Over time, that image of the shepherd, representing Jesus, who loves the one sheep out of a hundred, has been conflated with the image of the "good shepherd" who lays down his life for his sheep in John (10:11-16). Neither passage refers to the other, yet for many Christians, both seem powerfully linked to each other. In fact, this combined image has become so iconic and proverbial that any alternate understanding of this parable's meaning might seem bizarre or even outrageous. Nevertheless, we must look at this parable in Thomas as if we had never encountered it before, as if we had never before heard the story of the good shepherd and the repentant sinner.

As I have asserted before, this story may be compared to the parables of the wise fisherman (saying 8) and the merchant and the pearl (76). In both, the "one" is preferred over the many. In the former, the large fish is kept while the many small fish are thrown back into the sea. In the latter, we are told that the merchant is "shrewd." He returns the merchandise and buys the pearl for himself. Anyone possessing even a modicum of sense would say that this merchant is not shrewd, he is insane. Indeed, the fisherman seems odd as well, in throwing his huge catch of valuable fish overboard while keeping a large, unmarketable fish for himself. In this parable of the lost sheep, the shepherd does something that no sane shepherd would ever do: he abandons his ninety-nine sheep for the one. Then, he tells the one sheep that he loves or wants him more than all the others. All of these men appear to be detached from reality. That is to say, they appear to be detached from the so-called reality of the world. But here is the paradox: if we understand these parables as metaphorically illustrating the truth of the Kingdom, these men can then be seen as being quite wise and indeed shrewd.

This parable says that there are one hundred sheep. This is a very large number of sheep for one shepherd to look after. There is no mention of sheepdogs or other shepherds. This use of hyperbole prepares the reader to temporarily set aside his conventional view of reality and open his mind to alternate possibilities. The one sheep is said to be the "largest," yet the Coptic word for this is more accurately translated as the "greatest." The suggestion is that, in some sense, this sheep is seen as *greater* than any of the ninety-nine. The shepherd toils in his effort to find the sheep. When he does, he tells it that he *loves* it more than all the other sheep. Again, it is instructive to inquire how a Coptic word is used elsewhere in Thomas. In 109, the same word used here for "love" or "care" is generally translated as "wish" or "want." But here, most translators prefer "love' or "care"—perhaps because it supports the "good shepherd" idea in John (10:11-16). However, when "want" is used, the appropriateness of this word, as explained below, is more clearly understood.

Again, there is a definite pattern in Thomas regarding "the one." We find it repeatedly mentioned in this gospel. The "Kingdom" is a realm of unconditional oneness. In the previous saying (106), the power to move "mountains" results from making the "two one." In 75, it is the "whole one" who enters the bridal chamber. In 113, this Kingdom is "spread out upon the earth, and men do not see it." In other words, it is anywhere that men and women are willing to open their minds to it. In this saying, the one greater sheep is a metaphor for oneness. The shepherd wisely seeks this oneness, which, as the sheep had strayed from the flock, this awareness had strayed from his mind. In seeking the sheep, he makes a choice. This is what he "wants," not the ninety-nine, a metaphor for the world. It is not a matter of loving one sheep over the many sheep, but of choosing to identify with either the oneness of spirit or the world of separation. He chooses the one and abandons the many.

In Luke, the sheep is a metaphor for a sinner. The shepherd loves his sheep because it is lost and willing to repent of its sins. In Thomas, the shepherd is not necessarily Jesus but anyone who wants only the oneness of the Kingdom, represented by the one great sheep. He chooses oneness because oneness is his nature. In Luke, the sinner's offence is an attack on God and ultimately, only God can forgive him of this sin. In Thomas, "sin" is merely an impediment to spiritual vision in the same way that in saying 26, the beam is an impediment to inner vision. In the Bible, sin is a concept that stems from the belief that God's love is conditional. However, in Thomas, man's true home is a realm of unconditional love. It is in that realm where nothing, neither sin nor any other concept, can separate man from man or man from God.

Saying 108

> **(108) Jesus said, "Whoever drinks from my mouth will become like me. I myself will become he, and that which is hidden will be revealed to him."**

This saying reminds me of the lovely lines of "Checkmate," the poem by Jalal-al-Din Rumi, the 13th-century Sufi poet and mystic:

> "Borrow the beloved's eyes. Look through them and you'll see the beloved's face everywhere."[1]

To drink from the mouth of Jesus is essentially the same as to think with his mind and see with his eyes. It is not the same as listening passively to what he says. It is to align completely with his vision. Because Jesus is represented here as someone spiritually enlightened, drinking from his mouth is indeed equivalent to seeing through the eyes of God and consequently seeing the face of God in everything.

Here again is the theme of making the two one. Whoever drinks from the mouth of Jesus will become like him. Jesus will then become he, and by implication, Jesus will no longer be Jesus, but one not limited to Jesus. Whoever joins with Jesus, likewise, must abandon his own identity, so that neither he nor Jesus remains as a separate self. Such spiritual joining is not like physical joining in which elements of each continue to exist. In spiritual joining, nothing of the former self remains. And, if only for a brief moment, that self disappears and the Self is experienced. The Self is the true Self, the created Son of God, the wholeness of creation. This same idea can be seen in saying 19:

> Jesus said, "Blessed is he who came to be before he came to be. If you become my disciples and listen to my words, these stones will serve you."

To come into being before coming into being is to find the Self, the pristine oneness of creation that existed before time and which will never die. From this Self, man dreamed a dream of becoming something else, a separate self in a separate world. But with the help of Jesus, he can awaken to his true nature, as Jesus did. To become his disciple and surrender to his vision is to drink from his mouth and fully realize the oneness of his being. In that state of awareness, man rules over the all (2), and even the stones of the world, being illusions, will serve his will (19). Likewise, "that which is hidden"—that is to say, the immensity of God's love—"will be revealed to him." Only when the two become one can this revelation be experienced because oneness is a condition of the Kingdom.

---

1 Jalal-al-Din Rumi, *The Essential Rumi, New Expanded Edition*. Translation by Coleman Barks with Reynold Nicholson, A.J. Arberry, and John Moyne (New York: Harper Collins, 1995).

Saying 109

> **(109) Jesus said, "The kingdom is like a man who had a hidden treasure in his field of which he was unaware. And [after] he died, he left it to his [son]. The son, (as well) did not know (about the treasure). He took the field and sold it. And the man who bought it went plowing and found the treasure. He began to lend money at interest to whomever he wished."**

Here again, we have something "hidden" which is quite valuable. (See sayings 39 and 96.) It is hidden in a field, and the man who owns the field is unaware of it. Likewise, his son knows nothing of it either. There is no mention of these men working the field. The son, in fact, appears to sell the field as soon as he inherits it. By implication, the third man to own the field is the first of these three to plow it. So, by working the soil, the treasure is found. Notice here again, that some effort is required before it is discovered. As the shepherd in saying 107 "had toiled" in his search for the sheep, so too does this man work his field. This appears to say that some effort or dedication is required to discover what is most valuable.

The "field" is a metaphor for the mind. The "treasure" is God's love. It is hidden in the mind, not by God but by man himself. He hides it because he fears it. In fact, it is his greatest fear. He fears it more than death. Finding love would mean the loss of his ego identity, his counterfeit identity that God's love would threaten. Ironically, he fears what he needs the most to permanently banish all his excuses for fearing anything.

The first owners of the field represent those who believe that the answers to life's questions are found in the world, external to themselves. That is where their eyes are focused. Yet, what they look for is already theirs. The third man does not hesitate; he plows. He likewise has no idea of the wealth he owns, but he plows. And by laboring where the treasure is, he finds it. Such a treasure could never be anticipated by the ego-mind. This is because the ego insists on looking for value in the world, where there is no value. The third man represents the seeker of wisdom who dedicatedly probes his consciousness for meaning. Like the seeker of saying 2, he is astonished by what he finds. His ego-mind would never have anticipated such a find. It is the awareness of God's love for His Son. This is the ultimate treasure. Nothing outside of it means anything, and in truth, nothing outside of it is real.

The final line of this saying reads, "He began to lend money at interest to whomever he wished." This represents the idea that the treasure found hidden within the mind is not static but has, like the mustard seed of saying 20, enormous potential. Because it is love, it grows in the mind of the one who extends it to others. This is why it expands like interest expands. Some commentators have cited saying 95 as evidence that Jesus disapproved of this lending practice, and, therefore, this man should be seen as evil. However, the fact that lending at interest was not sanctioned by Jesus should not preclude him from using it as a metaphor. The man is not evil, and the Jesus of this gospel is not a moralizer. His focus is on seeking first the Kingdom, not on promulgating rules and standards of behavior. This final line demonstrates metaphorically how immeasurably profitable is the treasure of God's love and what spiritual wealth it brings to the one who labors for the Kingdom.

Saying 110

> **(110) Jesus said, "Whoever has found the world and become rich, let him deny the world."**

The key phrase in this saying is "Whoever has found the world." The word "world" in combination with "find" or "know" is encountered in only three Thomas sayings, 56, 80, and 110. Of these, the first two use the word "know" regarding the world, whereas in this saying "found" is preferred. Both words appear to convey a similar meaning, if not exactly the same. Consider the two other sayings:

> (56) Jesus said, "Whoever has known the world has found a corpse, and whoever has found (this) corpse, of him the world is not worthy."

> (80) Jesus said, "Whoever has known the world has found the body, but whoever has found the body, of him the world is not worthy."

In all three, there is the sense that what is found or known is the world as it really is, not as it seems to be. In all three, there is a revelation followed by or accompanied by a radical change in one's relationship with the world. In fact, there is a distinct pattern in Thomas that whenever anything is "known" or "found," there is a by-product, a revelation or major shift in perception. Another example comes in the next saying (111b): "Whoever has found himself, of him the world is not worthy." This time, what is found or known is not the world but oneself. For a person to find himself, like finding the world, is to know himself as he really is, not as he seems to be. Man *appears* to be a creature of the world and, rather convincingly, a victim of the world. Yet, as I shall argue in that saying (111), to find oneself is to find God's Son, the one Self who hides behind the veil of space and time. He shares God's divinity; therefore, "of him the world is not worthy." What he is worthy of is the glory and splendor of the Kingdom. That is his home and his birthright. Knowing the world as it is makes the fulfillment of this birthright possible.

In all four of the sayings mentioned above, the consequence of either "finding" or "knowing" is positive. In 56 and 80, the result of a person discovering the true nature of the world and the body is the realization that the "world is not worthy" of him. He is "superior" to the world. In short, he is superior because, as spirit, he is real and the world is not. In this saying (110), the result of having this same insight about the world results in both wealth and freedom from the world, two apparently compatible outcomes. Some have said that the "wealth" referred to here is worldly wealth and, therefore, not a positive quality. However, to take this position is to completely dismiss the above patterns and similar patterns found throughout Thomas. This wealth is spiritual wealth. The one who discovers the real truth about the world knows that this manifestation of the ego is nothing. His illusions about it are gone. He now realizes that it is a "corpse," something dead and certainly not his Source. He knows what is true and what is false; consequently, he is ready to deny the world entirely. The paradox is that only those who are aware of their spiritual wealth would dare deny the world.

The word "deny" in this saying is appropriate. Most translators have suggested the word "renounce," but in this gospel, the "world" is never simply renounced, it is utterly denied, just as duality is utterly denied in 22. The world is the physical representation of duality, and just as all dualities are meaningless in Thomas, so is the world.

Saying 111

> **(111a) Jesus said, "The heavens and the earth will be rolled up in your presence. And the one who lives from the Living One will not see [nor fear] death."**
> **(111b) Jesus said, "Whoever has found himself, of him the world is not worthy"?**

In Isaiah 34:4, it is written:

> "All the stars of the heaven will be dissolved and the sky rolled up like a scroll; all the starry host will fall like withered leaves from the vine, like shriveled figs from the fig tree."

Here are two passages about the heavens being rolled up like scrolls, one from Isaiah, the other from the Gospel of Thomas. It would have been quite natural for anyone listening to Jesus speak of a rolled-up scroll to be reminded of the Isaiah passage and conclude that both passages were heralding the end of something. In Thomas, what is rolled up is the entire world of form, both the heavens and the earth. The saying then adds that this upheaval will be accomplished in the presence of someone. That someone, therefore, cannot be of form, but spirit. If he were not of spirit, he would be part of that which is rolled up. Thus, here in this saying, Jesus makes the claim that man is not of this world, that he is made not of form but of spirit.

In Isaiah, we have the mixed metaphors of the stars dissolving, while falling like withered leaves, and the sky rolling up like a scroll. In contrast to our Thomas saying, it is an image of violence and destruction. It describes the wrath of God directed at the enemies of Israel. It is preceded in the same verse by such lines as this:

> "The Lord is angry with all nations…their dead bodies will send up a stench; the mountains will be soaked with their blood."

Sometimes referred to as the "Day of the Lord," this passage from Isaiah portrays God as inspiring the forces of Israel to wage war against their external enemies. It represents the settling of old scores by a people fed up and humiliated by centuries of domination. Though written much earlier, this prophecy would have nevertheless been fresh in the minds of first-century Jews suffering under the yoke of Roman occupation. It was no accident, I think, that Jesus chose to contrast Isaiah's horrific conception of violent retribution to his own vision of a peaceful loosening of the world's hold on man's mind.

In this saying, the world is overcome, not by violence but by living from the "Living One," a reference to the Father. The key phrase here is literally translated as, "the one who lives from the One who lives." The first "one" appears to be the one who witnesses the roll-up of the heavens and the earth, the one who will not see death, and also, the one who has found himself. It appears that living from the One who lives makes all these other phenomena possible. The question then is, what does it mean to "live from the One who lives"?

This first "one" appears to have the same relationship with God as the infant in saying 22 has with his nursing mother. The newborn child *lives from* his mother. He is wholly dependent on her, and between the two there is no sense of separation. He has not yet learned to focus his eyes on the world of form. In the same way, adult men and women must be like infants in their relationship with God and "live from the Living One."

For them, it is a decision to abandon the many (the world of duality) and embrace the oneness of God (sayings 8, 22, and 107). It is a realignment with spirit, made within the mind, in which the world of time and space is rolled up like an old script, a script no longer relevant or needed. Like a scroll that tells the story of man's isolation from the Father, it will be set aside. It is a scroll that man composed without consulting his Father, and now, with the Father's help, he is rolling it up. And with it goes the entire world of separation.

With the acceptance of this vision in Thomas, the world of Isaiah's prophecy is gone, and gone also is all sense of loss. Death in all its forms is gone, not only as the natural release of what is unessential but also as the perception of loss associated with the body. Man is not his body. With that realization the fear of death ceases to concern him. God's eternal and uncompromising love is acknowledged, and everything that is not of love is set aside.

The final line appears to be a separate saying amended to the first two lines by a later scribe. Nevertheless, it supports the saying by emphasizing the importance of Self-knowledge. It points out that when man understands who he is, that he is God's child, created as one, not many, he then will know his Father's love in all its fullness. Like one who wakes up from a bad dream, the world will then seem absurd to him, and, consequently, he will dismiss it from his mind forever. Surely, this world of pain and illusions is not worthy of such a one.

Saying 112

> **(112) Jesus said, "Woe to the flesh that clings to the soul; woe to the soul that clings to the flesh."**

The Coptic word that is translated here as "clings" is more often translated as "depends" or "hangs on." In this saying, any of these renditions is acceptable.

Indeed, this same word appears in saying 87 in a similar though slightly different context. In that instance, I prefer "depends." The determiner between shades of meaning is context, and here in 112, the word "clings" has a more active or assertive feel to it than does "depends." Additionally, a representation of being, such as the flesh or the soul, may "cling" in a constructive way or in a destructive way, depending on what clings to what. In contrast, the word "depends" has a more destructive connotation, as one representation that is subordinate to the other. That feature of the word in English may unnecessarily confuse the listener or reader. For that reason, "clings" appears to support more clearly the meaning of the saying.

Consider a man who is fixated on his body. We may compare his mental state to the "soul" that clings to the "flesh," representing the second half of our saying. He is not his body, but he believes he is. As he ages and appears to become ill, his obsession with his body becomes extreme. He tells himself that this flesh is all he is, and if it fails, he fails. If it dies, he dies. And so he clings to it, observing every ache and pain with the utmost concern. As this focus on his body sharpens, his identity as a soul grows dim. A soul, however, is what he truly is. He is a child of God, created perfectly in God's image. Could he but fully align his mind with this perfection, his body, being the outward manifestation of his thoughts, would be free to heal itself naturally. By not clinging to his soul, by clinging instead to his flesh, his soul is neglected. So we say, "Woe to the soul that clings to the flesh." (See sayings 3b and 29.)

If however, this man should change his mind and cling resolutely to what is whole in him, to his quiet center, to his soul, then the idea of a body with all its aches and pains would fade from his mind. It is a matter of focus. In Thomas, what is essential to man's ultimate freedom is his nakedness, his soul stripped of the body's defenses. He has no need of them (21a, 37). Man, as God created him in perfection, is free. There is nothing to hold him back. He is free of the body's problems the instant he firmly clings to his treasure—his soul, his true identity. It must be kept in mind also that this soul is not a separate soul, limited to an individual self. It is the whole Self, God's one Son, the entirety of creation. Outside of this perfection, there is only illusion, only a dream; but woe indeed to this dream when it clings to the truth. So we say, "Woe to the flesh that clings to the soul."

Saying 113

> **(113) His disciples said to him, "On what day will the Kingdom come?" <Jesus said,> "It will not come by watching for it. They will not say, 'Here it is' or 'There it is.' Rather, the Kingdom of the Father is spread out upon the earth, and men do not see it."**

His disciples ask Jesus, "On what day will the Kingdom come?" The assumption behind the question might be that the Kingdom represents an external remedy, a remedy that will somehow change the world for the better. The disciples might even be thinking that a new world order is coming, one in which the followers of Jesus might be rewarded and the world put right. More likely, though, if they had been listening to their teacher, the real question would be this: When will the oneness, of which you speak, be shown to us? Jesus's initial response is, "It will not come by watching for it." The literal translation of this is, "It is not coming in a look outward." The "Kingdom" is coming, but it will not be seen by looking outward, expecting a recognizable event to happen.

The saying continues: "They will not say 'Here it is' or 'There it is.'" The Kingdom cannot be located in space and time because the world of space and time has nothing to do with it. It cannot be seen with the body's eyes; therefore, "Men do not see it," though it is everywhere around them. It can only be experienced by a mind that is free of all attachments to the body and the world. Nevertheless, it is everywhere. That is what is meant by, "It is spread out upon the earth."

The Kingdom of the Father is a realm of spirit. It can only be experienced on that level. However, when the mind is quiet, when it stops reacting to images of fear and guilt, when it observes without judgment, and allows whatever comes to come and go, then, with the blocks gone to its awareness, the Kingdom of the Father can emerge in consciousness.

Consciousness is something that everyone experiences but no one understands. Experts on brain science admit that they have no clear idea what it is or how it works. All of the functions of the mind change, memories fade, sensations change, and what is thought important on one day may be completely dismissed the next. However, what does not change is consciousness. It appears to remain exactly the same from infancy to the death of the body and perhaps beyond. Indeed, some scientists suggest the possibility that consciousness is not a physical phenomenon but one arising from a parallel reality.

What appears to happen when the whole mind becomes conscious of the Kingdom is a profound upheaval (111). It permeates everything, and everything reflects its glory. It adds nothing to what is real; it simply reveals the incomparable wonder of what is happening (5). Jesus reveals in this saying (113) that it is "spread out upon the earth, and men do not see it." What that means is that the earth, which is not real but a projection of the mind, gives way to a vision of oneness that arises in consciousness. Accompanying that vision is the awareness that there is no distinction between inside and outside; the experience and the witness to that experience are one. Also, this is not an event in time but something that exists in the moment, in the eternal present. Men do not see it because they cannot shake off their blind and intoxicated attachment to the illusion of separation (29). When they wake up to the truth, however, they will be "astonished," and they will "rule" with their Father over everything (2).

Saying 114

> **(114) Simon Peter said to him, "Let Mary go forth from us, for women are not worthy of life."**
> **Jesus said, "Look, I myself will lead her in order to make her male, so that she too might become a living spirit resembling you males. For every woman who makes herself male will enter the Kingdom of Heaven."**

> **(114)** ***Simon Peter said to them, "Let Mary go forth from us, for women are not worthy of life."***
> ***Jesus said, "Look, I myself will lead her in order to make her male, so that she too might become a living spirit resembling you males. For every woman who makes herself male will enter the Kingdom of Heaven, and every male who makes himself female will see the Father." (My restored version)***

Some readers will no doubt object to my restoration of this saying, as seen above. Admittedly, there appears to be no evidence, external to this gospel, to justify this suggestion of an original, but lost, final clause. That clause reads, "And every male who makes himself female will see the Father." Yet, as we now have it, the dialogue in this saying is so extreme in multiple ways that it seems to beg for a concluding statement that would bring it back within the wisdom parameters of Thomas. Without it, this saying depicts an attack on women by Simon Peter that is wholly inconsistent with this gospel. Not only is his comment about Mary hateful and discriminatory, but Jesus himself seems to share his general assumptions. His reply suggests that women are inherently unequal to men, as they alone require guidance to become "living spirits" resembling males. The saying, as we have it, does two things. It inadequately responds to the brutal dismissal of Mary and women in general. Secondly, it proposes the idea that the Kingdom of Heaven is a male enclave, requiring for admittance certain unidentified male characteristics.

Clearly, the culture of that time was patriarchal. The perception that males and females had vastly different attributes was widely accepted. In his book *The Gospel of Thomas, The Hidden Sayings of Jesus*, Marvin Meyer makes this point about female-to-male transformations in ancient literature:

> Often the transformation of the female into the male involves the transformation of all that is earthly, perishable, passive, and sense-perceptible into what is heavenly, imperishable, active, and rational. In short, what is connected with the earth Mother is to be transformed into what is connected with the sky Father.[1]

Clearly there was a cultural penchant for such beliefs that saw women as less rational and therefore less capable of spiritual insights. The comment by Simon Peter, whether characteristic of the man himself or placed in his mouth for thematic purposes, fiercely reflects that bias. As for Jesus, it should be kept in mind that the central figure in this gospel is an extraordinarily independent thinker. Over and over we encounter him as an iconoclast and revolutionary visionary. In saying 14a he insists, "If you fast, you will give rise to sin for yourselves; and if you pray, you will be condemned; and if you give alms, you will do harm to your spirits." And in 14b Jesus says, "What goes into your mouth will not defile you," an audacious disavowal of the Jewish dietary laws. Such extraordinary dismissals or reinterpretations of what must have been sacred truths to his listeners reveal enormous insight and courage. Consequently, we cannot assume that he would freely align himself with the cruel, male-dominated attitudes of his day.

Moreover, as it stands, this saying contradicts Jesus's earlier denial of male/female duality in saying 22. In that key logion, one cannot enter the Kingdom unless "you make the male and the female one and the same," so that each loses its particular identity completely. That is not the same as saying that only females should shed their separate identities. It works both ways, equally for males and females. The message of 22 is not about exalting one gender over the other but of seeing such distinctions as meaningless. It is to abandon completely the belief that male and female are in any way separate in the eyes of God and, therefore, in the reality of the Kingdom.

Often overlooked in this saying is the phrase "living spirit," used by Jesus to describe the essential, non-physical identity of the males, while hinting that females might be made living spirits as well. This choice of words would seem misplaced in this connection if indeed he took the notion of separate and distinct bodies seriously. In fact, "living spirit" would seem to be the identity he claims for those who are, in essence, one and undivided. What is going on here? It is characteristic of Jesus in these sayings to invite the disciples to think he is leading them in one direction while slamming the door on their expectations in a final provocative line (16, 23, 37, and 101). But even within this ploy, he shrewdly plants the idea of an all-encompassing "living spirit" as a clue as to where he is leading them.

With my suggestion of a restored final clause, not only is Simon Peter's misogyny rejected, but the non-dualistic philosophy of Jesus is affirmed. The point of saying 22 is brought forward and dramatically applied. Some commentators have suggested that by making the female male, Jesus is suggesting some form of symbolic gender androgyny, but this is inconsistent with this gospel. Moreover, the phrase "living spirit" does not refer to someone having both male and female characteristics any more than does 22 refer to the blending of "outside" and "inside." All such dualities, as understood by the Jesus of this gospel, are equally meaningless.

In the "Kingdom" there is no inside and outside, nor is there male and female. Therefore, the suggestion by Jesus that he will make Mary a male is, in fact, a scheme intended to set up his disciples for a decisive puncture of their egocentric thinking. The statement that "every woman who will make herself male will enter the Kingdom of Heaven" is cleverly counterbalanced and given new meaning by the proposed clause that "every man who will make himself female will see the Father." The phrase "see the Father" was borrowed from saying 27, where finding the Kingdom is equated with seeing the Father. The stunning clash of these two statements is designed to remind the disciples of saying 22 and bring to mind again the central point of his message. That point is that only by making the "two one," by completely embracing the oneness of creation, beyond any idea of separate gender identities, will his disciples enter the Kingdom of the Father.

If, as I propose, such a cut was made from the original saying, then, one should ask why this happened. The handiwork of this ancient scribe (or scribes) has been seen before. A few examples are 6, 74, 90, and 106. When his superficial reading of a saying found a word or phrase to be contrary to what he considered Jesus-like or appropriate, he would change or discard it. It was subsequently replaced by what he thought was a more fitting word or phrase. Here, the final clause of this saying, that "every man who will make himself female will see the Father," was cut entirely. Unable to understand the implications of this line in relation to saying 22, he presumed it advocated homosexuality or, perhaps, castration. Consequently, this alarmed scribe erased the line completely, leaving us, indeed, with a very curious saying.

Because of the seemingly uncharacteristic and biased nature of this logion in Thomas, and because of the appearance of such bias in later Christian and Gnostic texts, many commentators have submitted that the entire saying was attached to this gospel at a later date and, therefore, not authentic. My response is less radical. I suggest that we save this saying with the recognition of my proposed conclusion. This is quite likely what this author had in mind. Not only does it restore wisdom to the saying in a typically Jesus-like fashion, but it also brings Thomas to a close in a way that is both humorously ingenious and consistent with this gospel as a whole.

---

1 Marvin Meyer, *The Gospel of Thomas, The Hidden Sayings of Jesus* (San Francisco: Harper Collins, 1992), 109.

Glossary

Advaita Vedanta A non-dualistic school of Hindu Vedantic philosophy. It is based on the idea that the true Self is identical to Brahman, the absolute reality. Advaita literally means "not-two."

Aphorism A terse but vigorously expressive statement of a truth or observation.

Clement of Alexandria Circa 150 to 215, Clement was a Christian theologian and Church Father. He was particularly well versed in Greek literature and philosophy.

Codex An ancient, handwritten manuscript in book form. The plural is "codices."

Coptic The final stage of the ancient Egyptian language. It was gradually replaced by Arabic beginning with the Islamic conquest in the seventh century CE and continuing for about a thousand years. Today, only the Bohairic dialect of Coptic is used in the rituals of the Coptic Christian Church. Our copy of the Gospel of Thomas is a translation from either Greek or Syriac into the Sahidic dialect of Coptic.

Demiurge A supernatural being adopted by some Gnostic sects as the fashioner and maintainer of the physical universe.

Dualism The belief that everything is divided into two opposed or contrasted elements. For the purposes of this book, I have included the philosophy of pluralism under the umbrella definition of dualism, as contrasted to acosmic monism or non-dualism.

Ego As used in this book, a set of beliefs that stem from a single belief that man is separate from God and from everything that truly exists. Man identifies with these beliefs and thus sees himself as a separate mind existing within a separate body. The beliefs of the ego are all unjustified and erroneous.

Ego-mind/ego-self The part of the mind that accepts and empowers the ego.

Enlightenment A state of awareness in which all things are seen as one. In Advaita Vedanta, it is revealed when the individual self (Atman) is seen as the ultimate universal reality (Brahman).

Eschatology The branch of theology that deals with death, judgment, and future states.

Eusebius of Caesarea Living circa 260 to 340 CE, he was a bishop of Caesarea Matima and a Church historian. He was the author of *Ecclesiastical History.*

Gnosticism This word does not appear in any of the ancient writings. It was first mentioned by Henry More in the 17th century in a commentary on the Book of Revelation. It very loosely refers to a Jewish/Christian set of beliefs that apparently arose in the first or second century among certain religious sects. They generally believed that the material world was the creation of a subordinate power or powers other than the perfect though remote supreme God. The world of matter was a kind of evil prison from which those seeking liberation labored to acquire knowledge or "gnosis." It is this knowledge that would make it possible for them to achieve freedom from this world, more often than not, in death. Though the Gospel of Thomas may be considered gnostic with a lowercase "g," it does not share the same interest in good/evil dualism as did many of these sects. It does not ascribe to a distant god or espouse complicated remedies for bridging the gap between man and God. Also, in Thomas there are no archons or supernatural beings other than the Father, the Holy Spirit, and possibly the undivided sonship of God's creation.

Hermetism A religious and philosophic tradition based primarily on the writings attributed to Hermes Trismegistus.

Hippolytus of Rome Believed to have lived from 170 to 235 CE, Hippolytus is chiefly known for his work *Refutation of All Heresies.*

Kingdom of the Father As suggested by the Gospel of Thomas, the Kingdom is the spiritual home of everything that lives in perfect oneness with its Source. It is a realm that is totally unlike the illusory realm of the world and completely incompatible with its values, laws, and limitations. Knowledge of this realm can be achieved by removing the blocks to its awareness.

Lacuna A gap or hole in a text.

Logion/logia A saying of Jesus, whether it be an aphorism, dialogue, or parable.

Messiah In Judaism, a messiah could be a king or high priest traditionally anointed with holy oil. It could also allude to a future leader that would unite the tribes of Israel, rebuild the Temple in Jerusalem, and usher in the Messianic Age. In Christianity, this title was assigned to Jesus as the Christ or anointed one. He was expected to fulfill his mission as the Christ in his Second Coming. It is not a term found in Thomas. In Thomas, however, no one, singular individual is THE son of God, but all are "sons of the Father" (3b) joined in oneness.

Mysticism In the limited sense in which I refer to it in this book, it is the tradition and practice of seeking union with Jesus or the divine in meditation, inquiry, or acts of selfless devotion. Its ultimate aim is the mystical experience of the divine.

Nag Hammadi A modern city in Egypt near the ancient site of Chenoboskion, an early center of Christianity. It was not far from this site that the so-called Nag Hammadi Library was discovered. In one of its codices was found the Gospel of Thomas.

Non-dualism An understanding that separation does not exist and that all apparent expressions of duality are illusions. Such expressions include form, space, and time.

Oneness The true nature of God's creation. A state in which separation of any kind is impossible. Any expression of space or time, subject or object, or inside or outside is therefore an illusion.

Origen of Alexandria Origen was an early theologian of the Church. He lived circa 184 to 253. In his writings is the earliest mention of the Gospel of Thomas, quoting what appears to be saying 82.

Orthodox As used in this book, this refers to both proto-orthodox and orthodox positions in the early Jesus movement from the time of Paul in the first century up to the mid-fourth century CE when this copy of the Gospel of Thomas was still accessible to its influence.

Oxyrhynchus An ancient city in Egypt where a large amount of papyrus texts were found in what once were trash dumps. These trash mounds dated from the Ptolemaic and Roman periods of Egyptian history. It was here between 1896 and 1907 that three separate fragments of the Gospel of Thomas were found, written not in Coptic but in Greek.

Parable A short allegorical story designed to reveal the truth by use of metaphor and hyperbole.

Plato A highly influential Greek philosopher (circa 347 BCE to 428 BCE). His ideas appear to have influenced the Jesus of this gospel, at least indirectly.

Pluralism The belief that that there are two or more substances or principles. Thus, the world is the sum of countless parts, all equally real. This contrasts with monism that holds that there is only one substance or principle that is real.

Q Part of the common material found in the Matthew and Luke gospels but not in Mark. A theory about this material asserts that this hypothetical collection of Jesus sayings was used in the composition of Matthew and Luke.

Sahidic A dialect of the Coptic language. It was the most widely spoken dialect in Upper Egypt prior to the Islamic conquest. It is the standard Coptic of the Nag Hammadi Library.

Separation The denial of oneness. The erroneous belief that life exists in a state where everything is separate from everything else. Thus, the world of space, time, and all physical phenomena, having the characteristic of separation, is unreal. From the viewpoint of non-duality, only the oneness of spirit is real, or as some would say, only consciousness is real.

Sepphoris A small city in Galilee, only a few miles from Nazareth where Jesus was reputed to have lived as a child and young man. In his time, Sepphoris was prosperous, cosmopolitan, and strongly influenced by Greek and Roman culture. It even had an amphitheater, though one can only speculate as to what was presented there.

Synoptic gospels The gospels of Matthew, Mark, and Luke. They are called synoptic because, unlike the Gospel of John, they share common material often in the same sequence and sometimes in identical wording.

Suggested readings

Davies, Stevan L. *The Gospel of Thomas and Christian Wisdom*. New York: Seabury Press, 1983.

Davies, Stevan L. *The Gospel of Thomas Annotated and Explained*. Woodstock, VT: Skylight Paths, 2002.

Doresse, Jean. *The Secret Books of the Egyptian Gnostics*. Rochester, VT: Inner Traditions International, Ltd., 1986.

Foundation for Inner Peace. *A Course in Miracles: Second Edition*. New York: Viking Penguin, 1996.

Funk, Robert W., Roy W. Hoover, and the Jesus Seminar. *The Five Gospels: The Search for the Authentic Words of Jesus; A New Translation and Commentary*. New York: Macmillan, 1993.

Hedrick, Charles W. *Unlocking the Secrets of the Gospel of Thomas: A Radical Faith for the New Age*. Eugene, OR: Cascade Books, 2010.

Leloup, Jean-Yves. *The Gospel of Thomas: The Gnostic Wisdom of Jesus*. English translation and notes by Joseph Rowe. Rochester, VT: Inner Traditions International, Ltd., 1986.

Meyer, Marvin. *The Gospel of Thomas: The Hidden Sayings of Jesus*. San Francisco: HarperSanFrancisco, 1992.

Pagels, Elaine. *The Gnostic Gospels*. New York: Vintage Books, 1981.

Pagels, Elaine. *Beyond Belief: The Secret Gospel of Thomas.* New York: Random House, 2003.

Patterson, Stephen J. *The Gospel of Thomas and Jesus.* Sonoma, CA: Polebridge Press, 1993.

Patterson, Stephen J., James M. Robinson with a New English Translation by Hans-Gebhard Bethge et al. *The Fifth Gospel: The Gospel of Thomas Comes of Age.* Harrieburg, PA: Trinity Press International, 1998.

Plisch, Uwe-Karsten. *The Gospel of Thomas: Original Text with Commentary.* Translated from the German by Gesine Schenke Robinson. Stuttgart: Deutsche Bibelgesellschaft, 2008.

Shibayama, Zenkei. *Zen Comments on the Mumonkan.* Translated into English by Sumiko Kudo. San Francisco: Harper & Row, 1974.

Skinner, Christopher W. *What Are They Saying About the Gospel of Thomas?* New York/Mahwah, NJ: Paulist Press, 2012.

Valantasis, Richard. *The Gospel of Thomas.* London and New York: Routledge, 1997.

Wapnick, Kenneth. *Love Does Not Condemn: The World, the Flesh, and the Devil According to Platonism, Christianity, Gnosticism, and A Course in Miracles.* Roscoe, NY: Foundation for "A Course in Miracles," 1989.

Winterhalter, Robert. *The Fifth Gospel: A Verse-by-Verse New Age Commentary on the Gospel of Thomas.* San Francisco: Harper & Row, 1988.

Lightning Source UK Ltd.
Milton Keynes UK
UKHW010801220722
406233UK00001B/128